Best Hikes Los Angeles

The Greatest Trails in the LA Mountains, Beaches, and Canyons

Second Edition

Allen Riedel and Monique Riedel

FALCONGUIDES

ESSEX, CONNECTICUT

FALCONGUIDES®

An imprint of Globe Pequot, the trade division of
The Rowman & Littlefield Publishing Group, Inc.
4501 Forbes Blvd., Ste. 200
Lanham, MD 20706
www.rowman.com

Falcon and FalconGuides are registered trademarks and Make Adventure Your Story is a trademark
of The Rowman & Littlefield Publishing Group, Inc.

Distributed by NATIONAL BOOK NETWORK

Photos by Allen and Monique Riedel
Maps by Trailhead Graphics Inc.

British Library Cataloguing in Publication Information available

Library of Congress Cataloging-in-Publication Data

Names: Riedel, Allen, author. | Riedel, Monique, author.
Title: Best hikes Los Angeles : the greatest trails in the LA mountains,
   beaches, and canyons / Allen Riedel and Monique Riedel.
Other titles: Best hikes near Los Angeles
Description: Second edition. | Guilford, Connecticut : Falcon Guides, 2022.
   | Revised edition of: Best hikes near Los Angeles. 2011.
Identifiers: LCCN 2022013992 (print) | LCCN 2022013993 (ebook) | ISBN
   9781493054848 (paperback) | ISBN 9781493054855 (epub)
Subjects: LCSH: Hiking—California—Los Angeles Metropolitan
   Area—Guidebooks. | Trails—California—Los Angeles Metropolitan
   Area—Guidebooks. | Los Angeles Metropolitan Area (Calif.)—Guidebooks.
Classification: LCC GV199.42.C22 L6569 2022 (print) | LCC GV199.42.C22
   (ebook) | DDC 917.94/93—dc23/eng/20220428
LC record available at https://lccn.loc.gov/2022013992
LC ebook record available at https://lccn.loc.gov/2022013993

∞™ The paper used in this publication meets the minimum requirements of American National
Standard for Information Sciences—Permanence of Paper for Printed Library Materials, ANSI/NISO
Z39.48-1992.

For Michael, Makaila, and Sierra

Contents

Acknowledgments viii
Introduction 1
    Weather 5
    Preparing for Your Hike 5
    Clothing, Shoes, Socks, and Gear 6
    Trail Regulations/Restrictions 8
    Leave No Trace 8
    Play It Safe 11
How to Use This Guide 13
Trail Finder 16
Map Legend 19

Wildwood Park 21
    1. Paradise Falls 23

Santa Monica Mountains National Recreation Area 27
    2. Mugu Peak and La Jolla Valley Loop 29
    3. Mishe Mokwa 34
    4. The Grotto 39
    5. Backbone Trail–Malibu Springs 44
    6. Nicholas Flat 48
    7. Charmlee Wilderness Park 52
    8. Paramount Ranch 57
    9. Calabasas Peak 63
    10. Solstice Canyon Rising Sun Loop 68
    11. Temescal Gateway Park 72
    12. Will Rogers State Historic Park 77
    13. Franklin Canyon 81
    14. Wilacre Park 85
    15. Runyon Canyon 89
    16. Griffith Park 93
    Honorable Mention
    A. Satwiwa–Rancho Sierra Vista 99

Angeles National Forest 100
    17. Echo Mountain 103
    18. Rubio Canyon 107
    19. Eaton Canyon Falls 111
    20. Sturtevant Falls 116
    21. Monrovia Canyon Falls 121
    22. Mount Hawkins 127
    23. Mount Baden-Powell 133

Overview

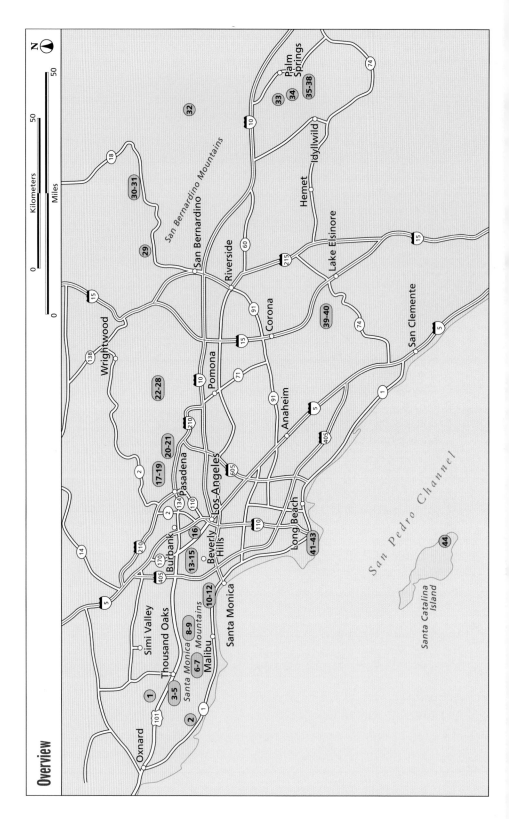

24. Big Horn Mine.. 139
25. Dawson Peak 145
26. Mount Baldy 150
27. Timber Mountain 155
28. Etiwanda Peak 160
Honorable Mentions
  B. Mount Islip... 165
  C. Mount Williamson 165

San Bernardino National Forest **167**
29. Heart Rock Falls... 169
30. Castle Rock... 173
31. Cougar Crest–Bertha Peak 177
32. Jepson Peak.. 181
33. San Jacinto Peak... 186
34. Suicide Rock 191
35. Ernie Maxwell Scenic Trail.. 195
36. Red Tahquitz 198
37. Spitler Peak.. 203
38. Lion Peak 208
Honorable Mentions
  D. Grays Peak 213
  E. Pine Knot Trail to Grand View Point... 213
  F. Fuller Ridge–Marion Mountain–Devil's Slide–Cactus to
     Clouds Trails to Mount San Jacinto 214

Cleveland National Forest.. **216**
39. Tenaja Falls 218
40. Chiquito Trail 222
Honorable Mentions
  G. San Juan Loop Trail.. 226
  H. Sitton Peak 226

Palos Verdes Peninsula **227**
41. White Point... 229
42. Portuguese Bend... 233
43. Point Vicente 237

Santa Catalina Island.. **241**
44. Avalon Canyon–Wrigley Gardens 243

Hike Index 247
About the Authors 248

Acknowledgments

I would like to especially thank my son, Michael J. Millenheft III, for being patient with us and joining us on many of these adventures whether or not he wanted to. To my wonderful stepdaughters, Sierra and Makaila Riedel, for being a constant source of inspiration and energy on the trails. And finally to my husband, best friend, and twin flame, Allen Riedel, for inspiring me to do things I never thought possible.

—Monique

I would like to first and foremost thank all of the people who have spent time hiking with me in the mountains, deserts, hills, forests, jungles, and coastal beaches. Many of you, my friends, have inspired me in countless ways, and I can't thank you enough.

I would also like to acknowledge my family: Monique, Michael, Sierra, and Makaila. All four of you have spent lots of time with me on trails that were great and some "not so much". . . I love you with all my heart.

I also owe a lot to my mom and dad, Barbara and Elmer Riedel, who raised me to believe in myself. Thanks! Thanks to my brother, Larry; my grandparents, Herbert and Vivian Ward, and Elmer and Lucille Riedel; I would like to thank the wonderful people at Globe Pequot Press.

Lastly, I would like to thank all of the students, administrators, teachers, and staff I have worked with over the past few decades. It has been a joy knowing all of you.

—Allen

Introduction

This book contains 44 hikes, and eight honorable mentions situated near the metropolitan region of Los Angeles. The hikes are located in a variety of areas ranging from county, city, or local parks to the surrounding national forests. This book highlights some of the best hikes in the region and covers a vast range of scenery, historical interests, and natural beauty.

Some of the best hiking in Southern California exists within a sixty- to ninety-minute drive from the city center of Los Angeles. The book is intended to be a sampling of the region and an introduction to the incredible wonders that the area has to offer. The hikes are also varied enough to provide interest for many disparate groups of people. There are hikes for waterfall lovers, peak baggers, the young, the young at heart, and even for those looking to get some quick exercise in the great outdoors. The hikes have been selected for their variety and their proximity to Los Angeles. Some are farther away than others, but even without assigning definitive borders to the city or county of Los Angeles, the greater Los Angeles area is a massive region.

Unbeknownst to many outside of the region, the Los Angeles area contains a great deal of austere and captivating pastoral beauty, from the chaparral-covered slopes of the Santa Monica Mountains to the lush alpine forests of the San Gabriel, San Bernardino, and San Jacinto ranges. Numerous nature preserves, reserves, and specially designated parks protect valuable ecosystems and wildlife around the southland.

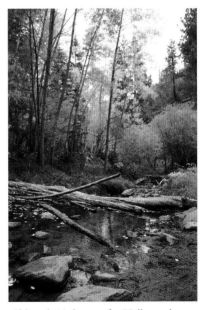

Los Angeles is the second-largest city/urban area in the United States. When people outside of the state think of Los Angeles, hiking is hardly the first subject to come to mind. Hollywood, beaches, celebrities, music, and fashion all supersede the thought of exploring the outdoors, and many people who live within the region fail to realize that high-altitude mountains exist just a short drive away. Many people walk down Sunset Boulevard in shorts while others are skiing down Mount Baldy's or Big Bear's slopes—merely an hour or so drive away. And the mountains aren't the only region ripe for hiking. The deserts, beaches, and local parks all have a uniquely Angelino feel to them. There are an infinite number of places to go when looking for a hike near Los Angeles, and there are no shortages on variety either.

Although it's known for Hollywood, movies, and stars, Los Angeles is a hiker's paradise with stunning natural beauty as well. Photo by Sierra Riedel.

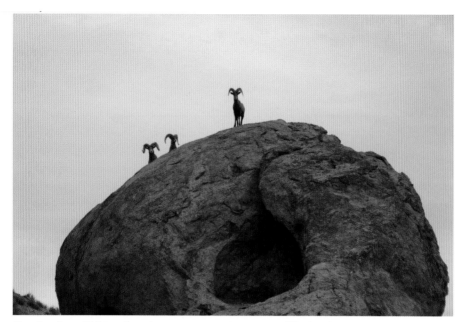

Spotting desert bighorn sheep is not very easy. Count yourself lucky if you see one. Photo by Allen Riedel.

Typically Southern Californian, the region is a semiarid Mediterranean ecosystem, ringed by the mountains uplifted by the tectonic forces of the San Andreas Fault. Seasonal arroyos dot the terrain and flow intermittently through steep rugged canyons. Varied species of mammals, reptiles, and amphibians inhabit the landscape. The flora of the region, mostly desert and coastal chaparral, can be magnificent in color, especially during certain times of the year and after a significant amount of rainfall. Oak, pine, and cedar forests grow into the upper elevations.

Mammals abound in the mountainous regions, with larger creatures such as black bear and mule deer inhabiting the higher reaches. Mountain lions and coyotes prowl throughout most of the foothill, park, and mountain areas, occasionally making their way into populated regions. Not really presenting much of a danger, attacks on humans are rare, and the danger can be reduced by traveling in groups of three or more. Smaller creatures and rodents such as squirrels, skunks, opossums, and mice are also abundant.

Several dams and waterways exist in the Los Angeles area, and while there are no major regional stopping points along the Pacific Flyway, there are opportunities for bird-watching. The region's mostly manufactured lakes offer sanctuary, recreation, and fishing, and more than 400 species of birds can be spotted throughout the year.

Hiking in the region is a popular activity, especially in the early morning and evening during summertime, and throughout the day during the fall, winter, and spring. Depending on the location, summer days can be pleasant at higher elevations and absolutely desiccating in lower climes. Winter temperatures are mild at lower

Garter snakes are harmless and can be found swimming in ponds and slinking along the trail. Photo by Allen Riedel.

elevations, but alpine conditions in the high mountains can lead to rapid hypothermia and death. Caution should be taken anytime you are hiking above 7,000 feet.

The COVID-19 pandemic has brought many to the mountains. This is both good and bad, in that many more folks are now enjoying the beauty of the natural world, but the human impact on our wildlands is now greater than ever. Take care to pack it in and pack it out. Wildfires have made some areas temporarily off limits, further crowding the trails in places that haven't suffered from a burn; some regions may never reopen or become the destinations that they once were.

Typically, the only animal that is dangerous to humans is the rattlesnake, and during hotter months they can be prevalent on certain trails. Do not walk through tall grasses or place hands and feet into locations unseen. Snakes are afraid of humans, and they understand the world through sensing vibrations. Typically, snakes will be alerted and flee long before a human approaches on the trail. Rattlesnakes will only strike if threatened, so the best thing to do is back away or walk in a wide berth around them on the trail. Mountain lions and bears can present an uncommon but real danger. Making noise as you walk along the trail and hiking in groups can significantly lessen the chance of encounters with these creatures, even though such encounters are already quite rare.

Insects are not normally a problem anywhere around Los Angeles, though after rains, ticks can present a small problem, as can mosquitoes and other pests. Flies and gnats can be slightly troublesome in wetter areas but are not normally a common problem. A mild insect repellent should do the trick for most hikes, and dogs should be protected with proper vaccinations and pet medicines.

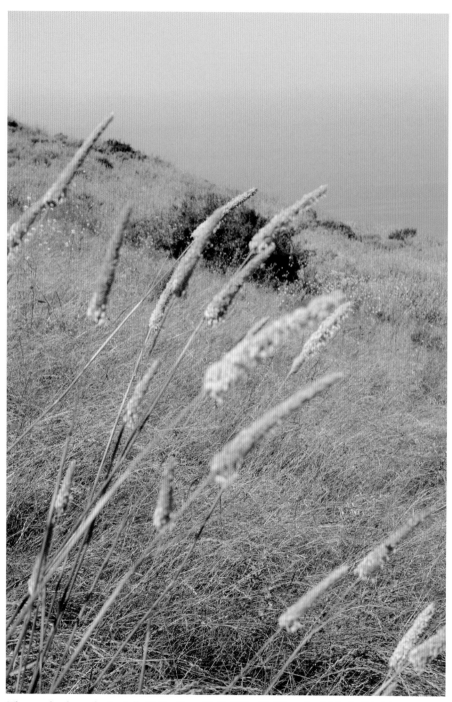

The grasslands on the La Jolla Valley Loop Trail (Hike 2). Photo by Makaila Riedel.

Weather

The Los Angeles metro area is mostly semiarid and the lower elevations can be stifling during June, July, August, and September. Heat can be a factor any time of the year, though late October through May is mild even in the hottest parts of the region.

Rain is not the normal state of affairs in Southern California, and the Los Angeles metro area is no exception, getting between 10 to 12 inches of rain annually. The rainy season is typically from November to February, though showers are more likely during December and January. Most rainstorms are over as quickly as they begin, though the region does see periods of continuing rainfall during the winter.

The mountains present an entirely different climate and create weather patterns that are separate from the rest of the region. Summer thunderstorms can be a common occurrence in the highest elevations, though rainfall does not typically occur elsewhere in the region during the summer.

Summer temperatures can reach triple digits, though the higher mountain ranges rarely reach above the 80s. The best times of year to hike in the Los Angeles metro area (outside of the mountains) are fall through spring, when the temperatures are mild during the day. Early morning, just before and after sunrise, and evening, just before and after sunset, are pleasant in the summer almost anywhere in the region.

Global warming has had an extreme impact on the forests of Southern California, which have suffered double repercussions from preventive forest fire practices for more than 100 years. Drought and blight have also contributed to a greater danger from fire, and as early as 1984, the US Congress doubted whether the pine forests of Southern California could be saved.

Preparing for Your Hike

Before you go hiking, always be prepared. Let someone know where you are planning to go and leave an itinerary of your hiking destination with a reliable friend. Give them an expected return time and the name of the trailhead you are visiting, along with specific routes you are taking. Be sure that your friend will contact authorities should you not return as expected.

Water is essential in desert environments. Hydrate before you leave and during your hike, and leave extra water in the vehicle so that you may hydrate on return. A good rule of thumb for hiking is one-half to one liter of water per hour of hiking. On hot days without shade you should drink as much as one gallon of water per hour of hiking. Salty snacks can help aid water retention. Hikers should avoid overexertion during the hottest part of the day. Make no mistake, the Los Angeles area is a dry one, and hikers should drink plenty of water even on cool days.

When you hike, you should always bring along the so-called 10 Essentials so that you can provide yourself with the basic necessities for survival should the unexpected occur. Hiking is a relatively safe activity, especially when care is taken, although it is always best to prepare for any eventuality. Minor mishaps like taking a wrong turn, getting back after dark, or being lost for a short while can be frightening, but as long as cool heads prevail, most outdoor mishaps can be easily rectified. The 10 Essentials are designed to keep people safe and provide a backup plan should something go wrong.

1. Navigation: map, compass, or GPS
2. Sun protection: hat, or sunscreen
3. Insulation: layered clothing
4. Illumination: headlamp or flashlight
5. First aid supplies: Band-Aids, bandages, gauze, tape, tweezers, etc.
6. Repair kit and tools: knife, duct tape, etc.
7. Nutrition: extra food
8. Hydration: extra water
9. Emergency shelter: tarp, tent, sleeping bag, or emergency blanket
10. Fire starter: necessary for life-threatening emergencies only

This is a basic list, and of course, other items may also be of use. The more time you spend on the trail, the more time you will have to modify and fine-tune this list. Some items may be more important than others.

Clothing, Shoes, Socks, and Gear

Clothing should be made up of layers to protect your body from the elements, whether wind, heat, rain, or cold.

An insulating layer of water- and sweat-wicking fabric (i.e., polyester, neoprene, Capilene, or other synthetic fiber) is best for a base layer. These fabrics wick sweat away from your body and keep you warm. On hot days cotton can be a good choice only because the sweat will remain on the fabric, keeping you cooler than a synthetic material. Cotton is a bad choice for cold and rainy days because the material retains water and loses its ability to insulate, which in even less than extreme circumstances can lead to hypothermia.

A fleece shell is good for an insulating layer because the material is lightweight and dries quickly. On days without a hint of precipitation, a fleece jacket may be the only necessary outerwear to bring along.

Last, a lightweight rain shell should be brought along in case of emergencies. Rain and snow can be deadly in the mountains. A waterproof shell and pants offer protection from the elements.

Improvements in lightweight hiking boots and shoes have revolutionized the sport. Boots no longer need to be bulky, heavy, cumbersome, Frankenstein-like appendages that cause blisters, chafing, and sore feet. Instead, many outdoor specialty shops can measure a hiker's feet and find a great-fitting shoe that can be worn immediately on

Many trails were once wagon roads such as the route that leads to Big Horn Mine (Hike 24). Photo by Allen Riedel.

the trail. These shoes are typically durable, sturdy, and excellent for short day hikes, though they may not be ideal for longer and more difficult trekking.

Socks made of wool or synthetic materials are best because they take moisture away from the feet, reducing chafing and blisters.

Backpacks for day hiking should be small, fit comfortably, and carry 10 to 20 pounds. Carrying more than 20 pounds on a day hike is actually kind of silly and will probably only serve to make the experience less enjoyable. In today's ultralight market, weeklong backpacking trips can be made carrying only 20 to 25 pounds (water and food included). Find a backpack that is large enough to carry what is needed but light enough to be comfortable. Hydration systems have become the norm, and drinking from a reservoir tube is pure bliss compared to the days of cumbersome canteens or stopping to retrieve water bottles from a pack when thirsty.

Other items may be fun to have along as well. Cameras or cell phones can be used to record an excursion for posterity. Binoculars can come in handy for wildlife viewing. Plant, bird, animal, and insect identification guides can prove to be informative and educational. Handheld GPS units are becoming increasingly inexpensive and are a great tool to use on the trail. Maps should be taken, but most trails are well marked. Many trail applications exist that mark your location and that of the trail; it is advisable to find a good one and learn how to use it.

CAUTION

The Los Angeles metro area is an extremely arid region, and wildfire is a constant danger and threat. Fires are not permitted in parks, forests, and hiking areas outside of designated campgrounds and "yellow post" campsites, which are specifically marked trailside campsites. If a life-threatening emergency requires building a fire, an area must be cleared 8 feet in diameter around the fire, and a rock ring should be constructed to contain the fire itself. Lighting a fire is not recommended nor endorsed by this book. Do not build new fire rings as these are destructive to a wilderness environment; use established rings.

With new technology comes a word of caution: Just because a trail exists does not mean you and your party are ready for it, nor the elements you may encounter. Always know your limits, and if you feel they are being pushed or even that they might be, remember that the trail will certainly be there another day. Take time to learn how to navigate using a map and compass, and carry a real map when hiking; cell phones, GPS, and even portable solar chargers can be unreliable. Always make sure that you are safe.

Trail Regulations/Restrictions

Trails in this guide are located in national parks, national forests, preserves, and local and regional parks. Trails in the national forests require an Adventure Pass for parking. Daily or annual Adventure Passes can be purchased at sporting goods stores, specialty outdoor shops, and in the local mountains. Some city parks and natural areas are free, and others require day-use fees. Fees for trailhead use are not required anywhere, though camping permits may carry fees.

Leave No Trace

Trails in the Los Angeles area and neighboring foothills are heavily used year-round. We, as trail users and advocates, must be especially vigilant to make sure our passage leaves no lasting mark. Here are some basic guidelines for preserving trails in the region:

Pack out all your own trash, including biodegradable items like orange peels and sunflower seeds. In the arid Southern California climate, items such as these take 10 or more years to decompose. If everyone who hiked these trails left peels and shells behind, the trails would look more like a waste dump than a forest or wild landscape. You might also pack out garbage left by less considerate hikers. Take a plastic bag and make the place better for your having been there.

Don't approach or feed any wild creatures; the ground squirrel eyeing your snack food is best able to survive if it remains self-reliant.

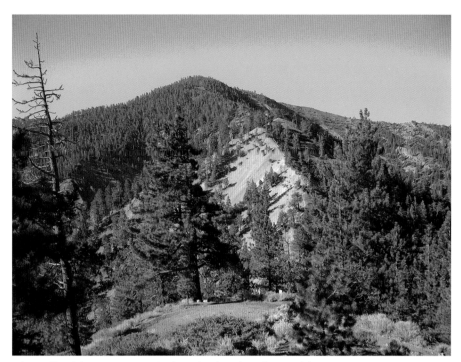

The trailhead from FR 3N06 (Hike 25). Photo by Allen Riedel.

Don't pick wildflowers or gather rocks, antlers, feathers, and other treasures along the trail. Removing these items will only take away from the next hiker's experience.

Avoid damaging trailside soils and plants by remaining on the established route. This is also a good rule of thumb for avoiding poison oak and stinging nettle, which are common regional trailside irritants.

Don't cut switchbacks, which can promote erosion. Be courteous by not making loud noises while hiking. Please do not bring portable speakers on the trail. If you must have music, wear earphones; people are enjoying solitude and the sounds of nature when hiking, and although your music might be the best playlist ever, it is better enjoyed as a personal choice. Hiking with earphones also lessens your sense of hearing, so take caution.

Many of these trails are multiuse, which means you'll share them with other hikers, trail runners, mountain bikers, and equestrians. Familiarize yourself with the proper trail etiquette, yielding the trail when appropriate. If in doubt, be courteous and simply let other users pass.

Hikers hiking uphill have the right of way. If someone is charging along uphill, it is more difficult for them to stop and get started again, so move to the side and let them pass. Bicyclists yield to hikers, horses, and other pack animals. Hikers should also yield to horses and pack animals. Announce yourself when approaching hikers from behind, and nod or say hello to hikers going the other way.

Small cascades dot creek beds after winter and spring rains. Photo by Allen Riedel.

Use outhouses at trailheads or along the trail.

Do not disturb wildlife.

Stay on the trail; a use trail up a peak is still a trail.

Be mindful of trail conditions.

As you take advantage of the spectacular scenery offered by the Los Angeles area, remember that our planet is dear, special, and fragile. All should do everything possible to keep it clean, beautiful, and healthy, including following the Green Tips you will find throughout this book.

Play It Safe

Generally, hiking in and around the Los Angeles metro area is a safe and fun way to explore the outdoors. Hiking is not without its risks, but there are ways to lessen those risks. Following a few simple steps and guidelines will help to make the activity as benign as possible.

It is a good idea to know simple first aid, including how to treat bleeding, bites, stings, fractures, strains, or sprains. Make sure to take along at least a basic first aid kit. It won't help to have the skills without any supplies.

The Los Angeles metro area—and Southern California, for that matter—is known for its sunny skies and warm climate. The sun can be powerful, especially at higher elevations; use sunscreen and wear a wide-brimmed hat.

Weather patterns can change abruptly, especially in the mountains and during winter and spring months (November through April). Carry layered clothing items to protect you from temperature changes and rain. Remember, summer thunderstorms aren't uncommon in the mountains and may bring dangers such as freezing temperatures, lightning, hail, and high winds.

The hills and mountains are home to a variety of wildlife. Some can be hosts to disease, and others may attack if prompted by hunger or the smell of food. Rattlesnakes may be found on any of the hikes described, particularly from early in the spring to the middle of fall. Be careful where you place your hands and feet.

Learn how to spot and identify poison oak. Its appearance will change throughout the year. During spring and summer, the distinctive three-pronged leaves are green and then turn to red and brown as the seasons progress through fall and into winter. In winter, the leaves may completely fall off the plant, leaving a hard-to-identify stalk that still contains and spreads toxins that may cause an itchy rash when touched by human skin. The noxious plant grows abundantly near water, in the canyons, and along the hillsides below 6,000 feet.

Ticks are another pest to be avoided. They are more likely to be found near water or after rains. They hang in the brush waiting to drop on warm-blooded animals. It is a good idea to check for ticks whenever stopping along the trail. Ticks will hang onto clothing or hair and not bite until the host has stopped moving. It is best to remove ticks before they have a chance to bite and latch on.

The Los Angeles metro area is almost a desert ecosystem and temperatures can soar. Bring more drinking water than you think you'll need. Any water you find on these hikes is considered unsafe to drink if untreated. Boil, filter, or treat before consumption.

How to Use This Guide

Start: This gives the general location of the trailhead and the parking area for the starting point or trailhead of each hike.

Distance: This is the total distance of the hike, whether out and back, around a loop, or one way with a car shuttle. Distances were measured by uploading a GPS track, where available, to topo-mapping software and free available topo-mapping websites, and then overlaying the track with a hand-drawn route line.

Hiking time: The approximate time for an average hiker to do the hike. These times err on the conservative side, estimating that the average hiker travels about 1 mile per 30 minutes. These estimations do not take into account rest stops, elevation gain, photography, and other nonhiking activities. Fast hikers will need less time, and slow, beginning, or out-of-shape hikers may use more time. In instances of difficult hikes, novice hikers may need double the time to complete hikes.

Difficulty: All hikes are rated as easy, moderate, or strenuous, with multiple reasons for the rating. Although this is necessarily a highly subjective rating, nearly anyone who can walk should be able to do an easy hike in just a few hours. Moderate hikes are longer—up to a full day—and may involve 1,000 feet or more of elevation gain and possibly cross-country hiking as well. Experienced hikers will have no problems; beginners should hike with someone more experienced and will have more fun if they are in reasonable shape. Strenuous hikes are long, requiring a full day of hiking by fit hikers and include possibly more than 2,000 feet of elevation gain. The hiking may involve cross-country hiking on faint, rough trails that require good map and compass skills, and some rock scrambling may be required on rough terrain. Only fit, experienced hikers should tackle these hikes.

Trail surface: Most trails in the Los Angeles region are dirt and rocks. Other trail surface conditions are described here, including hikes on old roads, paved trails, and cross-country.

Nearest town: This is the location of the nearest populated area from which to procure gas, supplies, and phone services. In populated areas, the nearest town may be redundant, but in the mountains, knowing where to stock up on a missing item may mean the difference between a 20-minute detour and a 2-hour drive up and down the mountain.

County: This is the county where the hike is located.

Other trail users: You may encounter horses, mountain bikers, and endemic wildlife such as rattlesnakes or mountain lions on some of the trails.

Canine compatibility: Many people like to hike with their furry friends, so this section mentions whether dogs are allowed and restrictions, if any. All areas that are open to dogs are subject to local and state statutes regarding leash laws. Some people are not amenable to interaction with dogs for personal reasons; therefore, it is important not only as a matter of law but as a common courtesy to leash your dogs.

Trailhead facilities/amenities: Availability or lack of water, restrooms, picnic tables, and so on.

Land status: National forest, national recreation area, city or state park, etc.

Fees and permits: If any fees, including entry fees, are required, they are mentioned here. Any permits required are also listed.

Schedule: If access is limited to certain times of the day for administrative reasons such as road closures, you'll find that information here. This area will also include best seasons to hike.

Maps: The National Geographic Topographical Map set covering the hike, the US Geological Survey (USGS) 7.5-minute series quads, and any other useful maps are listed here.

Trail contacts: Look here for the name and contact information of the agency or organization responsible for managing the land crossed by the hike. It's a good idea to call or email the land management agency before your hike to check on road and trail conditions. Where possible, the contact information includes the mailing and street address, phone number, and website. Email addresses are not included because they change frequently; check the agency website for an email address, generally found under a "Contact" link. Sometimes web addresses change as well, but you can usually find land management units on the web with a search engine.

Finding the trailhead: This section gives driving directions from Los Angeles freeways. We've also provided the GPS coordinates in latitude and longitude for the trailheads, which can be input into Google Maps.

The Hike: Here's the meat of the hike—a detailed description of the trail or route and the features and attractions along the way. We describe the route using landmarks as well as trail signs when possible because trail signs can be missing. Refer to the next section, "Miles and directions," for a description with distances between key points.

The high mountains of Southern California are an amazing escape. The San Jacinto range near Idyllwild are no exception. Photo by Monique Riedel.

California horned lizards are threatened by a dwindling food supply. Non-native ants and pesticides have caused a decline in their fodder of choice, the harvester ant. Photo by Allen Riedel.

Miles and directions: This table lists the key points, such as trail intersections, or turning points on a cross-country hike, by miles and tenths. You should be able to find the route with this table alone. The mileages in this book do not necessarily agree with distances found on trail signs, agency mileages, cell phone applications, and other descriptions because a variety of methods and personnel measure trail miles. All mileages were carefully measured using digital topographic mapping software for accuracy and consistency within the book.

Trail Finder

Hike No.	Hike Name	Best Hikes for Back-packers	Best Hikes for Water-falls	Best Hikes for Geology Lovers	Best Hikes for Children	Best Hikes for Dogs	Best Hikes for Peak Baggers	Best Hikes for Great Views	Best Hikes for Canyons	Best Hikes for Nature Lovers
1	Paradise Falls		•		•	•				
2	Mugu Peak and La Jolla Valley Loop	•					•		•	
3	Mishe Mokwa			•		•		•		
4	The Grotto		•	•					•	•
5	Backbone Trail–Malibu Springs							•		
6	Nicholas Flat							•		•
7	Charmlee Wilderness Park				•	•		•		•
8	Paramount Ranch				•					
9	Calabasas Peak			•	•		•	•		
10	Solstice Canyon Rising Sun Loop		•						•	
11	Temescal Gateway Park		•					•		
12	Will Rogers State Historic Park				•			•		
13	Franklin Canyon				•				•	
14	Wilacre Park					•				
15	Runyon Canyon					•				

Hike No.	Hike Name	Best Hikes for Backpackers	Best Hikes for Waterfalls	Best Hikes for Geology Lovers	Best Hikes for Children	Best Hikes for Dogs	Best Hikes for Peak Baggers	Best Hikes for Great Views	Best Hikes for Canyons	Best Hikes for Nature Lovers
16	Griffith Park				•			•		
17	Echo Mountain							•		
18	Rubio Canyon		•	•		•			•	
19	Eaton Canyon Falls		•			•			•	
20	Sturtevant Falls		•		•	•			•	•
21	Monrovia Canyon Falls		•		•	•			•	
22	Mount Hawkins	•					•	•		
23	Mount Baden-Powell						•	•		
24	Big Horn Mine				•	•				
25	Dawson Peak						•	•		
26	Mount Baldy						•	•		
27	Timber Mountain	•				•	•	•		
28	Etiwanda Peak	•				•	•	•		
29	Heart Rock Falls		•	•	•	•		•	•	•
30	Castle Rock			•	•	•		•		
31	Cougar Crest–Bertha Peak	•				•		•		
32	Jepson Peak	•					•	•		
33	San Jacinto Peak	•					•	•		

Hike No.	Hike Name	Best Hikes for Backpackers	Best Hikes for Waterfalls	Best Hikes for Geology Lovers	Best Hikes for Children	Best Hikes for Dogs	Best Hikes for Peak Baggers	Best Hikes for Great Views	Best Hikes for Canyons	Best Hikes for Nature Lovers
34	Suicide Rock			•	•			•		•
35	Ernie Maxwell Scenic Trail				•					
36	Red Tahquitz	•		•			•	•		
37	Spitler Peak					•	•	•		•
38	Lion Peak	•				•	•	•		
39	Tenaja Falls		•		•					
40	Chiquito Trail	•					•		•	
41	White Point				•	•		•		•
42	Portuguese Bend				•			•		•
43	Point Vicente			•	•	•		•		•
44	Avalon Canyon–Wrigley Gardens							•		•

Map Legend

Transportation

≡⬡5⬡≡ Freeway/Interstate Highway

─⬡101⬡─ U.S. Highway

═⬭23⬭═ State Highway

═▭1N05▭═ Forest/Other Paved Road

= = = = Unpaved Road

Trails

------- Selected Route

------ Trail

→ Direction of Route

Water Features

Body of Water

River or Creek

Intermittent Stream

Waterfall

Spring

Symbols

≍ Bridge

■ Building/Point of Interest

▲ Campground

Gate

Lighthouse

Lookout Tower

▲ Mountain/Peak

🅿 Parking

≍ Pass/Gap

🔼 Picnic Area

Ranger Station/Park Office

Restroom

Scenic View/Overlook

○ Towns and Cities

⑳ Trailhead

❓ Visitor Center/Information

Land Management

National Forest

Wilderness Area

State/Local Park

Wildwood Park

Wildwood Regional Park is an exercise mecca for those in the Conejo Valley. It is a favorite of hikers, mountain bikers, schoolchildren, and anyone looking for a little bit of outdoor adventure with a spectacular payoff. It is extensively marked and signed. There are many different trails and routes and lots of interesting things to see in Wildwood Canyon, but nothing is as outstanding as the 50-foot waterfall

The trails in Wildwood Canyon are well marked and easy to follow (Hike 1). Photo by Allen Riedel.

A lone columbine grows out of a rock. Photo by Allen Riedel. (Hike 35)

that pours over limestone into a large pool lined by oaks, sycamores, and cattails. There isn't as remarkable a waterfall anywhere else in the Conejo Valley, and there are only a few that cascade so vigorously and this beautifully in all of Southern California. Paradise Falls is a treasure that is unknown to most outside of the region, but it is heavily visited by those in the know.

The park contains two waterfalls, nearly 1,800 acres of open space, 60 species of birds, 37 different mammals, and 22 species of reptiles and amphibians. Consisting mostly of coastal chaparral and sage scrub, the park's ecology is decidedly Mediterranean. Wildflowers put on their best displays between February and May. The trails range from infrequently used, narrow, single-track ridgeline traverses to well-traveled open dirt roads that lead most visitors to the popular Paradise Falls.

Several notable movie and television programs were filmed here, including *Spartacus*, *Wuthering Heights*, *Wagon Train*, *The Rifleman*, and *Gunsmoke*.

1 Paradise Falls

Wander through a huge swath of open space wedged in suburban sprawl to find one of Southern California's most spectacular waterfalls. Marvel at the wildlife and untamed feel of a place so close to human settlement.

Start: At the corner of Avenida De Los Arboles and Big Sky Drive
Distance: 3.7-mile loop
Hiking time: About 2 hours
Difficulty: Easy
Trail surface: Single-track dirt trail and dirt road
Nearest town: Thousand Oaks
County: Ventura
Other trail users: Bicyclists, joggers, and equestrians
Canine compatibility: Leashed dogs permitted
Trailhead facilities/amenities: Restrooms, water, picnic tables along trail
Land status: City and regional parkland
Fees and permits: None

Schedule: Open year-round, sunrise to sunset, except during inclement weather; best to avoid the extreme heat of the day in summer or any season as most of the route is unshaded
Maps: USGS Newbury Park, CA; www.cosf.org/website/html/wildwood-map.html
Trail contacts: Conejo Open Space Foundation (COSF), P.O. Box 2113, Thousand Oaks, CA, 91358; www.cosf.org; 805-402-9550. Conejo Open Space Conservation Agency (COSCA), Administration: City Hall/Civic Arts Plaza, 2100 Thousand Oaks Blvd., Thousand Oaks, CA, 91362; 805-449-2345. Ranger Offices: 403 West Hillcrest Dr., Thousand Oaks, CA, 91360; http://conejo-openspace.org; 805-495-6471

Finding the trailhead: From Los Angeles take US 101 north. Take Exit 45 for Lynn Road, turn right onto Lynn Road, and drive for 2.5 miles. Turn left onto Avenida De Los Arboles and drive for 0.9 mile. Park in the lot on the left at the end of the road, at the intersection with Big Sky Drive. GPS: 34°13'12.8"N 118°54'09.6"W

The Hike

Head to the southeast end of the parking area and descend the stairs to take the Moonridge Trail. This is definitely the less traveled route through this portion of the park, though saying any trail is less traveled in Wildwood Canyon is like saying there aren't many people in the city of Los Angeles. There will be fewer people here though because this section is a bit tougher than (and not as straightforward as) the mostly fire road trails that traverse the Wildwood Park open space. It does meander up and down in some spots, losing and gaining elevation fairly rapidly. The trail wanders through mostly coastal chaparral and scrub sage. There is precious little shade, and it is advisable to bring extra water if the temperature is above 70 degrees.

Fewer people realize that a trail begins on the remote side of the parking lot, which also contributes to drawing fewer newcomers to this route. The Moonridge Trail crosses a public access road as it approaches 0.5 mile and continues on for another 0.4 mile before a T junction at North Tepee Trail.

Paradise Falls is a hidden treasure not known to many outside of the Conejo Valley. Photo by Allen Riedel.

Turn left and walk south and down for 0.1 mile along the North Tepee Trail, toward the giant replica of a modern man-made tepee, which will be of great interest to children but probably not anyone else. Turn right onto Tepee Trail and walk for about 0.1 mile to the junction with the Paradise Falls Trail. Here, you will catch glimpses of the falls, the overlook, and hear the falls if the water is flowing heavily. Everything is clearly marked, making it impossible to lose your way in the park. Turn left at the junction with the Wildwood Canyon Trail, although a short jaunt of 30 yards to the left provides an excellent vantage point and overlook of the falls. Turn right and follow the signs toward the waterfall.

The stream below the waterfall can be crossed during low and normal water runoff for a fantastic frontal vantage point of the 50-foot fall, but it should not be attempted during times of high runoff. At such times when the water level is dangerous, officials usually close the park. Use common sense and never cross deep or fast-moving water. In the previous decade, three deaths have been recorded below the falls. Although this is not normally a cause for concern, it is a caveat for hiker safety and caution.

From the waterfall, continue west on the Wildwood Canyon Trail, following it for 0.5 mile to the junction with the Lizard Rock Trail. Here the trail becomes wilder and definitely less traveled. There are some great vantage points along the way, and the canyon itself is especially lovely. It wraps around the Hill Canyon Water Treatment Facility and climbs 600 feet to the top of Lizard Rock. From afar, the rock looks strikingly like a giant lizard peeking its head over the Conejo Valley. From up close, Lizard

Paradise Falls

Rock provides an excellent view. The trail zigzags up the hillside for slightly more than 0.8 mile.

From the rock, follow the Stagecoach Bluff Trail for 0.2 mile to the connector to the Mesa Trail, which leads to the Mesa Trail in another 0.2 mile. Follow the Mesa Trail, which is an old dirt road, 0.6 mile back to the parking area.

While walking along these roads and trails, remember that some of your father's and grandfather's favorite Western movies and television shows were filmed right here. If you look hard enough, you might even recognize the landscape.

Miles and Directions

0.0 Start from the southeast corner of the parking lot on Avenida De Los Arboles on the Moonridge Trail.

0.5 Stay straight at the intersection with the road.

0.9 Turn left at the intersection with the road onto the North Tepee Trail.

1.0 Turn right onto the Tepee Trail at the tepee.

1.1 Turn left onto the Paradise Falls Trail.

1.2 Turn right onto the Paradise Falls Trail.

1.3 Arrive at Paradise Falls. Return via the same trail.

1.4 Turn left onto Wildwood Canyon Trail.

1.9 Turn right onto Lizard Rock Trail.

2.7 Arrive at Lizard Rock. Turn right onto Stagecoach Bluff Trail.

2.9 Turn left onto the connector trail that leads to the Mesa Trail.

3.1 Turn right onto Mesa Trail.

3.7 Arrive back at the parking area.

Hike Information

Local information: Conejo Open Space Foundation (COSF), P.O. Box 2113, Thousand Oaks, CA, 91358; www.cosf.org; 805-402-9550. Conejo Open Space Conservation Agency (COSCA), Administration: City Hall/Civic Arts Plaza, 2100 Thousand Oaks Blvd., Thousand Oaks, CA, 91362; 805-449-2345. Ranger Offices: 403 West Hillcrest Dr., Thousand Oaks, CA, 91360; http://conejo-openspace.org; 805-495-6471

Camping: Leo Carrillo State Park campgrounds, Malibu Creek State Park, Topanga State Park Campground, Point Mugu State Park Campground, McGrath State Beach, Emma Wood State Beach, California State Park campgrounds reservations, 800-444-7275; customer service, 805-488-1827; www.reservecalifornia.com

Santa Monica Mountains National Recreation Area

Part of the Transverse Ranges of Southern California, the Santa Monica Mountains run west to east from Point Mugu to Griffith Park. They are rimmed on the north by the Conejo and San Fernando Valleys, and to the south, they are entirely bound by the Pacific Ocean. Located in southeast Ventura County and western Los Angeles County, the mountains span 40 miles from end to end and are bisected by several roads and highways. The Santa Monica Mountains National Recreation Area (SMMNRA) is the world's largest urban national park. At nearly 240 square miles, the park encompasses a whopping 26 different zip codes and five separate area codes.

Established on November 10, 1978, the SMMNRA has been a beneficiary of land donations, private and public acquisitions, concerned citizens, generous donors, activists, and celebrity benefactors. To this day the Santa Monica Mountains Conservancy is working to buy back, preserve, protect, and restore land in the region for public access and wildlife habitat. The recreation area is made up of a conglomeration of nationally operated sites headquartered in Thousand Oaks, state parks, regional and local parks, and private lands, with more than 70 different parks and open space properties included.

Historically, the Santa Monica Mountains were home to the Chumash, Tataviam, and Gabrieleno/

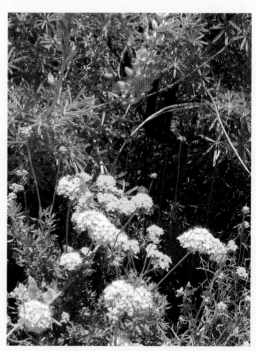

Buckwheat, lupine, and wallflower make for a fine canvas of wildflowers in the Santa Monica Mountains. Photo by Allen Riedel.

Tongva peoples. The Santa Monicas formed an overlap in the three cultures' territory. The 1542 arrival of explorer Juan Rodriguez Cabrillo brought the Spanish, Catholicism, the mission culture, and non-native plants, forever changing the mountains and ushering in modernization and urbanization of the region.

Despite being adjacent to the world's 30th-largest metropolitan area, much of the Santa Monica range has been protected. There are places that feel so remote it is difficult to believe the park is located in Los Angeles.

In November 2018, the Woolsey Fire burned nearly 100,000 acres, almost two-thirds of the entire SMMNRA, and a full 88 percent of the federally owned lands within the park. Many areas have changed, many have recovered and are recovering, some are thriving once again, but a few of the trails previously in this book have been closed, and after the fires, 2019 brought mudslides, further altering the landscape.

2 Mugu Peak and La Jolla Valley Loop

Hike up the oldest trail in Southern California, ascend to the top of a magnificent coastal peak with dynamite views, explore the beautiful flower-filled landscape, and walk through a historic valley where native Chumash thrived in the pre-Columbian era.

Start: Pacific Coast Highway 0.5 mile north of Mugu Rock across from the navy firing range
Distance: 6-mile lollipop
Hiking time: About 3 hours
Difficulty: Moderate
Trail surface: Single-track dirt trail and dirt road
Nearest town: Malibu
County: Ventura
Other trail users: Equestrians
Canine compatibility: No dogs permitted
Trailhead facilities/amenities: None

Land status: California state park
Fees and permits: None
Schedule: Open year-round; on hot days, the sun can be punishing, especially on the slope up the Chumash Trail and in the valley
Maps: USGS Point Mugu, CA; www.nps.gov/samo
Trail contact: Point Mugu State Park, 9000 W. Pacific Coast Hwy., Malibu, CA, 90265; www.parks.ca.gov/default.asp?page_id=630; 805-488-1827

Finding the trailhead: From Los Angeles take the Pacific Coast Highway/CA 1 for 31.5 miles north and west of Sunset Boulevard. The parking lot is on the right-hand side of the freeway, 0.5 mile north of Mugu Rock, across from the navy firing range. GPS: 34°05'29.7"N 119°03'56.9"W

The Hike

The Chumash Trail begins ignominiously from an unsightly dirt parking pullout across from the Point Mugu Naval Base's shooting range. Visitors to the area may hear early morning gunfire while ascending the vertical, cardio-blasting slope that gains 900 feet in elevation in 0.5 mile. Get there before the sun does, because even on a cool day in the morning, this trail can be hot if the sun is bearing down, and the initial climb is up, up, up. Half a mile of steep elevation gain isn't so bad though as it ends quickly and views of the mighty Pacific open up almost immediately. It does make for a heck of a workout. After the initial push, and the climb to the summit of Mugu Peak, the remainder of the trail is mostly an easy walk through a lovely valley that was spared by the 2018 Woolsey Fire.

Perhaps the coolest thing about the Chumash Trail is its age. The trail is purported to be anywhere from 5,000 to 9,000 years old, making this an old and established trail. One thing that is certain is that in October 1542, when the explorer Juan Rodriguez Cabrillo sailed through the region, he was greeted by local Chumash who called their village *muwu*, meaning "beach" or "seashore." The trail was then in use for bringing the bounty of the sea up to the teeming village that occupied a good portion of

Hiking through the grasslands on the La Jolla Valley Loop Trail. Photo by Makaila Riedel.

lush La Jolla Valley. Cabrillo's writings describe a bountiful population that thrived beneath the holy backdrop of Boney Mountain. Pondering Chumash life here and contemplating what their everyday existence must have been like is a great meditation for the hike.

After arriving on the plateau, a side trail/road takes off to the right; this is the Mugu Peak Trail. Ignore it; it leads around the base of the mountain, circumventing the summit. Instead, take the use trail that leads obviously upward just a short way ahead. At 0.8 mile, turn right onto the use trail that leads to the top of Mugu Peak. The trip up is pretty steep too, gaining 400 feet more of elevation in 0.4 mile. The plant life along the way is interesting and quite varied. Wildflowers are everywhere if timed right; spring can last here through late June. Atop the summit are a US flag, spectacular views of the Pacific Ocean, La Jolla Valley, as well as the ridgeline of Boney Mountain. From there, continue down the other side of the summit as the trail wanders through cacti and drops to the Y connector. Veer left and follow the trail down into the La Jolla Valley.

At 2.2 miles, the trail drops into a wooded canyon and connects with the La Jolla Loop. Turn right. The grasslands grow high here, so make sure to check for ticks whenever you stop. Follow the loop around the outside of the canyon. At 3.0 miles, the loop trail continues toward the pond on the northeast end of the loop; turn left to

JUAN RODRIGUEZ CABRILLO

Born in 1499, Cabrillo was a Portuguese explorer who led the first European expedition along the coast of California. He set sail from Mexico in June 1542. His three ships traveled up the coast with two years' worth of supplies exploring what is now San Diego, Santa Monica, San Pedro, Anacapa, Catalina, San Miguel, Point Conception, Point Reyes, and the Russian River.

Cabrillo's expedition missed San Francisco Bay entirely. The armada returned south to spend the winter in the Channel Islands after vicious storms threatened. There, the native Chumash population clashed with the conquistadors, and Cabrillo was injured going ashore. He fell leaving his ship and broke a bone. The bone became gangrenous, and he died on January 3, 1543.

The final resting place of Cabrillo is not known. It is reported that he was laid to rest on San Miguel, Santa Cruz, or Catalina Island.

Although many places in California are named for Spanish explorers, conquistadors, and missionaries, the history of the state and the world is constantly being reassessed. At least one California college named after Cabrillo is considering changing its name "due to his enslavement of Indigenous people and profiting from their genocide and exploitation." As the first European to set foot in California, Cabrillo earned his fame, seafaring was a difficult means of employment. As someone who took part in wholesale slaughter of unarmed Native Americans, perhaps his notoriety, bloodthirst, and inhumanity is justly why his role as a notable person is being rethought.

stay on the trail. The trail on the right leads to La Jolla Canyon, but this portion of the trail has been closed since 2015 due to rock and mudslides. The picturesque backdrop beneath Boney Mountain's spiny ridge is a photographer's and nature lover's dream.

Just after the pond, continue left at the trail junction. The route opens up here, and the views all look downward into the open valley grasslands. The navy's watchful communication dish sits atop Laguna Peak and moves every so often; those paying attention can even see it in action. For the remainder of the hike, stay straight and veer right at all junctions, enjoying the scenery and the serenity of this magical, peaceful, and historic place.

Miles and Directions

0.0 Start by heading northeast up the Chumash Trail.

0.8 Turn right onto the Mugu Peak use trail.

1.2 Arrive atop Mugu Peak. Continue southeast along the trail.

1.4 Veer left and straight at the Y junction.

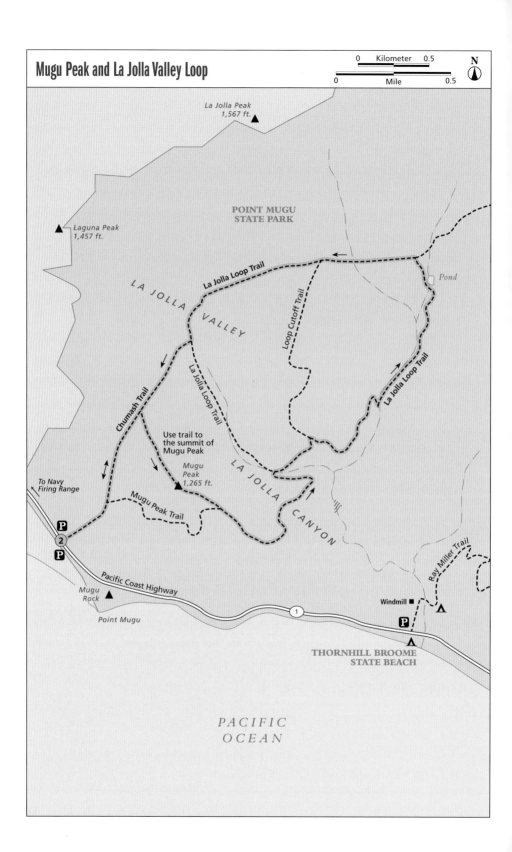

Mugu Peak and La Jolla Valley Loop

0   Kilometer   0.5

0   Mile   0.5

N

La Jolla Peak
1,567 ft.

POINT MUGU
STATE PARK

Laguna Peak
1,457 ft.

Pond

La Jolla Loop Trail

LA JOLLA VALLEY

Loop Cutoff Trail

La Jolla Loop Trail

La Jolla Loop Trail

Chumash Trail

Use trail to
the summit of
Mugu Peak

Mugu
Peak
1,265 ft.

LA JOLLA CANYON

To Navy
Firing Range

Mugu Peak Trail

Ray Miller Trail

P
2
P

Pacific Coast Highway

Windmill ■

Mugu
Rock

1

P

Point Mugu

THORNHILL BROOME
STATE BEACH

PACIFIC
OCEAN

2.2 Turn right onto La Jolla Loop Trail.

3.0 Turn left onto La Jolla Loop Trail.

3.6 Turn left to stay on La Jolla Loop Trail/Fire Road.

4.0 Continue straight on the La Jolla Loop Trail at the intersection with Loop Cutoff Trail.

4.9 Stay straight and to the right at the junction with La Jolla Loop Trail.

5.2 Stay right and continue down the Chumash Trail.

6.0 Arrive back at the trailhead and parking area.

Hike Information

Local information: California State Parks, 818-880-0363; Santa Monica Mountains National Recreation Area, 805-370-2301

Camping: Leo Carrillo State Park campgrounds, Malibu Creek State Park, Topanga State Park Campground, Point Mugu State Park Campground, McGrath State Beach, Emma Wood State Beach, California State Park campgrounds reservations, 800-444-7275; customer service, 800-695-2269; www.reservecalifornia.com

3 Mishe Mokwa

The showcase hike of the Santa Monica Mountains, this route has it all: spectacular vistas, strange geology, wildflowers, varying plant communities, and multiple eco-systems. Although not incredibly difficult, strenuous, or long, the hike is about the perfect length for those looking to get a sample of what the Santa Monica Mountains National Recreation Area has to offer. Children and adults alike will enjoy the points of interest scattered remarkably evenly along the route.

Start: At the Sandstone Peak parking lot 6.3 miles north of CA 1 on Yerba Buena Road
Distance: 6-mile lollipop
Hiking time: About 3 hours
Difficulty: Moderate
Trail surface: Single-track dirt trail and dirt road
Nearest town: Malibu
County: Ventura
Other trail users: Bicyclists and equestrian users allowed only on the Backbone Trail
Canine compatibility: Leashed dogs permitted
Trailhead facilities/amenities: Picnic areas at trailhead and Split Rock; no restrooms or water

Land status: National recreation area
Fees and permits: None
Schedule: Open year-round; bring ample water and protection from the sun, can be hot on summer days
Maps: USGS Newbury Park, CA, and Triunfo Pass, CA; www.nps.gov/samo/planyourvisit/loader.cfm?csModule=security/getfile&PageID=376833
Trail contacts: Circle X Ranch, 12896 Yerba Buena Rd., Malibu, CA, 90265. Santa Monica Mountains National Recreation Area, 401 W. Hillcrest Dr., Thousand Oaks, CA, 91360; www.nps.gov/samo; 805-370-2301

Finding the trailhead: From Los Angeles take the Pacific Coast Highway/CA 1 for 24.7 miles north and west of Sunset Boulevard. Turn right onto Yerba Buena Road and drive north for 6.3 miles. The Sandstone Peak parking lot is on the left-hand side of the road. GPS: 34°06'41.5"N 118°55'35.7"W

The Hike

The trail begins humbly, leading up and away from an unsightly dirt parking lot along a gated road toward what appears to be a set of barren summits. As unassuming as the intro to the hike is, the route quickly becomes breathtakingly beautiful. It climbs rapidly up the dirt road for the first 0.25 mile, gaining nearly 300 feet before the trail junction. At the junction, follow the branch to the right and walk along the more gentle Mishe Mokwa Trail. Here, the trail levels off, and the rest of the route follows an incredibly gentle incline, gaining only 700 feet over a 3-mile stretch.

As soon as the trail becomes single-track, the views begin to open up into the canyons that serve as a drainage for Lake Sherwood. From Triunfo Pass to the various outcroppings of Boney Mountain, the views are spectacular. As close to civilization as this hike is, it certainly does not feel that way. It is difficult to believe the machinations

The andesite breccia volcanic formations of the Boney Mountain region along the Mishe Mokwa Trail are eerily awesome. Photo by Allen Riedel.

of downtown Los Angeles are a mere 20 miles away, yet they are . . . and the beauty of this natural area is left to the hiker to enjoy.

Because people have begun hiking this trail in both directions, it feels a little more traveled than it really is. This trail is no secret, though if you are able to get away mid-week, you may get to have the trail mostly to yourself. On weekends, the parking lot can be full to overflowing, although on weekdays, one or two cars is the norm. This is a well-used trail, and many count it as an all-time favorite. It is easy to understand why. Time this trip for the spring and a fantastic wildflower display is sure to be in the works, though the lupine, wallflower, and buckwheat put on a pretty good show for much of the year.

The narrow trail hugs the side of the canyon and offers jaw-dropping views. Just before the trail hits the 1-mile mark and rounds a bend, the first point of interest comes into view. Across the canyon sits an enormous triangular rock reminiscent of Easter Island's giant Moai statues, and it just happens to be precariously balanced atop a smaller outcropping of stone. This natural acrobatic feat has earned the stone the painfully obvious appellation of "Balanced Rock." Although not creative in the naming department, the mammoth boulder is certain to garner everyone's favor and attention.

CHUMASH/TONGVA

The Native Americans of Southern California once thrived on the bounty of the land and the sea. With no immunological resistance to European diseases, entire populations were nearly wiped out by influenza and smallpox in the 1700s and 1800s.

The Chumash and Tongva tribes both navigated the Pacific Ocean in boats called *tomols*. When the Portuguese explorer Juan Rodriguez Cabrillo sailed up the California coast, Tongva and Chumash people sailed out to meet the ships. Whereas the Chumash settled more to the north, and the Tongva inhabited the region that is now Los Angeles County, the two tribes interacted and traded with one another and shared boundaries in what is now the Santa Monica Mountains.

The Spanish brought Christianity, missions, enforced acculturation, and diseases in the 1770s. The Native Americans, their languages, and their traditions have mostly been left to history, but traces remain. In many parks, there are exhibits and cultural centers where visitors can learn about the ways of the past and the amazing people who once inhabited these regions.

As the trail wanders away from Balanced Rock, it begins to enter a riparian canyon along an unnamed creek bed. The trees and bushes grow onto the trail and overhead, giving the route a "wild" feel, quite a bit different from the open cliff-side section that begins the hike. The remnants of the 2018 Woolsey Fire are everywhere in Circle X Ranch and along the Mishe Mokwa, but the streambeds were not wiped out and have recovered nicely to conditions before the fire.

At 1.75 miles, the trail opens into a small clearing near the creek, and a giant boulder that has cracked in half can be walked through, scrambled on, and photographed. This is the second point of high interest along the hike, especially for children, who will marvel at being able to maneuver through the crack. The split in the middle of the rock has also helped to generate another awe-inspiring name . . . wait for it . . . Split Rock. Yes, the names leave a lot to be desired, but hikers will find lots of joy in these simple pleasures. From Split Rock, the hike continues along some more jungle-esque trail for about another mile, at which point the trail opens up into a dirt road and leaves the canyon and its shadier confines.

On the road, the views and geology become the main attraction. Andesite breccia is the name for the volcanic rock that appears similar to sandstone—hence, one of the names given to a peak in the area. The region has a prehistoric feel to it, something akin to *Jurassic Park* or *The Land Before Time*. Pointed conical outcroppings are everywhere, and the scenery is just fantastic. Here, the route becomes convoluted with many road crossings; stay left at the first three, and follow the signs for Inspiration Point/Sandstone Peak when there are signs. The widest road is the main route.

Mishe Mokwa

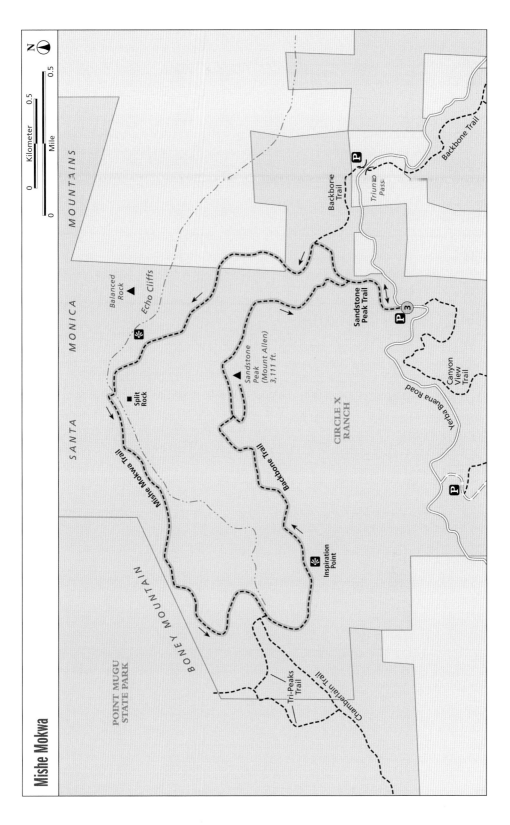

Stay left again at the junction with the Tri-Peaks Trail and follow the route as it curves around toward some water towers and back toward Inspiration Point and Sandstone Peak. At 3.5 miles, stay left again at the junction with the water tower road. At 3.7 miles take the small spur trail on the right and hike 0.1 mile to Inspiration Point. The views are incredible on clear days. The Pacific Ocean glimmers like a gem, and faraway peaks can be seen and even identified with the handy disk plaque affixed by the Boy Scouts.

Head back to the main trail and, at 4.2 miles, take the spur use trail to the top of Sandstone Peak. Alternately called Mount Allen, in honor of a local Boy Scout leader and SMMNRA benefactor (there is a plaque dedicated to his honor atop the summit), the naming request was denied by the USGS because Mr. Allen was still living at the time of the application.

Enjoy the magnificent views and then head down the trail back toward the dirt road leading into the parking area. The way is all downhill and steeply so. Those looking for invigorating uphill cardio workouts can turn the trip around and start backward around the loop.

Miles and Directions

0.0 Start north up the Sandstone Peak Trail.

0.4 Turn right onto the Mishe Mokwa Trail.

0.5 Stay left at the junction with the Backbone Trail.

1.0 Enjoy views of Balanced Rock.

1.75 Arrive at Split Rock and a picnic area.

2.9 Stay straight/left at the road junction.

3.0 Stay left at the junction with Tri-Peaks Trail onto the Backbone Trail.

3.5 Turn left at the junction, heading away from the water tanks.

3.7 Turn right to Inspiration Point. Check out the views and then return to the main trail.

3.9 Turn right onto the Backbone Trail.

4.2 Turn right onto the Sandstone Peak use trail.

4.4 Arrive atop Sandstone Peak (Mount Allen) at 3,111 feet. Return to the main trail.

4.6 Turn right onto the Backbone Trail.

5.6 Stay right onto the roadway, Sandstone Peak Trail, back to the parking area.

6.0 Arrive back at the trailhead and parking lot.

Hike Information

Local information: California State Parks, 818-880-0363; Santa Monica Mountains National Recreation Area, 805-370-2301

Camping: Leo Carrillo State Park campgrounds, Malibu Creek State Park, Topanga State Park Campground, Point Mugu State Park Campground, McGrath State Beach, Emma Wood State Beach, California State Park campgrounds reservations, 800-444-7275; customer service, 800-695-2269; www.reservecalifornia.com

4 The Grotto

Amble along shady trails, across creeks, and through meadows while enjoying scenic vistas of sandstone formations in a seemingly uninhabited portion of Southern California. This trail offers something for everyone: Verdant foliage, waterfalls, abundant wildlife, and boulder-hopping are a few of the perks associated with this trail. The most coveted aspect of this hike is The Grotto, a subterranean cave only attainable by scrambling down boulders. Personal skill is not going to be the only deciding factor in this endeavor because water levels and seasonal changes in the creek will be the preeminent element in your venture.

Start: At the parking lot for Circle X Ranch

Distance: 3 miles out and back

Hiking time: About 2 hours

Difficulty: Easy with some scrambling

Trail surface: Single-track dirt trail and dirt road

Nearest town: Westlake Village

County: Ventura

Other trail users: Joggers

Canine compatibility: Dogs not permitted in the streambed or grotto area

Trailhead facilities/amenities: Restrooms, water, and picnic area at trailhead and ranger station

Land status: National recreation area

Fees and permits: None

Schedule: Open year-round, sunrise to sunset, except during inclement weather; can be hot in the summer, bring ample water

Maps: USGS Triunfo Pass, CA; www.nps.gov/samo/planyourvisit/loader.cfm?csModule=security/getfile&PageID=376833

Trail contacts: Circle X Ranch, 12896 Yerba Buena Rd., Malibu, CA, 90265. Santa Monica Mountains National Recreation Area, 401 W. Hillcrest Dr., Thousand Oaks, CA, 91360; www.nps.gov/samo; 805-370-2301

Finding the trailhead: From Los Angeles, take the Pacific Coast Highway/CA 1 for 24.7 miles north and west of Sunset Boulevard. Turn right onto Yerba Buena Road and drive north for 5.3 miles. The parking lot and visitors' center are on the right-hand side of the road. GPS: 34°06'36.7"N 118°56'13.4"W

The Hike

The first part of the hike is primarily downhill, into what seems like a tunnel of trees heading into the unknown. The 2018 Woolsey Fire burned completely through Circle X Ranch, and the entire Grotto Trail shows the remnants of the fire. The area is recovering, and the natural ecology of fire is just another aspect to enjoy while hiking. Shortly after this downhill stretch, the trail opens up and offers little, if any, shade. The trail has recently been reworked, but, depending on the time of year, it may be a bit washed out and muddy because water naturally runs the course of the downhill trail. Some newer steps have been added at a particularly troubled area, which is just what the route needed.

Spectacular seasonal falls dot the landscape just after rains. Photo by Allen Riedel.

One of the first rewards you will come to around a significant bend is a stream (or brook, depending on the water level) to cross and a grand vista of a 30-foot waterfall when water is flowing. The trees become more abundant and the foliage more verdant. Though damaged by fire, many of the trees survived, especially in the wetter areas on and off the trail. Moss-covered rock walls provide for a unique ambience, feeling as if somehow the trail has taken you far away from the hustle and bustle of Los Angeles.

▶ **Fitness Tip: Use two trekking poles and the strength of your arms to help propel you along the trail for a better workout.**

Continuing up and down the winding trail, be prepared for more creek crossings. Again, depending on the season and water level, these may be a muddy hop over a trickle of water or a rock-balancing feat over a bubbling brook. Make sure to take a good look into the creek water because salamanders are endemic to these streams. You can see these mysterious creatures lounging in the cool water by rocks and sunken logs.

After crossing creeks, viewing waterfalls, and venturing into canopied forests, the trail opens up into a meadow teeming with wildflowers and winged creatures of all varieties, such as butterflies, dragonflies, and birds.

Once crossing the meadow, the trail really begins to give you a flavor of its namesake, The Grotto, as it leads into a tree-lined stream peppered with large and small boulders. The trail becomes a little more difficult to discern at this point, so keep in mind that this is natural for this part of the hike. Follow the trail over the creek bed, and you will see the trail continues on the other side. This part of the hike is where the jackpot lies. For some, the challenge of scrambling over 6- to 8-foot boulders presents a welcome thrill, whereas other, less-adventuresome souls may wish to sit and enjoy the mysterious beauty of the shady creek, perched safely on a boulder. Those who decide to boulder-hop down the creek bed a bit will be generously rewarded with a great watering hole and an underground grotto with a waterfall.

Keep in mind that this option is only ideal dependent on the season and the water level. Sometimes the water level is too high to scramble the boulders, and The Grotto may be out of reach while maintaining personal safety. At other times, the water level is too low and the creek bed may be too dry to enjoy the pool or absent waterfall.

This is definitely a hike that requires perfect timing to enjoy this part of the adventure. But no matter what season, it is certain that this hike will not disappoint. The otherworldly ambience and verdant scenery provides enough variety for everyone with or without a glimpse of The Grotto.

Miles and Directions

0.0 Start from the parking area and head south along the trail.

0.5 Continue straight at the junction with the Canyon View Trail.

1.5 Arrive at The Grotto. Return via same route.

3.0 Arrive back at the trailhead.

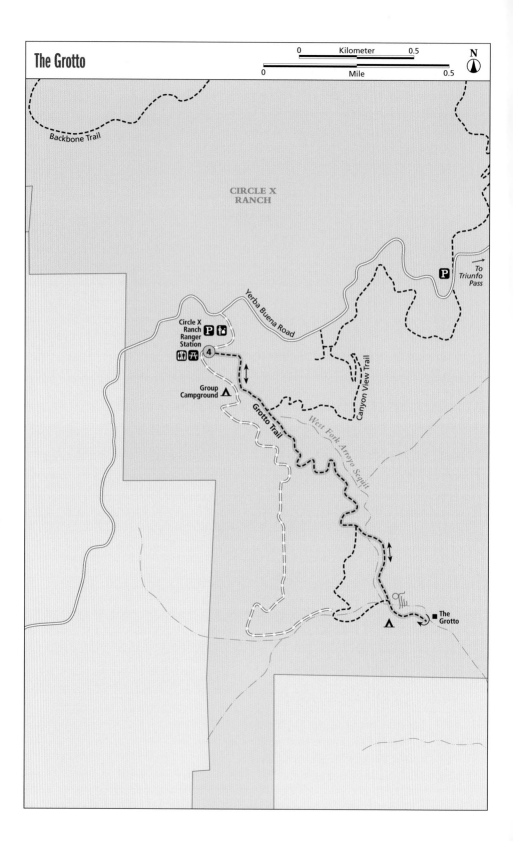

The Grotto

Backbone Trail

Yerba Buena Road

To Triunfo Pass

Circle X Ranch Ranger Station

4

Group Campground

Grotto Trail

Canyon View Trail

West Fork Arroyo Sequit

The Grotto

0   Kilometer   0.5
0   Mile   0.5

N

Bumblebees are effective pollinators of wildflowers like this snapdragon variety. Photo by Allen Riedel.

Hike Information

Local information: California State Parks, 818-880-0363; Santa Monica Mountains National Recreation Area, 805-370-2301

Camping: Leo Carrillo State Park campgrounds, Malibu Creek State Park, Topanga State Park Campground, Point Mugu State Park Campground, McGrath State Beach, Emma Wood State Beach, California State Park campgrounds reservations, 800-444-7275; customer service, 800-695-2269; www.reservecalifornia.com

5 Backbone Trail–Malibu Springs

Hike along the Santa Monica Mountains National Recreation Area's wondrous Backbone Trail, traversing a ridgeline with tremendous unimpeded views of the Pacific coastline. On clear days the vantage is unparalleled. This point-to-point hike requires a car shuttle and provides a fine workout.

Start: Triunfo Pass at the Backbone Trailhead on Yerba Buena Road
Distance: 4.25 miles point to point
Hiking time: About 2 hours
Difficulty: Moderate
Trail surface: Single-track dirt trail and dirt road
Nearest town: Westlake Village
County: Ventura
Other trail users: Bicyclists, joggers, and equestrians

Canine compatibility: Leashed dogs permitted
Trailhead facilities/amenities: None
Land status: National recreation area
Fees and permits: None
Schedule: Open year-round; hot in summer
Maps: USGS Triunfo Pass, CA; www.nps.gov/samo/planyour visit/upload/BBTMap.pdf
Trail contact: Santa Monica Mountains National Recreation Area, 401 W. Hillcrest Dr., Thousand Oaks, CA, 91360; www.nps.gov/samo; 805-370-2301

Finding the trailhead: From Los Angeles take the Pacific Coast Highway/CA 1 north, then turn right onto Yerba Buena Road. Drive north for 7.1 miles. Park in the lot on the right-hand side of the road. Drive a shuttle car 2.1 miles farther along Yerba Buena and park in the right-side turnout area. GPS: 34°06'51.4"N 118°55'05.6"W

The Hike

This hike is solely for people looking to enjoy a Southern California coastal view. It is best taken on clear winter days when the wind is sharp, the breeze is cool, and the visibility is perfect. Conversely, hiking in the heat is dangerous, and hikers should always be prepared with more than enough water and sun protection. It can be splendid to hike here in the fog as well, when the hazy quality gives off an effect similar to Brontë's *Wuthering Heights* and eternal callings for Heathcliff out on the moors. The ecosystem of the region is undoubtedly coastal chaparral, and only in the fog could one remotely consider it to be similar to English countryside. Wildflowers are common from February to May. During years of high rainfall, the period of full bloom transforms the hike into a marvelous jaunt, with golds and purples dominating the mountainsides. The 2018 Woolsey Fire blackened this section of the Santa Monicas, but the area has mostly recovered its former grandeur as coastal chaparral quickly returns to normal after a fire.

▶ **The Backbone Trail system extends nearly 70 miles across the Santa Monica Mountains, from Point Mugu State Park in the west to Will Rogers State Historic Park in the east.**

From the parking area at Triunfo Pass, take the Backbone Trail south. The trail loses elevation for the first 0.25 mile and stays fairly close to Yerba Buena Road, dropping just beneath the roadway. From the beginning, the views are nice but pedestrian compared with what will be coming later in the hike.

The trail meanders up and down for a bit before reaching a steep section that climbs a few hundred feet at the 0.5-mile mark. Here the trail bends westward and follows a long finger toward the end of the ridgeline and the ocean. As the route wraps around and turns southeastward, the views truly open up. To catch that unmatched 360-degree view, turn right (southwest) at 1.25 miles and take the short spur to the top of the mountain at 2,658 feet. The coastline sparkles in crystal blue where wave upon wave crashes on the beach. The spur trail is about 0.4 mile long and gains 300 feet of elevation rapidly.

Purple sage can be found on almost any trail in the Southern California lowlands. Photo by Allen Riedel.

Return to the Backbone Trail. It curves northward once more around 2.5 miles and nears the roadway once again at 3 miles, before heading east and south for more otherworldly vantage points.

At 3.5 miles, the trail turns northward again, heading back toward Yerba Buena Road and the drop-off point for the car shuttle.

Miles and Directions

0.0 Start by heading east and south along the Backbone Trail.

1.25 Reach the spur trail to the summit. Turn right and climb to the summit. Return via the same route.

2.0 Turn right (east) and continue on the Backbone Trail.

2.5 Curve toward the north.

3.0 Approach Yerba Buena Road.

3.5 Veer left (north), heading again to Yerba Buena.

4.25 Arrive at the end of the route and the drop-off point for your car.

Backbone Trail—Malibu Springs

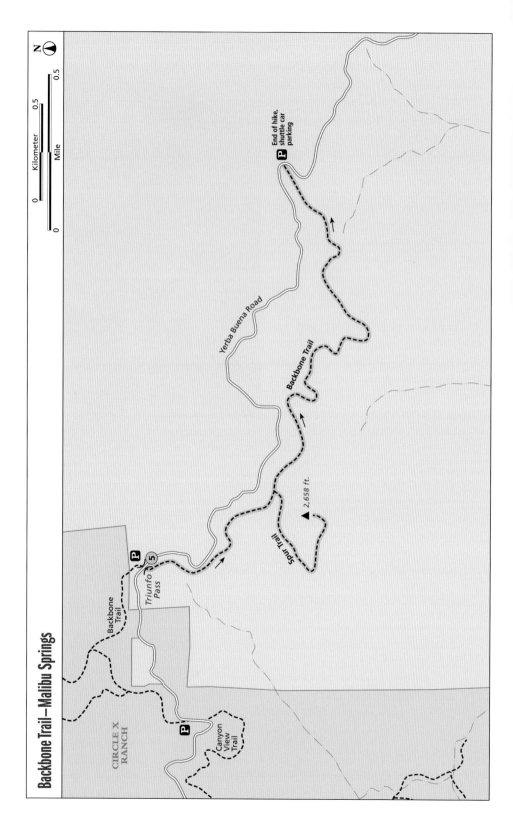

Yerba Buena Road

Backbone Trail

Backbone Trail

CIRCLE X RANCH

Triunfo Pass

Canyon View Trail

Spur Trail

▲ 2,658 ft.

End of hike, shuttle car parking

N

0   Kilometer   0.5

0   Mile   0.5

Hike Information

Local information: California State Parks, 818-880-0363; Santa Monica Mountains National Recreation Area, 805-370-2301

Camping: Leo Carrillo State Park campgrounds, Malibu Creek State Park, Topanga State Park Campground, Point Mugu State Park Campground, McGrath State Beach, Emma Wood State Beach, California State Park campgrounds reservations, 800-444-7275; customer service, 800-695-2269; www.reservecalifornia.com

6 Nicholas Flat

The beauty of Nicholas Flat Natural Park is understated, and the region is surprisingly undervisited. The 2018 Woolsey Fire burned over the entire region, but the mature oaks survived, and the area is recovering nicely. Ridgeline and ocean views here are phenomenal, as is the tranquility. Nicholas Flat feels like an escape from the hustle and bustle of modern life—and it is.

Start: At the end of Decker School Road
Distance: 3.6-mile loop
Hiking time: About 2 hours
Difficulty: Easy
Trail surface: Single-track dirt trail and dirt road
Nearest town: Malibu
County: Los Angeles
Other trail users: Joggers
Canine compatibility: No dogs permitted

Trailhead facilities/amenities: None
Land status: California state park
Fees and permits: None
Schedule: Open year-round; hot in summer
Maps: USGS Triunfo Pass, CA; www.parks.ca .gov/pages/616/files/LeoCarrilloPDF.pdf
Trail contact: Leo Carrillo State Park, 35000 W. Pacific Coast Hwy., Malibu, CA, 90265; www.parks.ca.gov/default.asp?page_id=616; 310-457-8143

Finding the trailhead: From Los Angeles take the Pacific Coast Highway/CA 1 north for 20.6 miles. Turn right onto Decker Road/Decker Canyon Road/CA 23 and drive for 2.4 miles. Turn left onto Decker School Road and drive for 0.2 mile. Veer right and stay on Decker School Road, and drive 1.4 miles to the parking area at the end of the road. Do not block the gate. GPS: 34°04'14.7"N 118°54'23.0"W

The Hike

From the parking area at the end of Decker School Road, continue south through the closed gate along the dirt road. Trails here aren't well marked and there are too many side and use trails to mention. Those with a poorly defined sense of direction and without a GPS device may want to stick solely to the roadways, but the route should be easy enough with the directions that follow. The 2018 Woolsey Fire completely engulfed the Nicholas Flat Natural Preserve and the entirety of Leo Carrillo State Park, but many of the mature oaks in the preserve survived. The park is recovering, though signs of the conflagration are everywhere.

The trail starts down a lovely, wooded oak path with a canopy overhead and poison oak below. An intermittent arroyo flows beside the roadway and the region is quaint and contemplative. The park is a sleepy remnant of erstwhile ranch life in the Santa Monicas, but for the views, this seldom-traveled little section of Leo Carrillo State Park is quite the hidden gem.

At the signed roadway for Nicholas Flat, continue straight toward lovely Nicholas Pond, follow its western contour and turn right, continuing along the trail to the

The views from the ridgeline around Nicholas Flat are glorious. Photo by Monique Riedel.

west. Turn right almost immediately at the fork and follow the route along the more open pathway and not into the arroyo.

The route skirts a hill around a meadow and joins back up with the roadway. Stay to the left at each Y intersection. The route heads south toward a smaller and usually dry pond, following a path sparsely lined with oaks. Turn left just before the pond to take a small detour to the top of a nice vista point. From the top, return to the main path and continue left past the depression/pond. The trail meanders and curves north again. At the next Y intersection, turn left and continue upward. The next vista point is the best one on the hike for taking in views of the Pacific Ocean. Turn left again at the T junction and continue uphill. Topping out at 1,737 feet, this is the tallest peak this far south, so the views are unparalleled. Take them in and return to the T junction, continuing straight ahead.

At times, the trail can be quite a bit overgrown and messy. When it meets back up with Nicholas Flat Road, turn right and then take an immediate left along the ridgeline. At this point, the route begins to climb to the top of a tremendous ridge with some ocean views, but the vistas here are mostly of the surrounding Santa Monica Mountains. Near sunset, this

▶ **Hiking Tip: Use a GPS to mark waypoints before hiking, and download trails and maps in hiking apps, making it easier to find difficult trail crossings and take the correct path.**

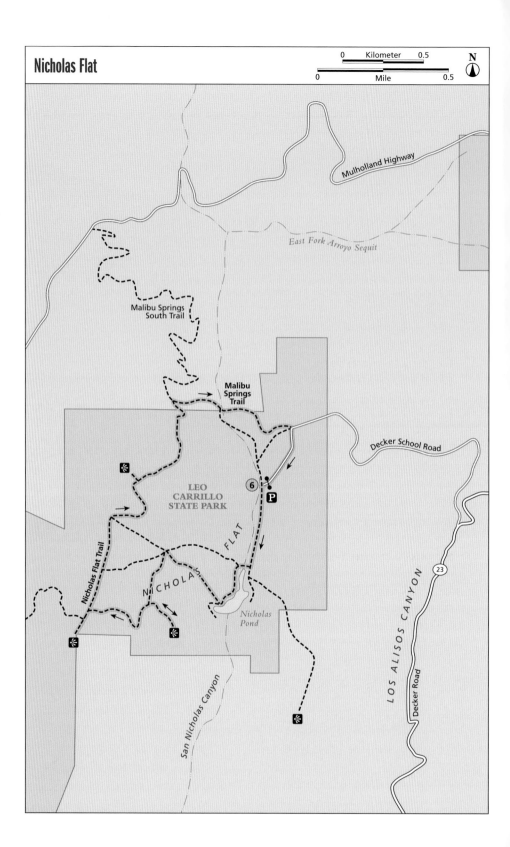

Mulholland Highway

East Fork Arroyo Sequit

Malibu Springs
South Trail

Malibu
Springs
Trail

Decker School Road

LEO
CARRILLO
STATE PARK

6

P

FLAT

23

Nicholas Flat Trail

NICHOLAS

Nicholas
Pond

LOS ALISOS CANYON

Decker Road

San Nicholas Canyon

can be quite the magical place. Hikers will understand the true meaning of "purple mountains majesty" for certain.

At 2.8 miles, the Malibu Springs Trail descends into the Arroyo Sequit sharply as it turns inward back toward Decker School Road. Turn sharply right here and return to the roadway, enjoying the views from this open field. Turn right again at the road and return to the parking area.

Miles and Directions

0.0 Start by heading south beyond the gate, continuing along Decker School Road.

0.3 Continue straight at the junction for Nicholas Flat Road.

0.4 Arrive at Nicholas Pond. Follow the western contour.

0.5 Turn right with the bend in the trail. Then turn right at the Y junction, following the open trail.

0.8 Continue straight and then veer left at the next two junctions. Follow the trail as it turns south.

1.0 Turn left and take a short spur trail to the top of a vista point.

1.2 Arrive at the top of a magnificent unnamed summit. Return to the main trail.

1.4 Turn left back onto the main route.

1.5 Reach a smaller (often dry) pond.

1.7 At the Y junction, veer left and up.

1.8 At the T junction, turn left and up. A bit farther on, continue straight at the main trail junction to the vista point above.

1.9 Arrive atop a spectacular 360-degree vista point with wide-ranging views of the Pacific Ocean. Return to the T junction.

2.0 Continue straight and avoid all turns until the elbow junction with Nicholas Flat Road.

2.2 Turn right onto Nicholas Flat Road. Then turn left onto Malibu Springs Trail.

2.8 Turn sharply right at the T junction for the Malibu Springs Trail. Head east.

3.3 Turn right onto Decker School Road.

3.6 Arrive back at the trailhead and parking area.

Hike Information

Local information: California State Parks, 818-880-0363; Santa Monica Mountains National Recreation Area, 805-370-2301

Camping: Leo Carrillo State Park campgrounds, Malibu Creek State Park, Topanga State Park Campground, Point Mugu State Park Campground, McGrath State Beach, Emma Wood State Beach, California State Park campgrounds reservations, 800-444-7275; customer service, 800-695-2269; www.reservecalifornia.com

7 Charmlee Wilderness Park

It isn't a coincidence that the name Charmlee evokes visions of a charming and magical place. Nestled on a meadowland bluff above the Pacific Coast Highway, Charmlee Wilderness Park is an idyllic setting for hikers of all ages.

Start: At the parking area for Charmlee Wilderness Park off Encinal Canyon Road
Distance: 2.1-mile loop
Hiking time: About 1.5 hours
Difficulty: Easy
Trail surface: Single-track dirt trail and dirt road
Nearest town: Malibu
County: Los Angeles
Other trail users: Joggers, bicyclists, and equestrians
Canine compatibility: Leashed dogs permitted
Trailhead facilities/amenities: All facilities available at trailhead

Land status: Malibu city park
Fees and permits: Parking fee is charged
Schedule: Open year-round, 8 a.m. to sunset daily; can be hot in summer
Maps: USGS Triunfo Pass, CA, and Point Dume, CA; www.ci.malibu.ca.us/download/index.cfm/fuseaction/download/cid/9197/
Trail contact: Charmlee Wilderness Park, 2577 Encinal Canyon Rd., Malibu, CA, 90265; www.ci.malibu.ca.us/index.cfm/fuseaction/Detail Group/CID/3801/NavID/174/; 310-457-7247

Finding the trailhead: From Los Angeles take the Pacific Coast Highway/CA 1 north for 20 miles. Turn right onto Encinal Canyon Road and drive for 3.8 miles. Turn left at the large stone sign onto Carmichael Road and drive for 0.2 mile to the parking area for Charmlee Wilderness Park. GPS: 34°03'32.8"N 118°52'45.5"W

The Hike

The Charmlee Wilderness Area comprises about 530 acres of meadowlands, oak woodlands, wildflower grasslands, and chaparral located conveniently on the coastal bluffs overlooking the Pacific Ocean. There are 9 miles of trails that meander throughout the park, providing an opportunity to stroll among an array of verdant wildflowers, view the remnants of a long-lost ranch house and water tower used during the days of cattle ranching, and revel in breathtaking ocean views. The entire park was consumed in the 2018 Woolsey Fire, but it is recovering nicely and most of the mature oak trees survived the fire, showing signs of life within their natural cycle.

It is said that when Leon and Charmian Schwartz purchased the land in the 1950s, they combined their first names to create the name "Charmlee" for their ranch. The two brothers built an A-frame ranch house, which to date is claimed to be the only residence ever built on the property. The ranch house was eventually destroyed by a wildfire in 1978, but the foundation remains as a relic from a not-so-distant past.

Beach views from the Old Reservoir at Charmlee Wilderness Park. Photo by Allen Riedel.

▶ Hiking Tip: Learn to
identify poison oak during
all seasons. Check for ticks
regularly, especially when
walking through tall grasses.

In June 2003, the City of Malibu obtained ownership of the property and dedicated it as Charmlee Wilderness Park.

The beauty of Charmlee lies not only in its name but also in the variety of choices offered to the casual hiker. This hike is perfect for young children, people with dogs on leashes, and those seeking a serene and relaxing experience. The hike described is only one of the multitude of variations to choose from. Depending on the time of year and climate, any of the trail options in the park will offer an incredible treat.

At the time of writing, the nature center is currently closed, but you may pick up a map and guide, and follow the trail northwest about 0.1 mile toward the old water tower that is made up of a concrete cistern used to provide irrigation and water for the old cattle ranch. The trail up to the old water tower presents an opportunity to spot an abundance of wildflowers. The water tower is perched above the park and offers an overview of the park grounds and the bluffs overlooking the ocean. From this vantage point, follow the main trail to Old Ranch Road and to the Old Ranch foundation. At the foundation, turn left at the junction and continue on Old Ranch Road across a grassy meadowland toward the Old Reservoir on a bluff overlooking the Pacific Ocean. The view from this bluff on a clear day bestows stunning ocean views. From the Old Reservoir, follow the trail east to the oak woodland area.

When you reach the shady woodland area, you will feel as if you have stepped into a different time and place. The oak grove provides a dark and mysterious backdrop in contrast to the openness of the rest of the park. This is a great chance to repose before heading onto the Fire Ecology Trail, which leads back to Old Ranch Road. Returning to the parking area, you can conclude your outing in the Oak Grove picnic area or the picnic area near the entrance of the park.

Due to the verdant nature of the flora and fauna on the trails, take special precautions to watch for ticks and rattlesnakes because this wonderland is teeming with wildlife species that call Charmlee Wilderness their home.

Miles and Directions

0.0 From the parking area, walk northwest toward the nature center.

0.1 Arrive at the nature center. Continue northwest.

0.2 Turn south along the fire road toward the water tower.

0.3 At the fork, veer left below and to the east of the water tower and follow the main route (no sign) to Old Ranch Road (no sign).

0.5 Arrive at Old Ranch Road and turn right toward the ocean, staying on the trail to reach the Old Ranch foundation.

0.6 Turn left at the T junction and stay on Old Ranch Road, following it south across an open meadow toward the Pacific Ocean.

1.1 Reach the Old Reservoir. Turn east and follow the loop trail through the oak woodland.

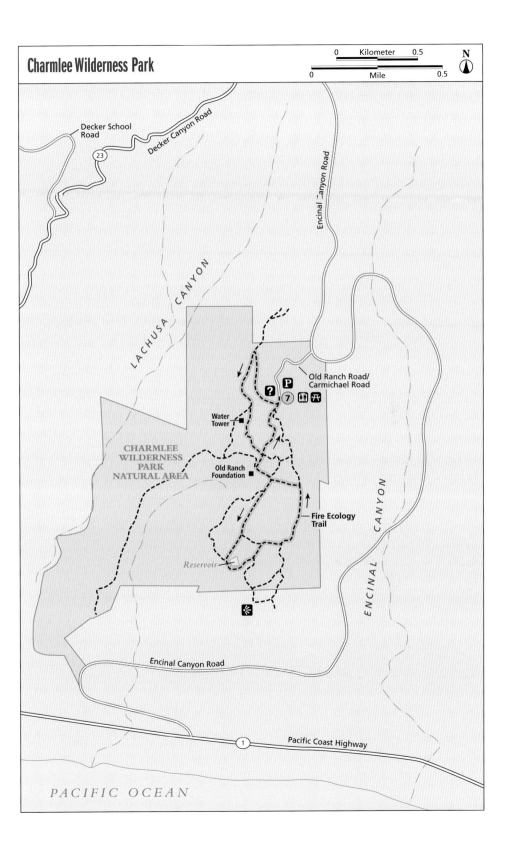

Charmlee Wilderness Park

Decker School Road

Decker Canyon Road

23

Encinal Canyon Road

LACHUSA CANYON

Old Ranch Road/
Carmichael Road

P

7

Water
Tower

CHARMLEE
WILDERNESS
PARK
NATURAL AREA

Old Ranch
Foundation

Fire Ecology
Trail

ENCINAL CANYON

Reservoir

Encinal Canyon Road

1

Pacific Coast Highway

PACIFIC OCEAN

0   Kilometer   0.5

0   Mile   0.5

N

1.4 Reach the oak woodland and turn north along the Fire Ecology Trail.

1.6 Turn left to get back onto Old Ranch Road and follow it back to the parking area.

2.1 Arrive back at the trailhead and parking area.

Hike Information

Local information: California State Parks, 818-880-0363; Santa Monica Mountains National Recreation Area, 805-370-2301

Camping: Leo Carrillo State Park campgrounds, Malibu Creek State Park, Topanga State Park Campground, Point Mugu State Park Campground, McGrath State Beach, Emma Wood State Beach, California State Park campgrounds reservations, 800-444-7275; customer service, 800-695-2269; www.reservecalifornia.com

8 Paramount Ranch

A stroll down Hollywood Boulevard is not your only option to walk in the footsteps of the stars; a visit to this movie ranch will conjure up visions of old Westerns and even more modern films. Paramount Ranch has been the site of a variety of films, from television to the big screen and is the only National Park unit dedicated to interpreting US film history. Though much of the park burned in the 2018 Woolsey Fire and only the church and the train station remain, the park still evokes images of film and television history.

Start: At the parking area for Paramount Ranch State Park

Distance: 1-mile lollipop

Hiking time: About 1 hour

Difficulty: Easy

Trail surface: Single-track dirt trail and dirt road

Nearest town: Malibu

County: Los Angeles

Other trail users: Joggers, bicyclists, and equestrians

Canine compatibility: Leashed dogs permitted

Trailhead facilities/amenities: All facilities available

Land status: National recreation area

Fees and permits: None

Schedule: Open year-round, 8 a.m. to sunset; can be hot in summer

Maps: USGS Point Dume, CA; www.nps.gov/ samo/planyourvisit/loader.cfm?csModule =security/getfile&PageID=376834

Trail contacts: Paramount Ranch, 2903 Cornell Rd., Agoura Hills, CA, 91301. Santa Monica Mountains National Recreation Area, 401 West Hillcrest Dr., Thousand Oaks, CA, 91360; www.nps.gov/samo/planyourvisit/ paramountranch.htm; 805-370-2301

Finding the trailhead: From the intersection of CA 134, US 101, and CA 170 in Los Angeles, take US 101 north and west for 21.6 miles. Take Exit 36 for Kanan Road. Turn left onto Kanan Road and drive for 0.2 mile. Turn left onto Sideway/Cornell Road and drive for 2.1 miles. Turn right at Paramount Ranch Drive and go 0.1 mile. Turn left onto Paramount Ranch Road and follow it 0.1 mile to the visitors' center and parking area. GPS: 34°06'57.9"N 118°45'17.0"W

The Hike

Paramount Ranch was purchased from the Rancho Las Virgenes land grant governed by the Treaty of Guadalupe Hidalgo in 1927 for use as a "movie ranch," a place developed by Hollywood filmmakers to create a variety of distant locations right in their own backyard. With the ability to fabricate locations such as San Francisco, Montana, Africa, a South Seas island, and even colonial Massachusetts, combined with the convenience and economic advantage of not having to pack up and travel to distant locales, filmmaking boomed at Paramount Ranch.

Despite the fact that the property changed ownership several times from 1957 to 1980, moviemaking continued. The National Park Service gained ownership of part

MOVIES IN THE MOUNTAINS

The Santa Monica Mountains are no stranger to the city to the south. The Hollywood film industry has used the mountains to represent nearly every continent of the world, from Africa to South America. Many of the more prominent locations have been used so many times that hiking within park boundaries creates a sense of nostalgia and déjà vu.

A list of some of the movies and TV shows filmed in the SMMNRA: *The Rifleman*; *Van Helsing*; *The Love Bug*; *Reds*; *Herbie Rides Again*; *Geronimo*; *Wells Fargo*; *The Adventures of Tom Sawyer*; *The Andy Griffith Show*; *Platoon*; *The Creature from the Black Lagoon*; *M.A.S.H.*; *Beau Geste*; *Bonanza*; *Spartacus*; *Planet of the Apes*; *Lassie*; *Dynasty*; *Murder She Wrote*; *True Blood*; *ER*; *How I Met Your Mother*; *Will and Grace*; *Star Trek*; *On Golden Pond*; *Kindergarten Cop*; *Minority Report*; *Rambo II*; *Bone Tomahawk*

of the original ranch in the 1980s and restored the old movie set. The list of stars that have graced the set is a genuine who's who of Hollywood's elite. Movie legends such as Cary Grant, John Wayne, and Gary Cooper, along with Lucille Ball, Marlene Dietrich, Diane Keaton, and Jane Seymour are among the hundreds of Hollywood A-listers who have walked the streets of Paramount Ranch. Even music legend Ringo Starr filmed his music video "Act Naturally" on location at the ranch. This is the only National Park site that doubles as a movie set. More contemporary films and TV series, such as HBO's *Carnivale* and *Westworld* and Showtime's *Weeds,* have been filmed on location at Paramount Ranch.

Sadly, in the 2018 Woolsey Fire, almost the entirety of the western town at Paramount Ranch burned, and only two notable buildings remain. Plans to rebuild at least a portion of the set are in the works, and fundraising is currently ongoing through the National Park Service.

The park offers several trails, many aptly named for the set for which it was built or for other activities that took place along the trail. Some of the most popular trails are the Hacienda Trail, the Backdrop Trail, and the Coyote Canyon Trail. Along the Paramount Ranch Trail, fans of *Dr. Quinn Medicine Woman* will recognize the train station used extensively in the series. The Backdrop Trail is famous for its ability to accommodate most any kind of shot because it lacks modern telephone poles and is famously generic in nature. The Coyote Canyon Trail is an easy stroll that travels through the heart of the now burned western town and onto the hillside above the town to a picnic overlook tucked away between the shrubs.

The visitors' center located at the parking area provides brochures and maps of the park that document its eclectic history. From the visitors' center, follow the road toward the remnants of the old western town, visible on the other side of a wooden bridge crossing a creek.

The open space around Paramount Ranch is pastoral and idyllic. Photo by Allen Riedel.

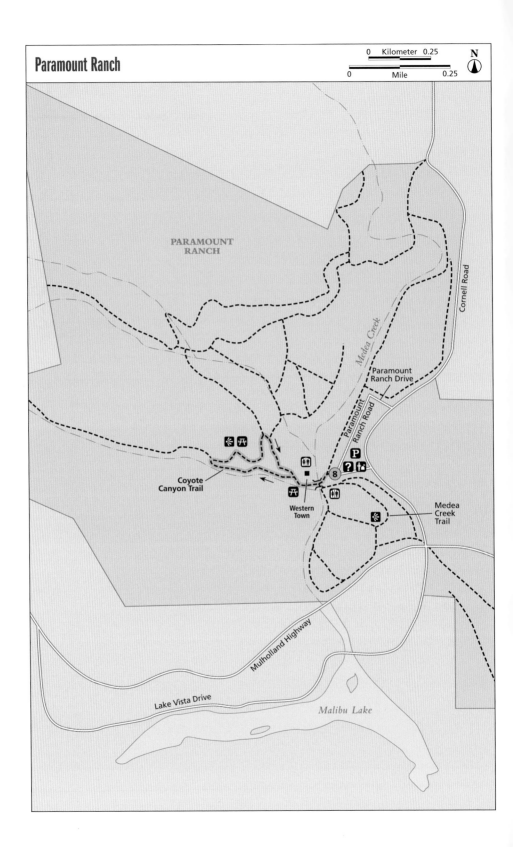

Paramount Ranch

N

0   Kilometer   0.25
0   Mile   0.25

PARAMOUNT
RANCH

Medea Creek

Cornell Road

Paramount
Ranch Drive

Paramount Ranch Road

Coyote
Canyon Trail

8

Western
Town

Medea
Creek
Trail

Mulholland Highway

Lake Vista Drive

Malibu Lake

Once you have walked through what is left of the town, turn left at the Coyote Canyon Trail sign. The trail follows along a tributary of Medea Creek.

At about 0.4 mile veer to the right at the unmaintained trail junction; here the public trail ends at a private property border. The trail is lined with shrubbery and chaparral; depending on the time of year, be aware that wildlife abounds, especially ticks, wasps, and bees. At about 0.5 mile, take a left turn where the trail ascends to the overlook that boasts an intimate picnic area.

From the overlook, continue down the Coyote Canyon Trail, turning left to follow the main trail loop. The trail gradually descends back toward the old western town and into the parking lot by the visitors' center. A short optional excursion along the Medea Creek Trail, up to the Western Town Overlook, displays the Old West set from a different vantage point and is a great photo opportunity to capture the park from a distance. Visitors are free to explore a multitude of trails in the park.

Western wallflower is common in mountain regions throughout Southern California. Photo by Allen Riedel. (Hike 31)

Miles and Directions

0.0 Start by heading south on the road from the visitors' center and walk west toward the creek.

0.1 Walk across the bridge to the western town film set.

0.25 Turn left down Coyote Canyon Trail. Follow along the creek bed.

0.4 Stay right at the unmaintained trail junction.

0.5 Turn left for the picnic overlook. Head back to the Coyote Canyon Trail.

0.6 Turn left to continue along the main trail loop.

0.75 Continue south on the road back to the western town set.

0.9 Walk across the bridge and back to the visitors' center.

1.0 Return to the trailhead and parking area.

Hike Information

Local information: California State Parks, 818-880-0363; Santa Monica Mountains National Recreation Area, 805-370-2301

Camping: Leo Carrillo State Park campgrounds, Malibu Creek State Park, Topanga State Park Campground, Point Mugu State Park Campground, McGrath State Beach, Emma Wood State Beach, California State Park campgrounds reservations, 800-444-7275; customer service, 800-695-2269; www.reservecalifornia.com

9 Calabasas Peak

Hike through the strange formations of Red Rock Canyon Park up to the high valley viewpoints of Calabasas Peak.

Start: At the end of Red Rock Road in the parking area for Red Rock Canyon Park
Distance: 5 miles out and back
Hiking time: About 2.5 hours
Difficulty: Moderate
Trail surface: Dirt road
Nearest town: Woodland Hills
County: Los Angeles
Other trail users: Joggers, bicyclists, and equestrians
Canine compatibility: Leashed dogs permitted
Trailhead facilities/amenities: Water, restrooms
Land status: Regional park

Fees and permits: Parking fee is charged
Schedule: Open year-round, 8 a.m. to sunset daily; hot in the summer and afternoons
Maps: USGS Malibu Beach, CA; www.lamoun tains.com/maps/redRock.pdf
Trail contacts: Red Rock Canyon Park, 23601 W. Red Rock Rd., Topanga, CA, 90290. Mountains Recreation & Conservation Authority, 570 West Avenue 26, Suite 100, Los Angeles, CA, 90065; 323-221-9944. Santa Monica Mountains National Recreation Area, 401 W. Hillcrest Dr., Thousand Oaks, CA, 91360; www .lamountains.com/parks.asp?parkid=47; 805-370-2301

Finding the trailhead: From Los Angeles, take US 101 north and west. Take Exit 27B for CA 27/South Topanga Boulevard; turn right and drive for 1.6 miles. Turn right onto Mulholland Drive and drive for 0.5 mile. Turn left onto Mulholland Highway and drive for 1.7 miles. Turn left onto Old Topanga Canyon Road and drive for 1.6 miles. Turn right and stay on Old Topanga Canyon Road for another 1.8 miles. Turn right onto Red Rock Road. Stay on Red Rock Road for 0.8 mile and park in the parking area. GPS: 34°06'21.8"N 118°38'15.0"W

The Hike

Red Rock Canyon as a namesake is about as common as park appellations come. The park isn't even the only Red Rock Canyon in California, let alone the dozen or so that share the title in the western United States. Regardless, this is quite a nice little park with some colorful sandstone outcroppings. There are side trails that lead to more exploration within the park, but this route follows Red Rock Road to a T junction with the Calabasas Peak Motorway and climbs to the summit of Calabasas Peak.

At 2,165 feet, the peak is one of the tallest along the eastern end of the Santa Monica mountain chain. As such, the views are fairly spectacular. One can make out a teeny portion of the Pacific Ocean. On clear days, the San Fernando Valley is almost entirely within view, along with parts of Los Angeles. The tall peaks of Saddle and Temescal are nearby, so the summit of Calabasas isn't prominently situated to view the

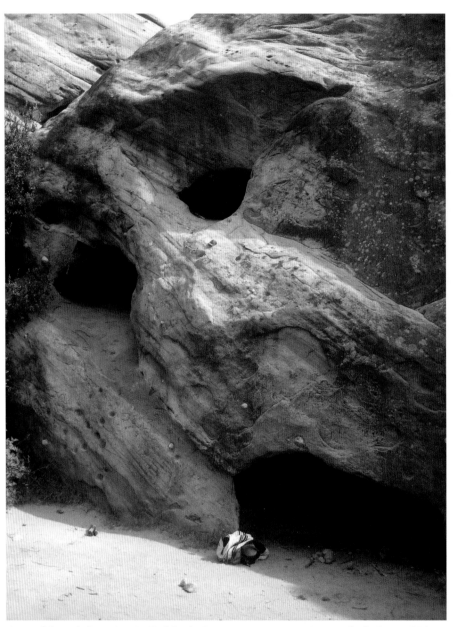

Some of the rock formations in Red Rock Canyon are quite stunning—and a little scary! Photo by Monique Riedel.

entire southland, but the views from on high are quite worthwhile, especially for the relative easiness of the hike itself.

From the parking area in Red Rock Canyon, follow the road past the restrooms and ranger residence into the canyon itself. After about 0.3 mile, a large, cave-filled,

Volcanic rock at Red Rock Canyon Park. Photo by Monique Riedel.

red rock formation appears on the left. This is a good place for a short side exploration, and a climb to the top reveals the entire canyon system and some good views to boot.

The route continues along the fire road, and the biggest problem with the hike is the unsightly aboveground wires that follow the roadway through the canyon. The road begins to climb and gains around 400 feet before reaching a bench high above the canyon. Here, an actual resting bench is placed at the overlook where the views aren't too bad.

Turn right and continue walking up Calabasas Peak Motorway toward the summit. The road travels through similar uplifted rocks that seem to jut from the earth as the route nears the peak. Once on top, the views of the surrounding countryside are fairly spectacular. Because this hike takes place in the valley, it is wise to go when temperatures are cooler; at those times the skies are clearer as well.

Enjoy the views and return via the same route.

▶ **Much of the parkland in the Santa Monica Mountains National Recreation Area was donated by private individuals and movie stars.**

Calabasas Peak

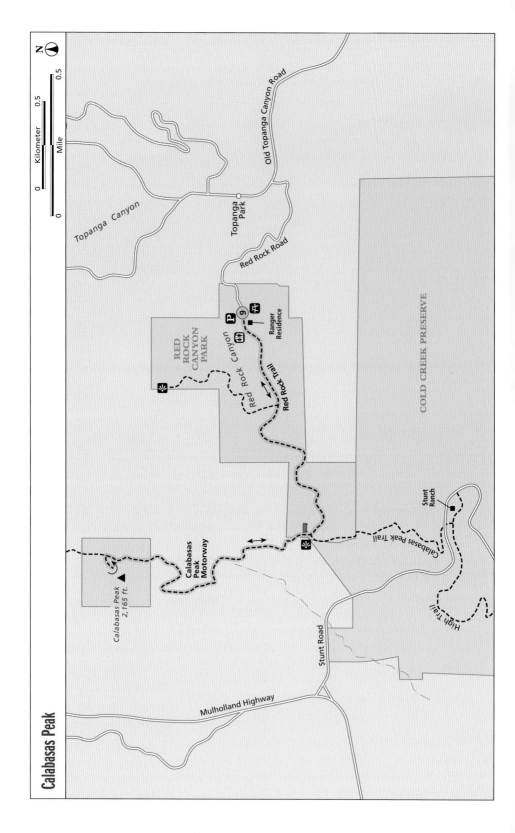

Topanga Canyon

Old Topanga Canyon Road

Topanga Park

Red Rock Road

RED ROCK CANYON PARK

Red Rock Canyon

Red Rock Trail

P

9

Ranger Residence

COLD CREEK PRESERVE

Stunt Ranch

Calabasas Peak Trail

High Trail

Calabasas Peak Motorway

Calabasas Peak 2,165 ft.

Stunt Road

Mulholland Highway

N

Kilometer

0   0.5

0   0.5

Mile

Miles and Directions

0.0 From the parking area, head west down Red Rock Road.

1.2 Turn right at the T junction toward the summit of Calabasas Peak.

2.5 Arrive on the summit of Calabasas Peak. Return via the same route.

5.0 Arrive back at the trailhead and parking area.

Hike Information

Local information: Red Rock Canyon Park, 23601 W. Red Rock Rd., Topanga, CA, 90290. Mountains Recreation & Conservation Authority, 570 West Avenue 26, Suite 100, Los Angeles, CA, 90065; 323-221-9944. Santa Monica Mountains National Recreation Area, 401 W. Hillcrest Dr., Thousand Oaks, CA, 91360; www.lamountains .com/parks.asp?parkid=47; 805-370-2301

Camping: Leo Carrillo State Park campgrounds, Malibu Creek State Park, Topanga State Park Campground, Point Mugu State Park Campground, California State Park campgrounds reservations, 800-444-7275; customer service, 800-695-2269; www .reservecalifornia.com

10 Solstice Canyon Rising Sun Loop

Climb up out of Solstice Canyon for ocean views and then descend to a waterfall and ruins in an historic Los Angeles canyon.

Start: At the Solstice Canyon Education Shelter and the TRW Loop Trailhead
Distance: 3 miles out and back
Hiking time: About 1.5 hours
Difficulty: Easy
Trail surface: Dirt road, trail, and pavement
Nearest town: Malibu
County: Los Angeles
Other trail users: Joggers, equestrians, and bicyclists
Canine compatibility: Leashed dogs permitted
Trailhead facilities/amenities: Water, restrooms

Land status: National Recreation Area
Fees and permits: None
Schedule: Open year-round, 8 a.m. to sunset daily; hot in the summer and afternoons
Maps: USGS Malibu Beach, CA; https://www.nps.gov/samo/planyourvisit/upload/Solstice-Canyon_v3.pdf
Trail contacts: Santa Monica Mountains National Recreation Area, 26876 Mulholland Hwy., Calabasas, CA, 91302; https://www.nps.gov/samo/planyourvisit/solsticecanyon.htm; 805-370-2301

Finding the trailhead: From Santa Monica, take CA 1 north and west. Turn right onto Coral Canyon Road for 0.2 mile, continue onto Solstice Canyon Road, and keep right for 0.3 mile. Park at the Education Shelter. GPS: 34°02'16.4"N 118°44'50.7"W

The Hike

Solstice Canyon is a popular coastal park right in the middle of the Santa Monica Mountains. Multitudes of visitors come to the canyon to hike, exercise, and get out into nature with friends. There certainly is splendor here, even though the canyon has been repeatedly stricken by fire, evidence of which can be seen all around, including the 2018 Woolsey Fire. The canyon itself was relatively unscathed from the last conflagration, unlike the surrounding hillside on the Rising Sun Trail and much of the surrounding wildlands and parks in the SMMNRA.

From the Education Shelter, hike up the hillside along the TRW Loop Trail for 0.2 mile to the signed junction with the Rising Sun Loop, turn right, and follow it for 1.3 miles along the hillside, which has nearly recovered from the fire. A shorter version of this hike can be had by staying on the TRW trail and going out and coming back on Solstice Canyon in an inverse lollipop. But if you are looking for views, and the day is cool, follow the walls of the canyon for some good cardio, until you are ready to descend onto Roberts Road. Getting off the main path will, without a doubt, decrease the number of people that you will see, but it will also greatly increase exposure to the midday sun.

Exploring the ruins in Solstice Canyon feels like walking through the past. Photo by Allen Riedel.

After descending, turn right up the canyon and hike 0.1 mile to the waterfall. Explore the ruins of the Tropical Terrace, built in 1952. Paul Williams, the famous Black architect, designed the ranch house, which burned to the ground in the 1982 Dayton Canyon Fire. The Roberts family called their dream house Tropical Terrace, and even from the ruins, it is easy to see how lovely a structure this was. Behind the house sits a charming little waterfall, and despite its diminutive stature, it is absolutely one of the most beautiful falls in all of Southern California. The canyon itself is lovely and lush, filled with a beautiful riparian habitat and a wonderful trickling stream. Return down the roadway for an easy and shaded stroll.

Miles and Directions

0.0 From the parking area, take the TRW Loop Trail north for 0.5 mile.

0.2 Turn right at the junction for the Rising Sun Trail.

0.6 Arrive at the junction with the El Nido Trail, stay right on the Rising Sun Trail.

1.8 Arrive at the junction with Roberts Road, turn right to head to the waterfall.

1.9 Stop at the waterfall.

2.0 Explore the Tropical Terrace ruins. Turn right and follow Roberts Road/Solstice Canyon Road south back through the canyon.

2.3 Pass an offshoot trail.

2.4 Pass the exit of the offshoot trail.

2.5 Take the spur trail and bridge to the Keller House Ruins.

2.6 Continue south on Solstice Canyon Road.

3.0 Return to the parking area.

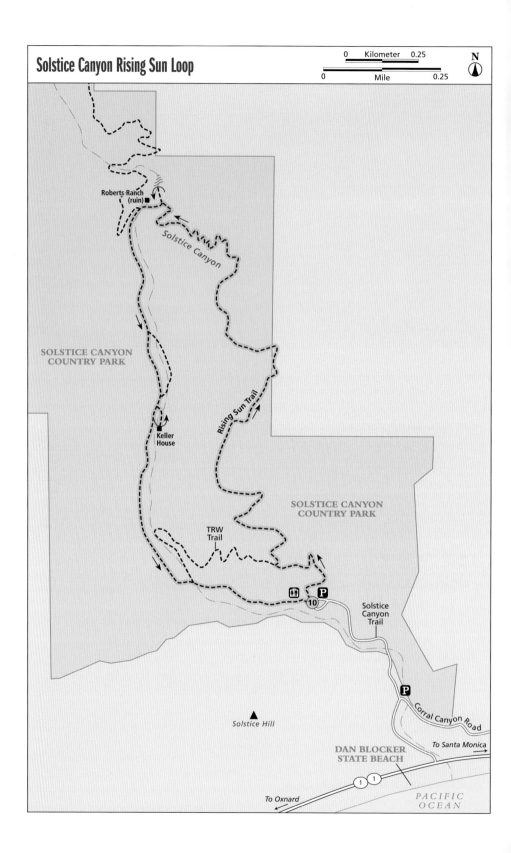

Solstice Canyon Rising Sun Loop

0   Kilometer   0.25

0   Mile   0.25

N

Roberts Ranch (ruin)

Solstice Canyon

SOLSTICE CANYON COUNTRY PARK

Rising Sun Trail

Keller House

TRW Trail

SOLSTICE CANYON COUNTRY PARK

10

P

Solstice Canyon Trail

P

Corral Canyon Road

Solstice Hill

DAN BLOCKER STATE BEACH

To Santa Monica

1   1

To Oxnard

PACIFIC OCEAN

A small waterfall delights behind the ruins of Roberts Ranch. Photo by Allen Riedel.

Hike Information

Local information: Santa Monica Mountains National Recreation Area, 26876 Mulholland Hwy., Calabasas, CA, 91302; https://www.nps.gov/samo/planyourvisit/solsticecanyon.htm; 805-370-2301

Camping: Leo Carrillo State Park campgrounds, Malibu Creek State Park, Topanga State Park Campground, Point Mugu State Park Campground, California State Park campgrounds reservations, 800-444-7275; customer service, 800-695-2269; www.reservecalifornia.com

11 Temescal Gateway Park

Located in the heart of Pacific Palisades, a prestigious community also known as "Where the Mountains Meet the Sea," Temescal Gateway Park presents a prodigious opportunity to escape to what seems like a million miles from civilization, while remaining only minutes from the hustle and bustle of Los Angeles, Santa Monica, and Malibu.

Start: At the large parking area at the park entrance on Temescal Canyon Road
Distance: 3.25-mile lollipop
Hiking time: About 2 hours
Difficulty: Moderate
Trail surface: Dirt road, single-track dirt trail, and pavement
Nearest town: Pacific Palisades
County: Los Angeles
Other trail users: Joggers
Canine compatibility: Leashed dogs permitted (dogs not permitted in Topanga Canyon State Park)
Trailhead facilities/amenities: All facilities available

Land status: Regional park, California state park
Fees and permits: Parking fee is charged
Schedule: Open year-round, 7 a.m. to sunset; can be hot in summer
Maps: USGS Malibu Beach, CA; www.lamountains.com/maps/temescal.pdf
Trail contacts: Santa Monica Mountains National Recreation Area, 401 W. Hillcrest Dr., Thousand Oaks, CA, 91360; Temescal Gateway Park, 15601 Sunset Blvd., Pacific Palisades, CA, 90272; 310-454-1395. Mountains Recreation & Conservation Authority, 570 West Avenue 26, Suite 100, Los Angeles, CA, 90065; 323-221-9944; www.lamountains.com/parks.asp?parkid=58

Finding the trailhead: From the intersection of I-10 and the Pacific Coast Highway/CA 1, drive 3.2 miles north on Pacific Coast Highway. Turn right onto Temescal Canyon Road and drive for 1.1 miles to the parking area on the left. GPS: 34°03'00.7"N 118°31'49.5"W

The Hike

What began as an enclave for intellectuals and luminaries, founded by Reverend Charles Scott in 1922 as part of the Chautauqua movement, has been transformed into one of the most popular destinations in the Santa Monica Mountains. The Chautauqua movement originated at Chautauqua Lake, New York, as a means to establish assemblies for families with stimulating topics concerning public issues, literature, art, science, and entertainment. This movement was highly popular in the early 1900s. In his desire to create one such community, Reverend Scott developed the area bound by the Santa Monica Mountains and the Pacific coastline, which became known as Pacific Palisades.

Despite that you may feel as if you are miles from civilization, there are a few reminders that you are still within the confines of the city. Be aware, while you are

Enjoy this charming waterfall before finishing your hike. Photo by Monique Riedel.

▶ **Fitness Tip: Set realistic goals for trip times and try to maintain them.**

in the parking area, which has plenty of space to park, that there are traffic cameras at each stop sign. The self-parking iron ranger is conspicuously placed in the parking area and requires a fee that must be placed in an envelope and dropped into the receptacle. Make sure to display your receipt properly in your vehicle as instructed on the envelope to avoid any costly parking violations. Because this is a popular trail, the parking regulations are strictly enforced by patrolling park rangers who are as tireless as automatons.

At the trailhead, there are informational placards with historical information and photos of the original Methodist settlement founded by the Reverend Charles Scott. There is also a visitors' center and a public restroom conveniently located at the onset of your journey. Aside from hiking, Temescal Gateway Park is host to a variety of activities, as well as home to several guest cabins and areas that may be reserved for private use.

The initial part of this trail is paved for a short bit, but don't be fooled: It quickly takes on the form of a traditional dirt road at 0.3 mile. Veer right at the intersection. Continue up the trail to the north, winding up a somewhat steep ridge along Temescal Canyon. Poison oak is abundant along this trail, so be cautious of your step and do not stray off the path.

Keep in mind that long stretches of the trail do not offer shade or respite from the heat. Bring plenty of water for hydration because the moderate ascent may seem extreme in hot weather. Once you have traversed the canyon ridge, through patches of dense foliage and open spaces, you will arrive at a charming waterfall and wooden footbridge. Boulders and strategically placed rocks are convenient for a tranquil interlude before forging on toward the next part of the trail.

After crossing the footbridge, the trail continues to ascend the other side of the canyon ridge, into a more dense area of vegetation lined with coastal chaparral, wildflowers, and of course, poison oak. The trail continues to wind upward; at 1.7 miles, veer left at the junction toward a windy plateau carpeted with profuse shrubbery. Here, you have reached the pinnacle of the trail. On a clear day you will be rewarded with magnificent 360-degree unimpeded views of the Pacific Ocean and the coastal communities to the north and south of Pacific Palisades.

From the plateau, the trail descends once again into dense foliage along the ridge of the canyon. Be mindful of trail etiquette during your descent as this is a moderate to heavily populated trail and others may be ascending. At this juncture, the trail is, at times, narrow enough to require descending hikers to step aside for those making their way up the ridgeline. Follow the trail down past the cabins and the visitors' center back to the parking area.

Miles and Directions

0.0   From the parking area, walk north up the paved road.

0.3   Turn right at the Y intersection to start the loop section of the hike.

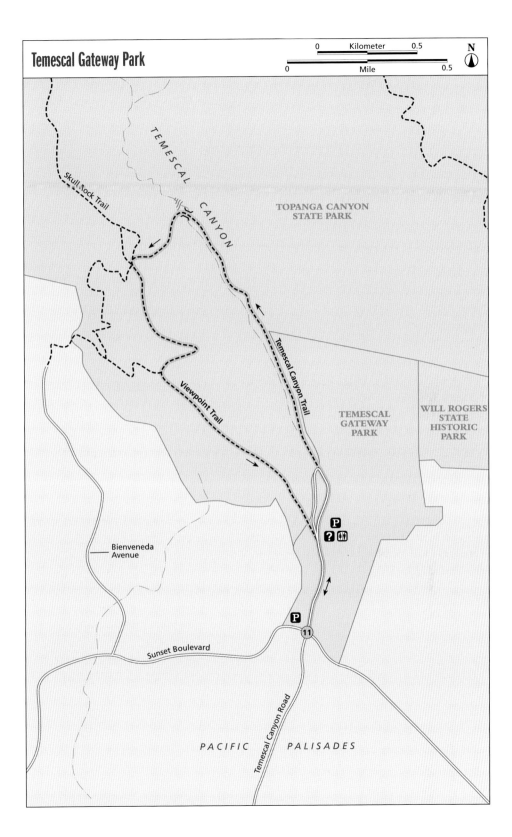

Temescal Gateway Park

0   Kilometer   0.5

0   Mile   0.5

N

Skull Rock Trail

TEMESCAL CANYON

TOPANGA CANYON
STATE PARK

Temescal Canyon Trail

Viewpoint Trail

TEMESCAL
GATEWAY
PARK

WILL ROGERS
STATE
HISTORIC
PARK

Bienveneda
Avenue

11

Sunset Boulevard

Temescal Canyon Road

PACIFIC   PALISADES

0.5 The road meets the trail; continue north.

1.0 Enter Topanga Canyon State Park.

1.4 Arrive at the waterfall and footbridge.

1.6 Stay left at the trail junction.

1.7 Turn left at the trail junction.

2.7 Rejoin the paved road and walk south to the parking area.

3.25 Arrive back at the trailhead and parking area.

Hike Information

Local information: California State Parks, 818-880-0363; Santa Monica Mountains National Recreation Area, 805-370-2301

Camping: Leo Carrillo State Park campgrounds, Malibu Creek State Park, Topanga State Park Campground, Point Mugu State Park Campground, California State Park campgrounds reservations, 800-444-7275; customer service, 800-695-2269; www .reservecalifornia.com

12 Will Rogers State Historic Park

Will Rogers State Historic Park is the 186–acre ranch where the renowned Hollywood personality lived and pursued his passions. Visitors to the park can visit his ranch, a small museum, and take a hike around the property to the majestic sweeping view at Inspiration Point.

Start: At the large parking area on Will Rogers State Park Road

Distance: 2.25-mile lollipop

Hiking time: About 2 hours

Difficulty: Easy

Trail surface: Dirt road and single-track dirt trail

Nearest town: Pacific Palisades

County: Los Angeles

Other trail users: Joggers

Canine compatibility: Leashed dogs permitted

Trailhead facilities/amenities: All facilities available

Land status: California state park

Fees and permits: A parking fee is charged

Schedule: Open year-round, 8 a.m. to sunset; can be hot in summer

Maps: USGS Topanga, CA; www.parks.ca.gov/pages/626/files/WillRogersPDF.pdf

Trail contact: Will Rogers State Historic Park, 1501 Will Rogers State Park Rd., Pacific Palisades, CA, 90272; www.parks.ca.gov/?page_id=626; 310-454-8212; Santa Monica Mountains National Recreation Area, 805-370-2301

Finding the trailhead: From the intersection of I-10 and the Pacific Coast Highway/CA 1, drive 2.1 miles north on Pacific Coast Highway. Turn right onto Chautauqua Boulevard and drive for 0.9 mile. Turn right onto Sunset Boulevard and drive for 0.6 mile. Turn left onto Will Rogers State Park Road and drive for 0.6 mile to the large parking area. GPS: 34°03'15.1"N 118°30'49.8"W

The Hike

From the parking lot follow the signs behind the visitors' center or the old ranch house to the Inspiration Loop Trail. Turn left and begin hiking on the fire road/trail that surrounds the property. The trail follows the dirt road through eucalyptus trees and gently climbs as it begins to circle the property. Old photos describe the route from 1929, as it was designed for riding horses around the property.

The route climbs to a plateau and the views only get wider with each step. The trail meanders on its way toward Inspiration Point. At 1.1 miles, take the short spur to the right that leads to the overlook. Here, visitors can survey the Los Angeles Basin from Long Beach and the entire Palos Verdes Peninsula to blue Santa Monica Bay. Certainly, the view on a clear day is one of the more fetching in all of the Los Angeles area, especially for such a simple walk. The payoff is well worth the price of admission. Those new to hiking and children will undoubtedly enjoy the view and the mild trail.

Rabbits are ubiquitous along Southern California trails. Photo by Monique Riedel.

From Inspiration Point, head back to the main trail and turn right, following the dirt road around and down and back to the visitors' center and ranch house.

There are several exhibits in the park, and visitors can take a guided tour Tuesday through Sunday at 11 a.m., 1 p.m., and 2 p.m. On weekends, visitors can also watch the Will Rogers Polo Club on the only regulation-size polo field in Southern California.

Miles and Directions

0.0 From the parking area, follow the trailhead sign to the Inspiration Loop behind the ranch house or visitors' center.

0.1 Turn left onto the main Inspiration Loop Trail/fire road.

1.1 Turn right to reach Inspiration Point. Return to the main trail and turn right.

2.25 Arrive back at the trailhead and parking area in front of the polo grounds.

Hike Information

Local information: California State Parks, 818-880-0363; Santa Monica Mountains National Recreation Area, 805-370-2301

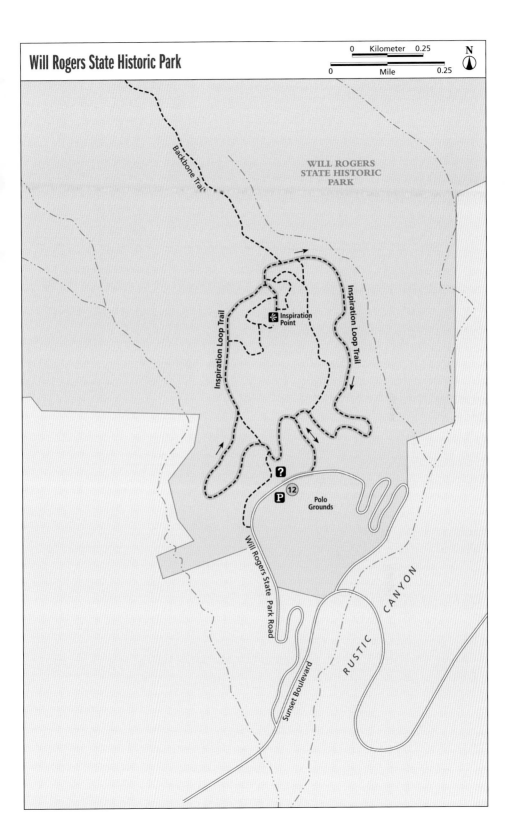

Will Rogers State Historic Park

0   Kilometer   0.25

0   Mile   0.25

N

WILL ROGERS
STATE HISTORIC
PARK

Backbone Trail

Inspiration Loop Trail

Inspiration Loop Trail

Inspiration
Point

Polo
Grounds

P 12

Will Rogers State Park Road

Sunset Boulevard

RUSTIC CANYON

WILL ROGERS

Will Rogers was born in 1879 in what is now Oklahoma on the Cherokee Nation. Rogers was a man of many talents, first gaining fame for his roping and cowboy skills. He became the most successful actor of his day, starring in 71 movies, some silent and some talking. He wrote books and more than 4,000 syndicated newspaper columns and was known for his humor and wit.

He had the ability to connect with the common person, and his political humor was regarded fair to all sides of the political spectrum. People admired his philosophy, his morals and ethics, and his simple down-home wisdom. Rogers's quote, "I have never yet met a man that I didn't like," seemed to be the key to his success. He had the grand ability to make people feel uplifted. Will Rogers died in an airplane crash in 1935.

The property he owned with his wife, Betty, was donated to the State of California and became a state park when she passed away in 1944.

Camping: Leo Carrillo State Park campgrounds, Malibu Creek State Park, Topanga State Park Campground, Point Mugu State Park Campground, McGrath State Beach, California State Park campgrounds reservations, 800-444-7275; customer service, 800-695-2269; www.reservecalifornia.com

Local organizations: Will Rogers State Historic Park Docents, 310-454-8212

13 Franklin Canyon

Hike through the lovely, shaded splendor of Franklin Canyon, the quieter and more peaceful alternative to Runyon Canyon. Franklin Canyon is one of the most popular filming parks in Los Angeles; movie and television buffs will undoubtedly recognize some of its more prominent locations.

Start: At the parking area on Franklin Canyon Drive

Distance: 3.5-mile double lollipop

Hiking time: About 2 hours

Difficulty: Easy

Trail surface: Dirt road and single-track dirt trail

Nearest town: Studio City

County: Los Angeles

Other trail users: Joggers

Canine compatibility: Leashed dogs permitted

Trailhead facilities/amenities: All facilities available

Land status: Regional park

Fees and permits: None

Schedule: Open year-round, sunrise to sunset; can be hot in summer

Maps: USGS Beverly Hills, CA; www.lamountains.com/maps/franklinCanyon.pdf

Trail contact: Franklin Canyon Park, 2600 Franklin Canyon Dr., Beverly Hills, CA, 90210; www.lamountains.com/parks.asp?parkid=14; 310-858-7272

Finding the trailhead: From Los Angeles, take US 101 north and west. Take Exit 15 for Coldwater Canyon Avenue, turn left (south), and drive for 2.5 miles. At the intersection with Mulholland Drive, make a 90-degree right turn onto Franklin Canyon Drive (to the southwest). There is no sign for Franklin Canyon Drive; the sign says ROAD CLOSED 800 FEET. Park in the parking area. GPS: 34°07'24.7"N 118°24'34.4"W

The Hike

Franklin Canyon is the kind of park that families take their little ones to. Native Angelenos will want to bring out-of-state visitors here too, so that they can point out the famous pond from the opening of *The Andy Griffith Show* or the lagoon from *The Creature from the Black Lagoon*. It is a place for picnics, enjoying the scenery, and taking in a few of the grand vistas down into Century City and over the Pacific Ocean (if the day is clear). Franklin Canyon isn't necessarily the place to get away from it all, but it is a huge swath of open land right next to Los Angeles and a pretty quick drive for most people living in the region.

The duck pond and reservoir are both fairly picturesque, and birders also flock to Franklin Canyon. The watering holes are both stops on the Pacific Flyway, so many migrating birds have layovers in Franklin Canyon. It is entirely possible to just laze around the pond and visitors' center, which has some wonderful attractions and exhibits for children, but people who really want a hike can take one as well. The

Springtime brings wildflowers and bees. Photo by Allen Riedel.

following loop is designed to get the maximum out of Franklin Canyon, taking in views, exploring the park, and getting some cardio in while doing it.

From the parking area, walk down Franklin Canyon Drive between Upper Franklin Reservoir and Heavenly Pond. Follow the road as it continues down canyon, losing 250 feet in elevation toward the lower section of the park. The route is wooded and shaded for the most part, making this a peaceful stroll.

▶ **The reservoir at Franklin Canyon was famously featured in many movies and television shows.**

Franklin Canyon Drive splits at a Y intersection at 0.75 mile. Take the left fork and continue down Lake Drive. At around 1 mile, the Hastain Trail branches to the left; take it and follow it as it loops around to a pretty viewpoint at 1.75 miles, looking down into Beverly Hills. The viewpoint sits right at the junction with the Hastain Fire Road, which climbs steeply to the left. Continue along the Hastain Trail to the right, and rejoin Lake Drive at 2.1 miles. Follow the road back to the intersection with Franklin Canyon Drive and take the trail on the left at 2.8 miles, which leads above Heavenly Pond. Follow this trail for 0.7 mile back to Franklin Canyon Drive and the parking area.

Miles and Directions

0.0 Start by heading south down Franklin Canyon Drive.
0.75 Turn left down Lake Drive.

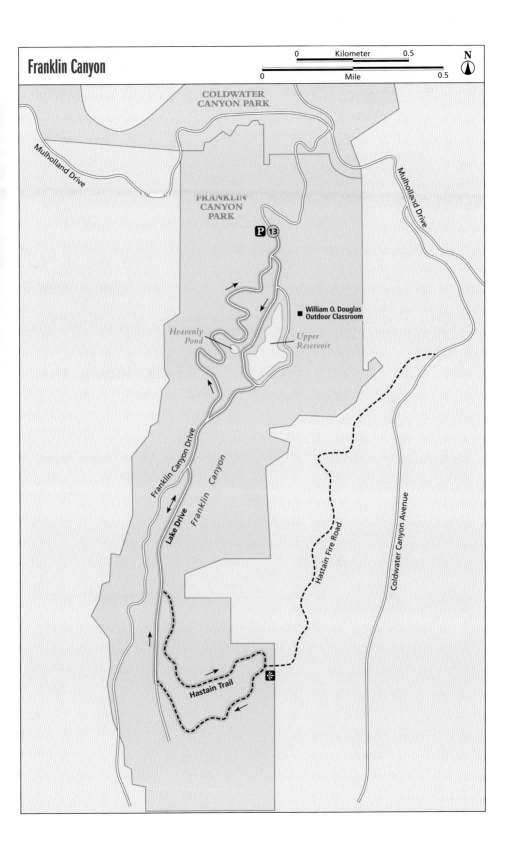

Franklin Canyon

COLDWATER
CANYON PARK

Mulholland Drive

FRANKLIN
CANYON
PARK

Mulholland Drive

P 13

William O. Douglas
Outdoor Classroom

Heavenly
Pond

Upper
Reservoir

Franklin Canyon Drive

Lake Drive

Franklin Canyon

Hastain Fire Road

Coldwater Canyon Avenue

Hastain Trail

N

0   Kilometer   0.5

0   Mile   0.5

1.0 Turn left onto the Hastain Trail.

1.75 Intersect with the Hastain Fire Road at the viewpoint. Continue right along the Hastain Trail.

2.1 Turn right and rejoin Lake Drive.

2.35 Complete the southern loop. Continue north on Lake Drive and then Franklin Canyon Drive.

2.8 Take the trail branch on the left above Heavenly Pond.

3.5 Return to Franklin Canyon Drive, and arrive back at the trailhead and the parking area.

Hike Information

Local information: Santa Monica Mountains National Recreation Area, 805-370-2301; Mountains Recreation & Conservation Authority, 570 West Avenue 26, Suite 100, Los Angeles, CA, 90065; 323-221-9944; www.lamountains.com/parks; Franklin Canyon Park, 310-858-7272; https://mrca.ca.gov/parks/park-listing/franklin -canyon-park/

Camping: Leo Carrillo State Park campgrounds, Malibu Creek State Park, Topanga State Park Campground, Point Mugu State Park Campground, California State Park campgrounds reservations, 800-444-7275; customer service, 800-695-2269; www .reservecalifornia.com

14 Wilacre Park

Wilacre Park is a wonderful slice of nature with open-air views of the San Fernando Valley. It is a great place to get out into the outdoors with family or just to get a bit of exercise.

Start: At the parking area on Fryman Road
Distance: 1.8-mile lollipop
Hiking time: About 1.5 hours
Difficulty: Easy
Trail surface: Dirt road, paved road, and single-track dirt trail
Nearest town: Studio City
County: Los Angeles
Other trail users: Joggers and equestrians
Canine compatibility: Leashed dogs permitted
Trailhead facilities/amenities: All facilities available
Land status: Regional park

Fees and permits: Parking fee
Schedule: Open year-round, sunrise to sunset; can be hot in summer
Maps: USGS Van Nuys, CA; www.lamountains .com/maps/wilacre.pdf
Trail contacts: Santa Monica Mountains Conservancy, 310-589-3200. Mountains Recreation & Conservation Authority, 570 West Avenue 26, Suite 100, Los Angeles, CA, 90065; 323-221-9944. Wilacre Park, 3431 Fryman Road, Studio City, CA, https://mrca.ca .gov/parks/park-listing/wilacre-park/

Finding the trailhead: From Los Angeles, take US 101 north and west. Take Exit 14 for Laurel Canyon Boulevard. Turn left (south) onto Laurel Canyon and drive for 1.5 miles. Turn right (west) onto Fryman Road. The parking lot is on the right. GPS: 34°08'01.0"N 118°23'30.3"W

The Hike

Wilacre Park is fairly popular despite parking fees, and it's just a great place to get out, stretch your legs, and take an urban hike. The best time to hike in Wilacre Park is during the winter months when views are clear and the air is crisp. Summer is not such a good time due to smog and heat, but mornings and evenings are pleasant even during the hotter months.

The trail is composed of asphalt and dirt, and like the four other parks connected by Mulholland Drive, it is a simple yet powerful example of conservation within an urban area sorely in need of open space and outdoor recreation. It is possible to connect to all four parks (Wilacre, Coldwater Canyon, Fryman Canyon, and Franklin Canyon) along trails without being mindful of borders. This trail, however, takes the popular route up the Betty B. Dearing Trail and returns to the parking area along the U-Vanu Trail.

There will be lots of people along the trail; they will have their dogs and cell phones. Some people will be running and jogging, but overall, the park does not feel crowded. Surprisingly, it is quite peaceful and free

▶ **Hiking Tip: Getting out on shorter trails more often builds stamina for longer, more difficult trails.**

This wild phlox is one of the many fine examples of lovely wildflowers and photographic opportunities in the Santa Monica Mountains. Photo by Allen Riedel.

from the noise of the city. Hikers can take a variety of trails and string together a long exercise routine or a simple short jaunt. The best reasons to hike here are because the park is close, it is good for families, and it is good for exercise.

From the parking area, walk through the gated entrance to the Betty B. Dearing Trail. Follow it up the hill to a viewpoint 0.75 mile from the entrance. The trail climbs 300 feet for wonderful clear-air views of the surrounding cityscape. At 1 mile, turn left and take the dirt path of the U–Vanu Trail, following it back down to the junction with the Betty B. Dearing Trail. Turn right and continue back to the parking area.

Miles and Directions

0.0   Start by heading west through the gated entrance to the Betty B. Dearing Trail.

0.15 At a Y intersection take the right fork to walk the north side of a small loop around a picnic area.

0.2   At a four-way intersection stay to the right.

0.3   At a four-way intersection continue straight west on the Betty B. Dearing Trail.

0.45 Pass the U-Vanu Trail on the right.

0.75 Reach a viewpoint of the San Fernando Valley.

1.0   Make a sharp hairpin turn to the left and return on the U-Vanu Trail.

1.4   Turn right (south).

Wilacre Park

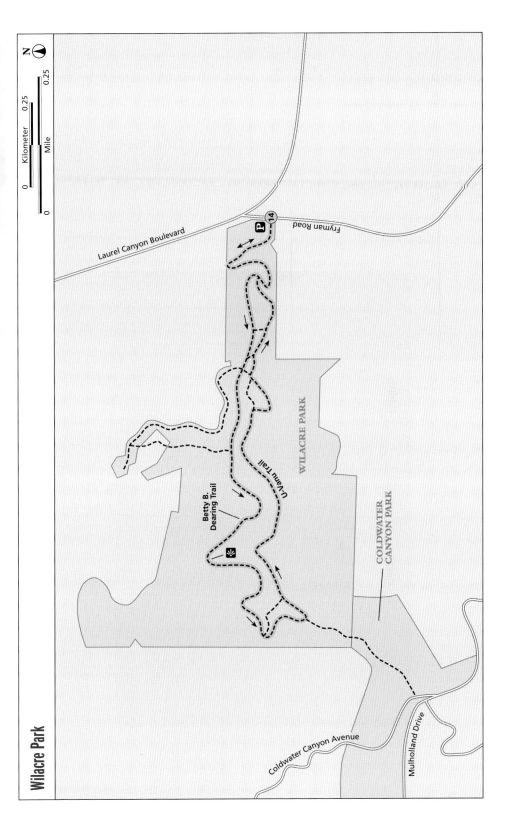

N

0   Kilometer   0.25
0   0.25
                                    Mile

Laurel Canyon Boulevard

P
14
Fryman Road

WILACRE PARK

Betty B.
Dearing Trail

U-Vanu Trail

COLDWATER
CANYON PARK

Coldwater Canyon Avenue

Mulholland Drive

1.5 At the next three intersections, stay to the right.

1.65 Complete the loop and stay to the right.

1.8 Arrive back at the trailhead and parking area.

Hike Information

Camping: Leo Carrillo State Park campgrounds, Malibu Creek State Park, Topanga State Park Campground, Point Mugu State Park Campground, California State Park campgrounds reservations, 800-444-7275; customer service, 800-695-2269; www .reservecalifornia.com

Snow plants are not really plants at all, but fungi; they are red because they lack chlorophyll. Photo by Allen Riedel. (Hike 33)

15 Runyon Canyon

Though not wilderness-like and full of people and dogs, this is the quintessential Los Angeles urban hike, and there are no two ways about it. Hike here for networking, fitness, to walk a dog, just to get outside, to take in some pretty darned good views, or to simply witness the freak show if you are so inclined.

Start: At the parking area just off Mulholland Drive
Distance: 2.5-mile loop
Hiking time: About 1.5 hours
Difficulty: Easy
Trail surface: Dirt road, paved road, and single-track dirt trail
Nearest town: Hollywood
County: Los Angeles
Other trail users: Joggers, equestrians, bicyclists, and influencers
Canine compatibility: Dogs permitted off leash in designated areas

Trailhead facilities/amenities: None
Land status: Los Angeles city park
Fees and permits: None
Schedule: Open year-round, sunrise to sunset; can be hot in summer
Maps: USGS Hollywood, CA; www.ci.la.ca.us/rap/dos/parks/facility/runyonCanyonPk.htm
Trail contacts: Runyon Canyon Park, 2000 N. Fuller Ave., Los Angeles, CA, 90046; www.laparks.org/dos/parks/facility/runyonCanyonPk.htm; 323-666-5046. Santa Monica Mountains Conservancy, www.lamountains.com/parks.asp?parkid=122, 213-485-5572

Finding the trailhead: From Los Angeles, take the 101 freeway north. Take Exit 11A toward Barham Boulevard. Merge onto Cahuenga Boulevard east, drive 0.1 mile, and turn right onto Lakeridge Place. Turn right onto the overpass toward Mulholland Drive and drive over the 101 freeway. Turn left onto Mulholland Drive and drive for 1.5 miles to the parking area for Runyon Canyon Park. GPS: 34°07'10.9"N 118°21'09.3"W

The Hike

Without a doubt, Runyon Canyon is not the greatest hiking destination in Los Angeles—not even close. Runyon Canyon is the place where it seems nearly everyone who wanted to go for a walk in Los Angeles decided to go, and they brought their dog along too. Now, if you are a dog or have a dog, Runyon Canyon is the place to be; there are a multitude of off-leash areas, and even those areas that aren't so designated are effectively nonleash zones as well. There are dogs everywhere; this place is a great bet for dog owners, for sure. Hikers might even run into a famous dog or two . . . or three or four. Yes, the reason to go to Runyon Canyon is to see what Los Angeles is all about.

People who are working on their résumés or their acting chops are walking here. People who are writing their first, second, and third blockbusters all spend some time on the trail. The cast of *Friends,* before they were the cast of *Friends,* probably spent

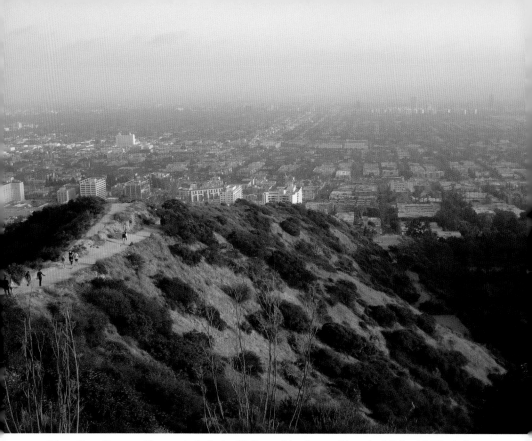

Views from Runyon Canyon include the Hollywood landscape. Photo by Michael Millenheft III.

time walking up and down Runyon Canyon. When waiters and busboys get a break from the action, they all seem to head to Runyon Canyon to keep up with someone.

Now, with that said and all Hollywood jokes aside, the canyon is a pretty decent place to hike. A fantastic cardio workout can be had for sure, there are some really nice vista points, especially on clear days, and there are a lot of people. People-watching in the park is second nature—or maybe first nature. The trail is really close to the city and it is fairly easy to get to for a whole lot of people, which is another reason for the crowds. There are also some cool Hollywood homes, some right on the trail. Although a multitude of routes can be taken in the park, this path highlights the best.

From Mulholland Drive, take the path on the left that heads down into Runyon Canyon. Follow the road for 0.6 mile to a high promontory. The road continues down on the right, and the trail continues straight, veering left ahead. Follow the trail. The route passes above some old ruins and a tennis court and then leads right by them. The way gets a little confusing at the bottom, and there are a multitude of trails and roads. Turn left at the bottom of the hill to get back onto Runyon Canyon Road, and head for the ridgeline to the west. When the road intersects a dirt trail leading upward, take it. This path has the best views and leads back up to Mulholland Drive.

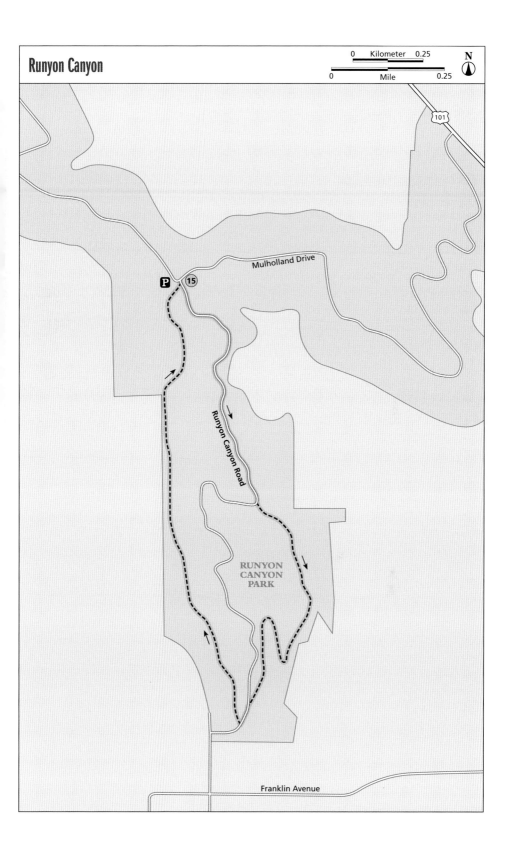

Runyon Canyon

101

Mulholland Drive

P 15

Runyon Canyon Road

RUNYON
CANYON
PARK

Franklin Avenue

Miles and Directions

0.0 Start down Runyon Canyon Road toward the city.

0.6 Take the dirt path that continues straight and to the left.

1.3 Turn left onto Runyon Canyon Road and head for the ridgeline. Turn right onto a dirt trail.

2.5 Arrive back at the trailhead and parking area.

Hike Information

Local information: California State Parks, 818-880-0363; Santa Monica Mountains National Recreation Area, 805-370-2301. Runyon Canyon Park, 2000 N. Fuller Ave., Los Angeles, CA, 90046; www.laparks.org/dos/parks/facility/runyonCanyonPk .htm; 323-666-5046

Camping: Leo Carrillo State Park campgrounds, Malibu Creek State Park, Topanga State Park Campground, Point Mugu State Park Campground, California State Park campgrounds reservations, 800-444-7275; customer service, 800-695-2269; www .reservecalifornia.com

16 Griffith Park

This hike highlights some magical Hollywood hotspots, from the Griffith Observatory to the views from Mount Hollywood to an overlook that takes hikers to the back of the Hollywood sign atop Mount Lee. There is something for everyone on this trip.

Start: Griffith Observatory
Distance: 8-mile lollipop
Hiking time: About 3.5 hours
Difficulty: Moderate
Trail surface: Dirt road, paved road, and single-track dirt trail
Nearest town: Hollywood
County: Los Angeles
Other trail users: Joggers, equestrians, tourists, and bicyclists
Canine compatibility: Leashed dogs permitted

Trailhead facilities/amenities: All facilities available
Land status: Los Angeles city park
Fees and permits: None
Schedule: Open year-round, sunrise to sunset; can be hot in summer
Maps: USGS Hollywood, CA; www.latrails.com/hike/gp.html
Trail contact: Griffith Park, 4730 Crystal Springs Dr., Los Angeles, CA, 90027; www.laparks.org/dos/parks/griffithPK/gp_location.htm; 323-913-4688

Finding the trailhead: From Los Angeles, take I-5 north. Take Exit 141A for Los Feliz Boulevard and turn left (west). Drive for 1.3 miles on Los Feliz Boulevard. Turn right onto Hillhurst Avenue and drive for 0.2 mile. Turn right onto Vermont Canyon Road and drive for 1.1 miles. Stay to the right (straight) onto Mount Hollywood Drive and drive through the tunnel. The road becomes Observatory Avenue. Follow it 0.3 mile to the parking lot for the Griffith Observatory. GPS: 34°07'12.6"N 118°18'00.1"W

The Hike

Hiking within Griffith Park is not as easy as it seems. There are trails galore, and some of them are incredibly steep and hot. The finest seasons to hike here are from fall to spring. It is best to avoid the summertime for two reasons: The heat can be oppressive and the smog makes visibility poor. With that said, visitors should realize that the sun is present year-round, and anyone attempting this hike should be duly prepared with sunblock and water. This isn't an easy leg stretcher to take the kids on. This hike gains 1,400 feet of elevation on three separate uphill climbs, and hiking 8 miles round-trip is nothing to shake a stick at. Part of the trip is on pavement, making it a little bit tougher on the feet and knees than dirt roads or trails alone.

Visitors with children wishing only to climb Mount Hollywood (not the trip to the Hollywood sign) north of the observatory can do so, and children will more than likely enjoy the trip up and back. The observatory has been redesigned and the

GRIFFITH J. GRIFFITH

Industrialist, philanthropist, city father, and convicted felon, Griffith J. Griffith was born in Wales in 1850. He immigrated to the United States at the age of 15. In the 1870s he worked for the California newspaper *Alta California* as a mining correspondent. From this job he learned the ins and outs of mining and succeeded in making a fortune with mines in Mexico.

He moved to Los Angeles in 1882 as a wealthy man. He used some of his fortune to acquire the majority of the Rancho Los Feliz Mexican land grant, purchasing two-thirds of the original land and then donating more than 3,000 acres to the city of Los Angeles so that an urban park could be built in the same vein as New York's Central Park. When Griffith donated the original 3,015 acres to the city in 1896, it was the largest city park in the world. His plans included building an observatory and science center. He called the donation a "Christmas present" and wanted it to be a place of serenity where the people of Los Angeles could relax and enjoy the outdoors.

The city passed an ordinance to name the park after its donor. Further plans for Griffith Park were placed on hold when he was convicted of shooting his wife in the face at the Arcadia Hotel. As the story goes, he handed her a prayer book and pulled out a revolver. Christina Griffith then threw herself out of a window, landed on an awning, and reentered the hotel through a window. She was left disfigured and blind from the incident.

The sensational trial that followed found Griffith's defense being insanity by reason of alcohol. He was found guilty of assault with a deadly weapon and sent to San Quentin for two years. He returned to Los Angeles and lived out his remaining years trying desperately to remake his image in the mind of Angelenos. He was unable to do so. The city and its populace would not take his money or let him reinvent himself. Because of his notoriety and crimes, he was unable to improve the park that bore his name. In death, he bequeathed most of his wealth to the city, which funded the construction of the Griffith Observatory and the Greek Theater.

revamped features are intriguing to both young and old. Take a visit to the observatory first and then start hiking north along the road.

Where the main parking lot ends, there is a curb with an obvious wide trail heading straight north as it parallels Observatory Avenue. Head north, and after about 0.3 mile, the trail crosses a concrete overpass. Continue along the main path and ignore all of the smaller side routes. These trails will get to the summit faster but are steep in spots and lead to erosion.

The trail winds westward, and views of Mount Lee and the Hollywood sign open up. It hairpins back to the east and begins working its way steeply up the slope.

The iconic Hollywood sign can be seen up close but not touched. Photo by Monique Riedel.

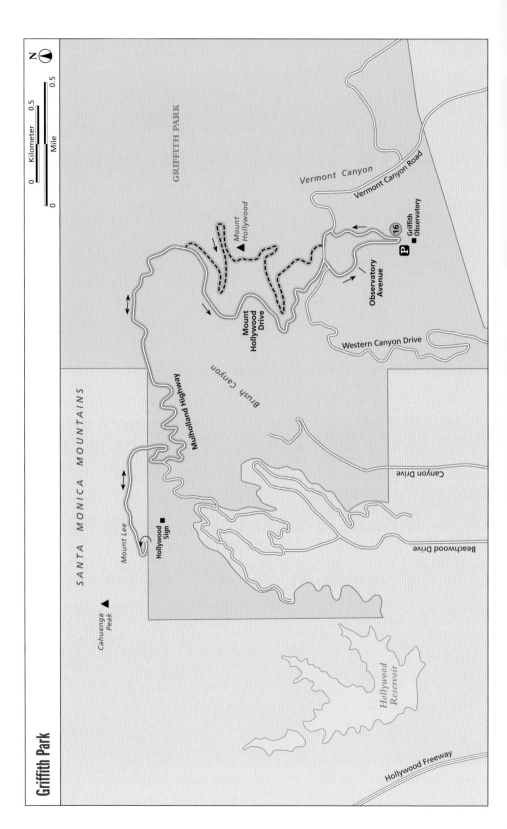

Griffith Park

SANTA MONICA MOUNTAINS

GRIFFITH PARK

Cahuenga Peak

Mount Lee

Hollywood Sign

Mulholland Highway

Mount Hollywood

Mount Hollywood Drive

Brush Canyon

Vermont Canyon

Vermont Canyon Road

Observatory Avenue

Western Canyon Drive

16 Griffith Observatory

Canyon Drive

Beachwood Drive

Hollywood Reservoir

Hollywood Freeway

Kilometer
0   0.5
0   0.5
Mile

N

At 1.1 miles, the path splits in three directions; take the far left fork and wrap around the backside of Mount Hollywood, following the graded road/trail beyond a water tower. Turn right, ascend the final push to the summit, and take in a grand vista of the Los Angeles Basin, the San Gabriel Mountains and valley, and the Hollywood sign.

At this point, the route gets a little convoluted. Head back down the main trail, which is the farthest road on the right. Pass an intersection and come immediately to a four-way intersection where trails lead off in the cardinal directions. Turn west along the roadway/trail. Follow the road as it turns and hairpins and meets up with Mount Hollywood Drive. Turn right at the Y intersection at 2.25 miles. At 2.5 miles, the trail meets another Y intersection; veer left off the pavement and onto the dirt road/trail. This is Mulholland Highway. In 0.25 mile, there is another Y intersection; head right and continue upward toward the antennae atop Mount Lee.

▶ **Drink plenty of water while hiking—take a drink every 15 minutes.**

At 3.25 miles, the trail meets yet another Y intersection. This time veer right and continue along Mulholland Highway. The last intersection is at 3.7 miles, where the dirt road reaches a T junction with Mount Lee Drive. Turn right and follow the roadway up steeply behind the Hollywood sign. The famous letters cannot be touched or even walked up to, but visitors can catch a glimpse from behind a chain-link fence protected by electronic security and cameras.

Enjoy the views of the sign, the Los Angeles Basin, and the Hollywood Reservoir, and then turn around and follow the road back to Mount Hollywood Drive. Instead of taking more ups and downs by returning along the same route, stay on the road until it intersects with Observatory Avenue at the tunnel. Turn right and follow Observatory Avenue back to the observatory.

Miles and Directions

0.0 Start north from the Griffith Observatory.

0.2 Head up the trail at the northern end of the parking area.

0.3 Cross over Mount Hollywood Drive on a concrete overpass. Stay on the main road/trail.

1.1 Take the far left fork around the back of Mount Hollywood.

1.2 Turn right and ascend the summit of Mount Hollywood. Head back down the large road on the right.

1.3 At the four-way intersection, head west along a fire road.

2.25 Turn right onto Mount Hollywood Drive.

2.5 Turn left onto the dirt road/trail (Mulholland Highway).

2.75 Stay right at the Y intersection to continue on Mulholland Highway.

3.25 Veer right at the Y intersection to continue on Mulholland Highway.

3.7 Turn right onto paved Mount Lee Drive.

4.5 Arrive behind the Hollywood sign atop Mount Lee. Return via Mulholland Highway.

6.5 Turn right onto Mount Hollywood Drive. Follow it to Observatory Avenue.

7.5 Turn right and follow Observatory Avenue back to the observatory and parking area.

8.0 Arrive back at the observatory trailhead and parking area.

Hike Information

Local information: City of Los Angeles Department of Parks and Recreation, 221 N. Figueroa St., Suite 1550, Los Angeles, CA, 90012; 213-202-2633; Griffith Observatory, 2800 East Observatory Rd., Los Angeles, CA, 90027; 213-473-0800

Camping: Malibu Creek State Park, Topanga State Park Campground, California State Park campgrounds reservations, 800-444-7275; customer service, 800-695-2269; www.reservecalifornia.com

Honorable Mention

A Satwiwa–Rancho Sierra Vista

Satwiwa/Rancho Sierra Vista is a lovely parcel of land on the western end of the Santa Monica Mountains at the border of the National Park, situated on the eastern escarpment of the range. The land had been used by the Chumash peoples for as long as 10,000 years. With the arrival of the Spanish and their missions and land grants, this portion of Southern California became the sprawling Rancho El Conejo. The surrounding area is still pastoral, though subdivisions and strip malls have cropped up nearby over the past 50 years. The park contains a couple of waterfalls and a nature center, complete with a Native American demonstration area where a Native American docent/park ranger is available for presentations and questions on Saturday and Sunday from 9 a.m. to 5 p.m. Art shows and interactive exhibits will fascinate the historically curious and children of all ages. Several hikes can be taken through the lovely little park. Wildlife seems to abound here, especially early in the morning. The park can feel like the land that was forgotten by time. Enjoy the loop trail or take a walk to the waterfall. Bring the family; all are certain to enjoy Satwiwa/Rancho Sierra Vista. Satwiwa/Rancho Sierra Vista is located off Lynn Road between Thousand Oaks and Malibu. Many hikes from short to epically long can be taken on the park's multitude of trails or connect with the larger Point Mugu State Park. Satwiwa is the only parcel of land in the western portion of the SMMNRA that was left untouched by the 2018 Woolsey Fire.

Angeles National Forest

The Angeles National Forest stretches from the Newhall Pass in the west to San Bernardino County in the east, covering more than 650,000 acres with more than 800 miles of hiking trails. The San Gabriel Mountains continue into the Cajon Pass and

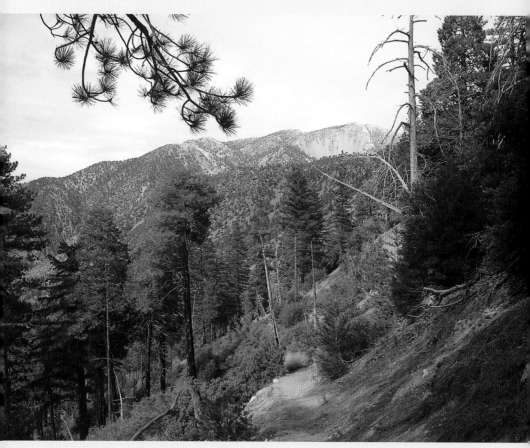

The Angeles National Forest is a beautiful and rugged range filled with fantastic vistas and lush forests. Photo by Allen Riedel.

to I-15. The mountain range comprises two sets of mountains, a taller northern range and the front range, which looms high above the Los Angeles metro area. Since 1956, the 66-mile-long Angeles Crest Highway/CA 2 has bisected a path nearly straight through the mountains from west to east, from La Canada Flintridge to Wrightwood. Construction began in 1929, and from that date, travelers and visitors were able to more easily flock to the higher regions of the forest. Because of its proximity to Los Angeles, the forest is one of the most heavily visited in the nation.

Historically, the front range was quite the hiking destination for those living in Los Angeles and in the Los Angeles metro area. Resorts flourished in the front range from the late 1800s to the 1930s, the remains of which can still be explored. Cabins cropped up along popular streams and rivers. Even naturalist and conservation hero John Muir tried his hand at hiking in the San Gabriel Mountains, calling the spiky chaparral and steep slopes, "Most ruggedly, thornily savage. Not even in the Sierra have I ever made the acquaintance of mountains more rigidly inaccessible." After the construction of the Angeles Crest Highway, the lower reaches lost their favor and their trappings of remoteness, though many of these areas are absolute treasures today, especially due to the preponderance of waterfalls along the front range.

The back range is known for its lofty heights and peaks above 9,000 feet, including Mount Baldy (also known as Mount San Antonio—the highest peak in the forest at 10,046 feet), Mount Dawson, Pine Mountain, Mount Baden-Powell, and Throop Peak. The views of the Los Angeles Basin and the high deserts are unmatched, and hiking in the high mountains can be a mystical and religious experience. There are numerous peaks above 8,000 feet, and most of the summits require little more than walking skills during the spring, summer, and fall months. However, the range can be dangerous in winter, and the foolhardy and unprepared often underestimate the high country's potential for disaster. Unprepared hikers go missing in the winter almost every year. Higher elevations are not to be trifled with in bad weather conditions, and the inexperienced should descend at the slightest hint of severe weather and danger. Caution should always remain the better part of safety when hiking in these parts.

The San Gabriel Mountains were named for the river of the same name that flows out of the mountains 75 miles to the Pacific Ocean. The Angeles Crest Highway enters the mountains in La Canada Flintridge just north and west of Pasadena and divides the mountains in half, exiting onto CA 138 near I-15 in the high desert. Ample opportunity for outdoor activity exists along the highway. The hikes in this book are only a sample of what the lower country close to Pasadena has to offer and a few in the high country, but no matter the destination, wild adventure awaits.

In September 2020, the Bobcat Fire burned more than 115,000 acres of the 700,000-acre Angeles National Forest, cutting a swath from south in Santa Anita and Sierra Madre and burned in a cornucopia shape all the way to the high desert in the north. The forest was effectively cut in half with nearly 20 percent of its total landmass consumed by flames. Coupled with the 2002 Curve Fire and the 2009 Station Fire, nearly half of the wildlands in the national forest have burned in this millennium.

The Curve and Station Fires burned some beloved hiking spots, but the Bobcat Fire burned brightest in the high country from Mount Waterman to the Vincent Gap. These areas will regrow, will experience a rebirth, and will also gradually reopen to hikers.

---

17 Echo Mountain

Experience vistas of the Los Angeles metro area while ascending to the ruins of a historic Victorian chalet and follow the trail of the only scenic mountain electric traction railroad ever built in the US.

Start: At the corner of Lake Avenue and Loma Alta Drive

Distance: 5 miles out and back

Hiking time: About 3 hours

Difficulty: Moderate

Trail surface: Dirt road and single-track dirt trail

Nearest town: Altadena

County: Los Angeles

Other trail users: Joggers, equestrians, and bicyclists

Canine compatibility: Leashed dogs permitted

Trailhead facilities/amenities: Picnic tables atop Echo Mountain

Land status: National forest

Fees and permits: None

Schedule: Open year-round; can be hot in summer

Maps: USGS Mount Wilson, CA; www.mtlowe .net/MtLoweTrail.htm

Trail contact: Angeles National Forest, 701 N. Santa Anita Ave., Arcadia, CA, 91006; https:// www.fs.usda.gov/angeles/; 747-322-6574 or 626-574-1613

Finding the trailhead: From Los Angeles, take CA 110/Pasadena Freeway north. Drive to the end of the Pasadena Freeway. Continue north on Arroyo Parkway for 1.3 miles. Turn right onto Colorado Boulevard and drive for 0.9 mile. Turn left onto Lake Avenue and drive 4 miles to its end and the intersection with Loma Alta Drive, where you'll find parking. GPS: 34°12'14.8"N 118°07'49.4"W

The Hike

You will begin your expedition through a stone gateway at the top of Lake Avenue. It seems apropos to begin the journey through this seemingly otherworldly gateway of ancient stones. Follow the trail east about 0.2 mile toward the Sam Merrill Trail. Follow the Sam Merrill Trail, which descends into a creek bed. After this short descent, the trail quickly begins the ascent up the eastern ridge of the Los Flores Canyon. The trail is well maintained and relatively wide at most points early in the hike. As you make your ascent, you will be rewarded with breathtaking views of the Los Angeles metro area.

This is a relatively popular trail so prepare to come upon other visitors making the trek. This pet-friendly trail hosts many travelers with leashed dogs. The trail is lined with various local foliage and chaparral, and it is home to an array of fauna.

As you reach the summit, the trail begins to narrow and become rockier for a short length of time. About 0.5 mile after you passed the 2-mile marker, you will see the rail bed of the Mount Lowe Railway. This was the historic rail line established by

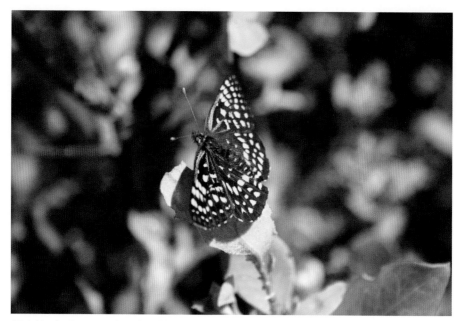

Variable checkerspot. Photo by Allen Riedel.

Professor Thaddeus S. C. Lowe on July 4, 1893, the third scenic railroad of its kind to be established in the US.

Whether or not one believes in ghosts, the awe of the grand panoramic view at the concrete stairs that remain and the slab of the Echo Mountain House or White City ruins contain an aura and presence of the recent past. The resort at the summit was aptly referred to as the "White City" because all of the buildings and even the railcars were referred to as the "white chariots." This provided a stark contrast to the hillside, such that any passerby could see the tiny white railcars climbing the mountainside from miles away.

The summit provides various opportunities to appreciate grand vistas of the Los Angeles metro area, the ruins, and the landscape of Echo Mountain. During its heyday, the Echo Mountain House provided its visitors with "echo phones," with which to bellow through toward the "sweet spot" in the canyon that can resonate a sound up to nine times. Take time to wander through the ruins of the old resort, which included a zoo, an observatory, and a tavern. Scattered throughout the site are placards and informational postings about the historic site, which is on the *National Register of Historic Places*.

Miles and Directions

0.0 From Lake Avenue, walk east beyond the stone gateway along a chain-link fence.

0.1 Ignore the fire road and stay straight to enter the Sam Merrill Trail. Continue toward the top.

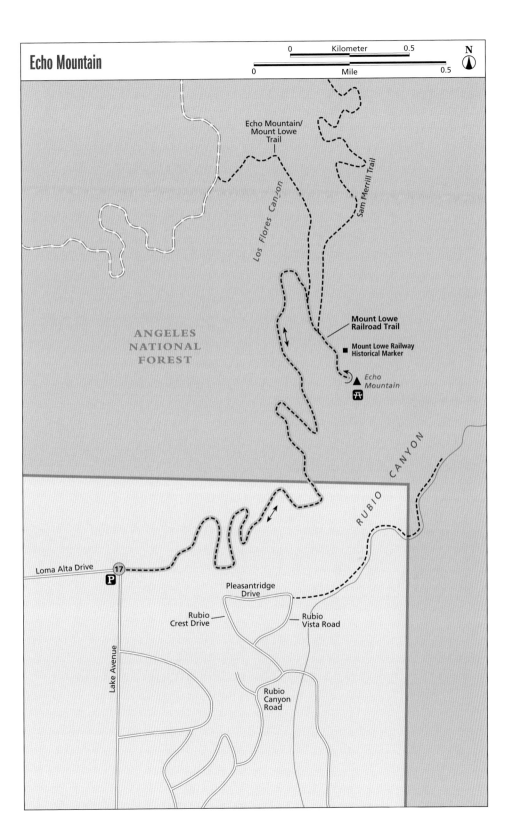

Echo Mountain

0   Kilometer   0.5

0   Mile   0.5

N

Echo Mountain/
Mount Lowe
Trail

Sam Merrill Trail

Los Flores Canyon

ANGELES
NATIONAL
FOREST

Mount Lowe
Railroad Trail

Mount Lowe Railway
Historical Marker

▲ Echo
Mountain

RUBIO CANYON

Loma Alta Drive   17

Pleasantridge
Drive

Rubio
Crest Drive

Rubio
Vista Road

Lake Avenue

Rubio
Canyon
Road

ECHO MOUNTAIN—THE WHITE CITY AND THE MOUNT LOWE RAILWAY

The Mount Lowe Railway was created as a tourist attraction by Thaddeus Lowe, a man of some fame and fortune in the Pasadena area, and David MacPherson, a civil engineer. The two spoke of Lowe's vision of a railcar leading up to the crest of the San Gabriel Mountains and began making plans for the railway. They hiked and fished in the region, enjoyed the spectacular waterfalls, and finally developed Southern California's most visited landmark, opening the railway on July 4, 1893.

The railway led a half mile up through the "Great Incline" of Rubio Canyon to Echo Mountain, where two hotels, a zoo, an observatory, and a casino awaited passengers. Riders could go farther to the top of Mount Lowe and on to Inspiration Point, where travelers were dazzled by the lights of the city and the mountain views from on high. Here, visitors could stay at the Alpine Tavern and enjoy the majesty of the Mount Lowe Railway.

While Lowe's vision sounds fantastic, the reality is that he went broke funding it. He couldn't pay back the debt that he owed on the railway's construction, and despite its popularity, he lost the railroad in slightly less than seven years. Other owners came and went, and so did the buildings and eventually the railway itself. All were lost to fire, winds, rains, storms, and general calamity. The Mount Lowe Railway made its last run on December 5, 1937. What remains now is simply a magnificent relic of the past.

2.2 Turn right and follow the Echo Mountain/Mount Lowe Railroad Trail to the ruined foundations of the "White City."

2.5 Arrive at the summit of Echo Mountain. Return via the same route.

5.0 Arrive back at the trailhead and the Lake Avenue parking area.

Hike Information

Local information: Angeles National Forest, 701 N. Santa Anita Ave., Arcadia, CA, 91006; 747-322-6574 or 626-574-1613

Camping: Angeles National Forest campgrounds (first come, first served; 14-day stay maximum): Appletree, Bear, Bear Canyon, Big Rock, Blue Ridge, Chilao, Coldbrook, Crystal Lake, Gould Mesa, Guffy, Horse Flats, Idlehour Trail Camp, Little Jimmy Trail Camp, Los Alamos, Lupine, Manker, Messenger Flats, Millard Trail Camp, Monte Cristo, Mount Lowe Trail Camp, Oak Flat, Pacifico, Peavine, Sawmill, South, Sulphur Springs; https://www.fs.usda.gov/main/angeles/home

18 Rubio Canyon

Scramble across boulders and traverse narrow footpaths to historic Rubio Pavilion and majestic Ribbon Rock Falls. With unprecedented scenery and panoramic vistas of the Los Angeles metro area, Rubio Canyon is a worthwhile endeavor for hiking enthusiasts of all skill levels.

Start: Between two houses on Pleasantridge Drive
Distance: 1.5 miles out and back
Hiking time: About 2 hours
Difficulty: Moderate for steep and loose footing as well as creek crossings
Trail surface: Packed dirt and rock
Nearest town: Altadena
County: Los Angeles
Other trail users: None
Canine compatibility: Leashed dogs permitted

Trailhead facilities/amenities: None
Land status: National forest
Fees and permits: None
Schedule: Open year-round; can be hot in summer
Maps: USGS Mount Wilson, CA; www.altadenatrails.org/multimedia/rubiotrailsmap.jpg
Trail contact: Angeles National Forest, 701 N. Santa Anita Ave., Arcadia, CA, 91006; https://www.fs.usda.gov/angeles/; 747-322-6574 or 626-574-1613

Finding the trailhead: Take CA 110/Pasadena Freeway north. Drive to the end of the Pasadena Freeway. Continue north on Arroyo Parkway for 1.3 miles. Turn right onto Colorado Boulevard and drive for 0.9 mile. Turn left onto Lake Avenue and drive 3.4 miles. Turn right onto East Palm Street and drive for 0.2 mile. Continue straight as Palm becomes Maiden Lane for 0.3 mile. Make a slight right onto Rubio Canyon Road. Drive for 0.1 mile and veer left to stay on Rubio Canyon Road. Continue for 0.2 mile. Turn left onto Rubio Crest Drive. Drive for 0.3 mile. At the sharp right, Rubio Crest Drive becomes Pleasantridge Drive. Continue for 0.2 mile to the corner. Park on the street. The signed trailhead is between two houses. GPS: 34°12'10.6"N 118°07'22.5"W

The Hike

Rubio Canyon is part of the historic site of Professor Thaddeus S. C. Lowe's intricate rail system, debuting in 1893 as Mount Lowe Railway. The Rubio Pavilion and hotel was located at the lower terminal of the incline of the railway that traversed the hillside to the top of Echo Mountain. Passengers could board the "white chariots" at the pavilion for a thrilling ride up to any number of destinations along the Mount Lowe rail line. During its heyday, the pavilion boasted a complex system of stairways and walkways brilliantly lit by thousands of Japanese lanterns leading to nine of the magnificent waterfalls of Rubio Canyon. Unfortunately, the grand pavilion was short lived, because in 1909 a severe storm destroyed it and

> **Rubio Canyon was buried under countless tons of rock during a preventable accident while blasting in 1998. Heavy rains in 2004 uncovered five of the glorious waterfalls in the canyon.**

the hotel. All that is left today are the concrete slabs of the foundation, easily visible along the trail.

The trailhead is located on an easement between two homes on Pleasantridge Drive and Rubio Vista Road; here the trail follows between the two houses toward the western ridge of Rubio Canyon. There is little shade along the trail, so during hot weather, it is advisable to prepare for extreme sun exposure.

At 0.5 mile you will begin your descent into the creek bed that the trail will ascend into the canyon. Here you will spot the first in a series of water pipes that follow along the trail. Just beyond an oak tree you will see the site of the Rubio Pavilion. Continue to veer right along the trail, which becomes a bit narrow in patches and requires some traversing, to the concrete foundation of the Rubio Pavilion.

Rubio Canyon is rugged and beautiful. Photo by Allen Riedel.

From the foundation, follow the creek bed north up into the canyon. Here the trail disappears and, depending on the time of year, may require some criss-crossing over water running down the canyon. At 0.75 mile you will find yourself at the base of charming Ribbon Rock Falls and just below Moss Grotto Falls. The beauty of Rubio Canyon is the dynamic nature of these falls. Prior to a prodigious landslide, there were several other falls in the lower canyon. Ribbon Rock Falls had, at one time, been obstructed by massive boulders as well. Due to the ever-changing nature of this area, it is advisable to note that some of the boulders may be capricious, so be cautious when exploring the area around the falls.

Today, Ribbon Rock Falls is once again flowing and provides for a delightful conclusion to this part of the trail. When you have had your fill of exploring the falls, head back down the creek bed toward the trail you came up on, and follow the same trail back to the trailhead.

Miles and Directions

0.0   Park on Pleasantridge Drive. Walk between the two houses on the signed trail.

0.5   Descend to the creek bed and follow the canyon upward.

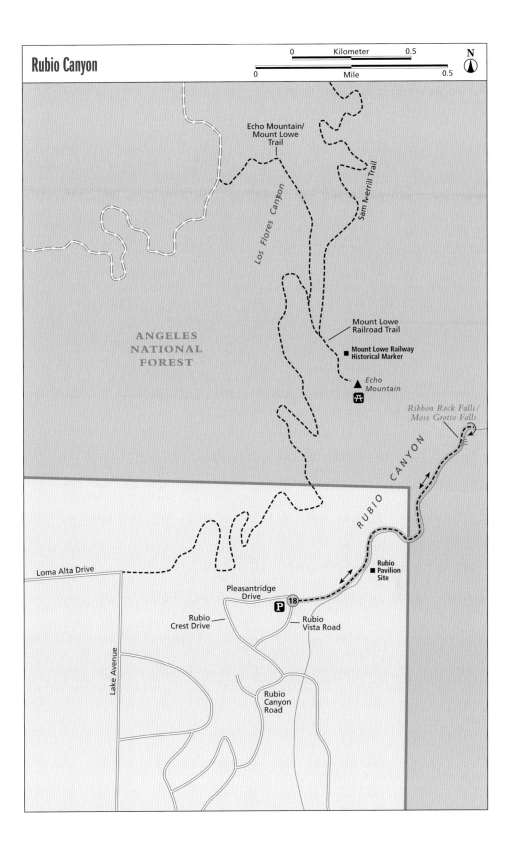

Rubio Canyon

0   Kilometer   0.5

0   Mile   0.5

N

Echo Mountain/
Mount Lowe
Trail

Los Flores Canyon

Sam Merrill Trail

ANGELES
NATIONAL
FOREST

Mount Lowe
Railroad Trail

■ Mount Lowe Railway
Historical Marker

▲ *Echo
Mountain*

Ⓐ

*Ribbon Rock Falls/
Moss Grotto Falls*

RUBIO CANYON

Rubio
■ Pavilion
Site

Loma Alta Drive

Pleasantridge
Drive

Ⓟ (18)

Rubio
Crest Drive

Rubio
Vista Road

Lake Avenue

Rubio
Canyon
Road

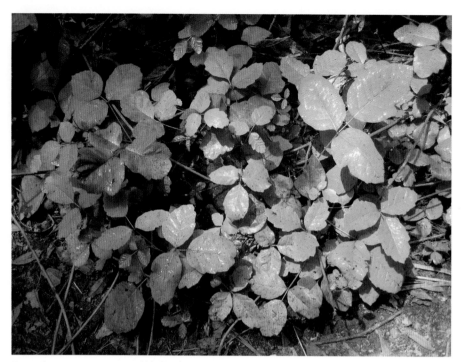

Learn how to spot poison oak before hiking! Photo by Monique Riedel.

0.75 Arrive at the base of Ribbon Rock Falls. Return via the same route.

1.5 Arrive back at the trailhead on Pleasantridge Drive.

Hike Information

Local information: Angeles National Forest, 701 N. Santa Anita Ave., Arcadia, CA, 91006; 747-322-6574 or 626-574-1613

Camping: Angeles National Forest, 701 N. Santa Anita Ave., Arcadia, CA, 91006; 747-322-6574 or 626-574-1613. Angeles National Forest campgrounds (first come, first served; 14-day stay maximum): Appletree, Bear, Bear Canyon, Big Rock, Blue Ridge, Chilao, Coldbrook, Crystal Lake, Gould Mesa, Guffy, Horse Flats, Idlehour Trail Camp, Little Jimmy Trail Camp, Los Alamos, Lupine, Manker, Messenger Flats, Millard Trail Camp, Monte Cristo, Mount Lowe Trail Camp, Oak Flat, Pacifico, Peavine, Sawmill, South, Sulphur Springs; https://www.fs.usda.gov/main/angeles/home

19 Eaton Canyon Falls

If you are looking for variety and challenge, Eaton Canyon is for you. This trail is a leisurely stroll that, at times, presents a moderate challenge and an even greater reward in the form of one of Southern California's most picturesque waterfalls and mirrored pools.

Start: At the end of Veranda Avenue in the Eaton Canyon Natural Area parking lot
Distance: 3.7 miles out and back
Hiking time: About 2.5 hours
Difficulty: Moderate for steep and loose footing and creek crossings
Trail surface: Paved road, dirt road, and packed dirt and rock
Nearest town: Pasadena
County: Los Angeles
Other trail users: None
Canine compatibility: Leashed dogs permitted

Trailhead facilities/amenities: Available
Land status: National forest
Fees and permits: None
Schedule: Open year-round, sunrise to sunset; can be hot in summer
Maps: USGS Mount Wilson, CA; www.ecnca .org/hiking_trails/hiking_trails.html
Trail contact: Eaton Canyon Natural Area Park and Nature Center, 1750 N. Altadena Dr., Pasadena, CA, 91107; www.ecnca.org; 626-398-5420; https://parks.lacounty.gov/ eaton-canyon-natural-area-and-nature-center/

Finding the trailhead: From Los Angeles, take CA 110/Pasadena Freeway north. Drive to the end of the Pasadena Freeway. Continue north on Arroyo Parkway for 1.3 miles. Turn right onto Colorado Boulevard and drive for 2.6 miles. Turn left onto Sierra Madre Boulevard and drive for 0.4 mile. Turn left onto Altadena Drive and drive for 1.8 miles. Turn right onto Veranda Avenue into the signed parking lot for Eaton Canyon Park. GPS: 34°10'39.6"N 118°05'47.8"W

The Hike

Eaton Canyon, formerly known as "El Precipio" by the Spanish due to its precipitous fissures and extreme terrain, is named for Judge Benjamin Eaton. Judge Eaton resided not far from Eaton Canyon at Fair Oaks Ranch House in the late 1800s and was one of the founders of the historic Mount Wilson Toll Road. Today, Eaton Canyon is governed by several different agencies and comprises 190 acres of land that lie between San Gabriel Peak and Mount Markham along the San Andreas Fault in the San Gabriel Mountains. The park offers a variety of activities, from challenging to leisurely.

Eaton Canyon has a visitors' center you do not want to miss. The visitors' center provides fantastic amenities, including a restroom, gift shop, historical information, and an interactive learning center complete with live animals. This is a must-see for all ages. You won't be disappointed.

The rocky gorge of Eaton Canyon. Photo by Sierra Riedel.

From the visitors' center, follow the pavement to the north end of the parking area. The trailhead begins on the other side of a bright yellow gate. Follow the trail past the yellow gate; you are on Park Road Trail.

Park Road Trail is a wide dirt path that resembles more of a road than a hiking trail. Continue into the creek bed and follow the trail over the creek. Depending on the season, the water level will vary. Beyond the creek, follow the trail veering to the left. This part of the trail consists of a wide, dusty path with patches of intermittent tree groves but is predominantly open and exposed to sunlight. Follow this wide trail 1.3 miles to a bridge at the Mount Wilson Toll Road.

Continue under the bridge toward Eaton Falls Trail. Here the trail takes on a new appearance because you will be entering the canyon. It becomes narrower and uneven in constitution and is highly affected by the water level in the canyon, which will fluctuate with the season. The trail begins its windy course upward into the steep gorge of the canyon. Just underneath the bridge, a few feet up the canyon, you will come to the first of several creek crossings. There are strategically placed rocks and logs for crossings during high water, and the trail is easy to find on the other side of the creek bed. Continue upward into the canyon, following the intricate zigzag of the trail toward the falls for about 0.5 mile to Eaton Canyon Falls.

JOHN MUIR

John Muir, born in Scotland in 1838, is the founder of modern conservation and the Sierra Club. He is credited with being responsible for preserving wilderness in the western US and for being the impetus for the foundation of Yosemite and Yellowstone National Parks. His writings and philosophies influenced presidents, other leaders, and the entire conservation movement.

As a young man, Muir was injured in an industrial accident, and it was feared that he would not regain his sight. Immediately, he felt a sense of purpose, deciding that he would explore the wonders of the natural world and "study the inventions of God." He left his home and walked from Indiana to Florida, taking the most forested path he could find. In Florida, he caught malaria and immediately booked transport to California. Upon arrival in California, Muir promptly traveled to Yosemite, where he found his life's passion. His was a kindred spirit with the natural world and he relished its magnificence, feeling a spiritual connection with nature and the beauty that surrounded him.

Muir's ideas differed from those of many of his contemporaries. To explain the scientific formation of Yosemite Valley, Muir argued for glaciation as the reason for the carved granite walls, whereas his chief rival, Josiah Whitney, head of the California Geological Survey, said that Yosemite was created by massive earthquakes. He also differed in his conservation strategies. Muir believed the forests to be a temple (though he saw a need for sustained use), whereas most of his contemporaries saw the forests as simply needing to be preserved for utilitarian purposes and nothing more.

Muir's ideas have influenced the foundation with which we today look at nature. In the late 1800s civilization was encroaching upon the wildlands but had not yet engulfed them. Muir's voice was the centralizing force that led to the preservation of our national parks and wild areas; his leadership as a wilderness prophet was exactly what was needed at the right time for this nation and the world.

Though Muir had many forward-thinking ideas, and his philosophy evolved later in life, the Sierra Club has recently reexamined his legacy in light of racist comments and viewpoints he held toward those of African descent and Indigenous populations. While heroes of the past are seldom without flaws, John Muir's legacy remains, but the truth must be told so that future generations can understand the dangerous snare of racism and its lasting effects upon humanity.

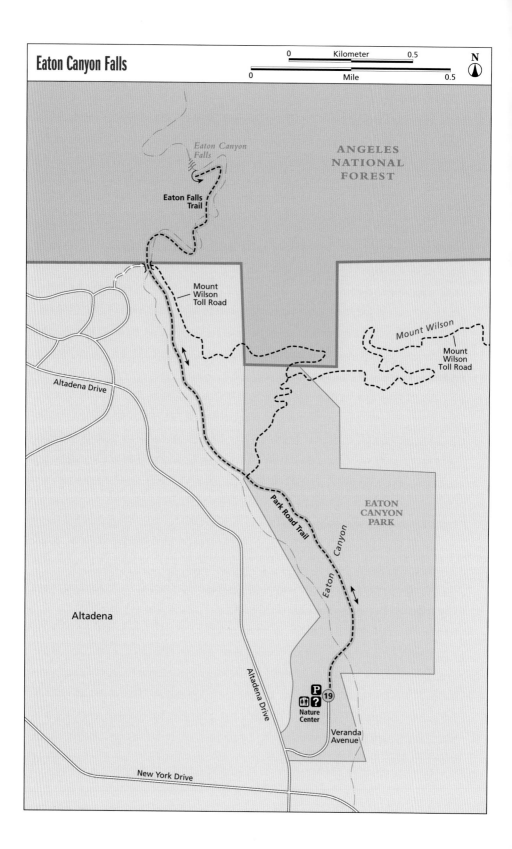

Eaton Canyon Falls

0 Kilometer 0.5
0 Mile 0.5

N

Eaton Canyon Falls

ANGELES
NATIONAL
FOREST

**Eaton Falls
Trail**

Mount
Wilson
Toll Road

Mount Wilson

Mount
Wilson
Toll Road

Altadena Drive

Park Road Trail

Eaton Canyon

EATON
CANYON
PARK

Altadena

Nature
Center

19

Veranda
Avenue

Altadena Drive

New York Drive

These falls are indubitably one of Southern California's most enchanting. John Muir is quoted as describing these falls as "a charming little thing, with a low, sweet voice, singing like a bird, as it pours from a notch in a short ledge, some thirty or forty feet into a round mirror-pool." The base of these falls is a popular destination for picnickers, sunbathers, and photographers, and, for the more adventuresome, swimmers. In 2014, due to the large numbers of rescues/injuries from inexperienced hikers above the falls, exploring beyond the falls is no longer allowed. Exploring beyond the falls is dangerous and punishable by a $5,000 fine and/or six months' imprisonment.

When you have concluded your excursion, follow the same trail back down into the canyon to the parking area and visitors' center.

Miles and Directions

0.0 Start from the visitors' center in Eaton Canyon Park and walk north through the parking area along Veranda Avenue.

0.2 At the yellow gate, cross over and walk north along the wide dirt path known as Park Road Trail. Stay on the main, widest path.

1.3 Arrive at the bridge on Mount Wilson Toll Road. Continue on the Eaton Falls Trail, underneath the bridge. Follow the trail as it winds through the canyon.

1.8 Arrive at Eaton Canyon Falls. Return via the same route.

3.7 Arrive back at the trailhead, visitors' center, and parking area.

Hike Information

Local information: Eaton Canyon Natural Area, 1750 N. Altadena Dr., Pasadena, CA; 626-398-5420; Angeles National Forest, 701 N. Santa Anita Ave., Arcadia, CA, 91006; https://www.fs.usda.gov/angeles/; 747-322-6574 or 626-574-1613

Camping: Angeles National Forest, 701 N. Santa Anita Ave., Arcadia, CA, 91006; 747-322-6574 or 626-574-1613. Angeles National Forest campgrounds (first come, first served; 14-day stay maximum): Appletree, Bear, Bear Canyon, Big Rock, Blue Ridge, Chilao, Coldbrook, Crystal Lake, Gould Mesa, Guffy, Horse Flats, Idlehour Trail Camp, Little Jimmy Trail Camp, Los Alamos, Lupine, Manker, Messenger Flats, Millard Trail Camp, Monte Cristo, Mount Lowe Trail Camp, Oak Flat, Pacifico, Peavine, Sawmill, South, Sulphur Springs; https://www.fs.usda.gov/main/angeles/home

20 Sturtevant Falls

Sturtevant Falls is slated to reopen in April 2023. It remains in this book because it is an incredible area and waterfall and historically important to the San Gabriel Mountains. Though changed, the canyon demonstrates the true power of regrowth in the forest.

Start: Chantry Flat Recreation Area
Distance: 3.5 miles out and back
Hiking time: About 2.5 hours
Difficulty: Easy, but with a few creek crossings
Trail surface: Paved road, dirt road, and single-track dirt trail
Nearest town: Altadena
County: Los Angeles
Other trail users: Bicyclists
Canine compatibility: Leashed dogs permitted
Trailhead facilities/amenities: Located at the trailhead and along the hike; water must be filtered on trail

Land status: National forest
Fees and permits: Adventure Pass required for parking
Schedule: Open year-round; FR 2N40 open 6 a.m. to 8 p.m.
Maps: USGS Mount Wilson, CA; www.bigsanta-anitacanyon.com/Chantry_map.htm
Trail contact: Angeles National Forest, 701 N. Santa Anita Ave., Arcadia, CA, 91006; https://www.fs.usda.gov/angeles/; 747-322-6574 or 626-574-1613

Finding the trailhead: From Los Angeles, take I-5 north. Exit 139A for CA 2 North/Glendale Freeway north toward Glendale, driving for 3.5 miles. Take Exit 17A to merge onto CA 134 east toward Pasadena, and drive for 5.3 miles. Continue on I-210 east for 6.4 miles. Take Exit 32 for Santa Anita Avenue; turn left and drive 4.9 miles. Santa Anita Avenue becomes FR 2N40 and Santa Anita Canyon Trail/Santa Anita Canyon Avenue. Park in the lot or along FR 2N40. GPS: 34°11'44.3"N 118°01'21.2"W

The Hike

The trail to Sturtevant Falls follows the Gabrielino National Recreation Trail, a classification assigned to existing trails that contribute to "health, conservation, and recreation goals" in the US, for most of the route. Only the last portion follows the Sturtevant Falls Trail.

From the 1880s to the 1930s, the "Great Hiking Era" boomed throughout the Angeles National Forest, causing an upswing in a need for trail accommodations as thousands of visitors were finding their way into the Big Santa Anita Canyon. Wilbur M. Sturtevant was one such hiking enthusiast, establishing Sturtevant's Camp in 1892, located in a shady grove in upper Big Santa Anita Canyon. Today, Sturtevant's Camp is the only remaining resort in the area. Private cabins can be seen nestled among alder trees and live oak groves along the trail's stream. These cabins are for recreational use only and are operated by private owners under a "special use permit" to keep "improvements" on federal land. Enjoy the charm and delight of these quaint cabins,

Shade cools the trail. Photo by Makaila Riedel.

but be mindful and respectful of the owners' or occupants' privacy. The 2020 Bobcat Fire rushed through Big Santa Anita Canyon and destroyed 17 of the 81 historic cabins; only 64 now remain. It is undecided if the Forest Service will allow owners to rebuild after the fire.

Parking at Chantry Flat is limited, so be prepared to find a spot along the narrow roadway leading into Chantry Flat. At the trailhead, there is a visitor kiosk and restrooms.

The first part of the trail is a wide, paved portion of the Gabrielino Trail. You will descend about 400 feet into Santa Anita Canyon via this road. At 0.5 mile you will arrive at a wooden footbridge crossing a stream and a rest area with restrooms. From here, follow the trail to the right at the junction with Winter Creek Trail and continue up Santa Anita Canyon to the north.

The trail begins to lose its lackluster appearance and emerges into a landscape teeming with vegetation, water, and wildlife. Damage from the fire is evident, but the beauty remains. Here you will be greeted by the sounds of nature—several different species of birds, insects, and babbling brooks. Where nature did not always provide conveniently placed rocks for a rippling stream, Los Angeles County has helped out by placing concrete weirs strategically along the creek, which when covered with moss and foliage add to the rustic appeal. At this juncture, the trail becomes narrow and follows the stream up into the canyon. Here you walk through a canyon damaged by the natural process of fire, but many of the trees that survived and the surrounding forest will completely regrow and thrive in time.

At 1.25 miles, at the Fern Lodge Junction, follow the trail straight up toward the falls. The trail to the left leads to a picnic area and campground. Just a few minutes past the junction, veer to the right at a cabin marked FIDDLERS CROSSING, and follow the easily definable trail over the creek. There are strategically placed rocks and boulders for crossing but be prepared for a bit of adventure as water levels vary depending on season.

The trail winds back up to the left and to another similar creek crossing, which brings you to a shady grotto area canopied by trees and large boulders. Follow the trail straight uphill, veering to the right and into the alcove, where you will find the enchanting Sturtevant Falls.

Beginning at 50 feet up the canyon precipice, the falls provide a wondrous cascade into a shimmering pool at the base of the canyon wall. Large boulders, small rocks, and some shade trees offer a perfect ambience for those seeking to revel in the fragrant air and ethereal environment of Sturtevant Falls. When departing, be mindful that the last stretch of the hike requires a 400-foot ascent back up to Chantry Flat.

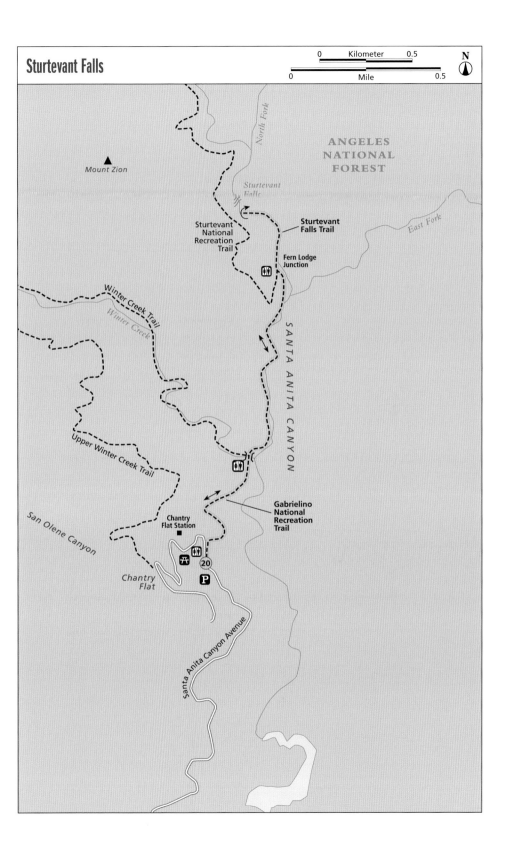

Sturtevant Falls

0   Kilometer   0.5

0   Mile   0.5

N

Mount Zion

North Fork

ANGELES
NATIONAL
FOREST

Sturtevant
Falls

Sturtevant
Falls Trail

East Fork

Sturtevant
National
Recreation
Trail

Fern Lodge
Junction

Winter Creek Trail

Winter Creek

SANTA ANITA CANYON

Upper Winter Creek Trail

Gabrielino
National
Recreation
Trail

Chantry
Flat Station

San Olene Canyon

Chantry
Flat

20

P

Santa Anita Canyon Avenue

Miles and Directions

0.0 From the lower parking area, cross the road and head down the paved section of the Gabrielino Trail.

0.5 Turn right at the bridge and junction with the Winter Creek Trail and follow Santa Anita Canyon north.

1.25 Turn right at Fern Lodge Junction and head to the base of Sturtevant Falls.

1.75 Arrive at the base of the falls. Return via the same route.

3.5 Arrive back at the trailhead at Chantry Flat.

Hike Information

Local information: Angeles National Forest, 701 N. Santa Anita Ave., Arcadia, CA, 91006; https://www.fs.usda.gov/angeles/; 747-322-6574 or 626-574-1613

Camping: Angeles National Forest, 701 N. Santa Anita Ave, Arcadia, CA, 91006; 747-322-6574 or 626-574-1613. Angeles National Forest campgrounds (first come, first served; 14-day stay maximum): Appletree, Bear, Bear Canyon, Big Rock, Blue Ridge, Chilao, Coldbrook, Crystal Lake, Gould Mesa, Guffy, Horse Flats, Idlehour Trail Camp, Little Jimmy Trail Camp, Los Alamos, Lupine, Manker, Messenger Flats, Millard Trail Camp, Monte Cristo, Mount Lowe Trail Camp, Oak Flat, Pacifico, Peavine, Sawmill, South, Sulphur Springs; https://www.fs.usda.gov/main/angeles/home

21 Monrovia Canyon Falls

An easy jaunt through a primeval-looking riparian rainforest culminates at a charming waterfall resplendent with alluring flora and fauna at its bubbling crest. Monrovia Canyon reopened in August 2021 after the 2020 Bobcat Fire.

Start: At the Monrovia Canyon Park middle parking lot
Distance: 2 miles out and back
Hiking time: About 1.5 hours
Difficulty: Easy but with a few creek crossings
Trail surface: Paved road, dirt road, and single-track dirt trail
Nearest town: Santa Anita
County: Los Angeles
Other trail users: None
Canine compatibility: Leashed dogs permitted
Trailhead facilities/amenities: All facilities available
Land status: City park, national forest
Fees and permits: Parking fee is charged; reservations required for hiking in the park until further notice. To make trail reservations visit the web page: https://cityofmonroviarecreation .org/CourseActivities.aspx?id=2005&cat=3
Schedule: Open year-round, 8 a.m. to 5 p.m., gate closes and locks at 5 p.m. sharp; closed Tuesday
Maps: USGS Azusa, CA; www.ci.monrovia.ca .us/images/content/community_life/bro_wild guide_mcc.pdf
Trail contacts: Angeles National Forest, 701 N. Santa Anita Ave., Arcadia, CA, 91006; https:// www.fs.usda.gov/angeles/; 747-322-6574 or 626-574-1613. Monrovia Canyon Park, 1200 N. Canyon Blvd., Monrovia, CA, 91016; 415 South Ivy Ave., Monrovia, CA, 91016; 626-932-5550; www.ci.monrovia.ca.us/ community-life/parks/342-monrovia-canyon -park; 626-256-8282

Finding the trailhead: From Los Angeles, head north on CA 110. Drive to the conclusion of CA 110. Continue onto Arroyo Parkway for 1.3 miles. Turn right onto Colorado Boulevard; drive for 3.8 miles. Turn left onto Sierra Madre Villa Avenue and drive for 0.1 mile. Turn right to merge onto I-210 east. Drive for 2.8 miles. Take Exit 32 for Santa Anita Avenue toward Arcadia. Turn left onto Santa Anita and drive for 0.2 mile. Turn right onto Foothill Boulevard. Drive for 2 miles. Turn left onto Canyon Boulevard and drive for 0.4 mile. Turn right to stay on Canyon Boulevard and continue for 0.8 mile to the parking lot and trailhead. GPS: 34°10'21.4"N 117°59'30.5"W

The Hike

The Monrovia Canyon watershed is sustained by a variety of water sources high in the San Gabriel Mountains. The falls at Monrovia Canyon are a result of these springs nourishing the watershed at a 30-foot waterfall nestled in the canyon. The landscape and foliage surrounding the canyon are verdant any time of year and provide for a lush, canopied traverse from the trailhead into the canyon to the streamside habitat at the base of the falls. Though the canyon was burned and damaged in the 2020 Bobcat Fire and the area has changed, it still retains much of its beauty. Bobcats and bears have returned, and wildflowers and new growth are emerging everywhere.

Monrovia Canyon Falls spills 30 feet over a double cascade. Photo by Michael Millenheft III.

SAN ANDREAS FAULT

The San Andreas Fault is the 810-mile sliding boundary between the Pacific and the North American plates that extends from the northwest part of California into Mexico and the Gulf of California. It has been responsible for the two major quakes in San Francisco: the 1906 disaster that nearly leveled and burned the entire city and the 1989 Loma Prieta Quake, or the World Series Quake, which caused substantial damage as well.

Everything to the west of the fault line is moving to the northwest, and the converse is true for the eastern side. Even though the plates only move a little more than an inch in each direction every year, the pressure exerted on the tectonic plates is enough to cause major earthquakes when the two sides jar back into place. All the mountain ranges of Southern California, from the Santa Lucias in Big Sur to the San Jacintos, were uplifted from the pressure and movement of the two plates. The fault is notable in that rocks on one side share no common geological component with the rocks on the other side of the fault line. One famous example is in the Pinnacles National Monument near Salinas, where the volcanic outcropping of rocks that makes up the park has a geologic twin in the remnants of the Neenach Volcano, which sits 200 miles to the south in the city of Lancaster.

Anyone wishing to see the power or the evidence of the fault line itself can travel to Devil's Punchbowl Natural Area, Vasquez, or Mormon Rocks, where colossal angular sedimentary rocks jut out from the earth's crust. The fault line is also visible from the ground in the Carrizo Plain in central California, and the familiar pictures in science books are taken here.

While the San Andreas Fault is not going to suddenly push California into the sea, it will, one day, after millions of years of movement, push Southern California into San Francisco—in fact, it has already done so. The geology at Point Reyes is the same as that of the Tehachapi Mountains, which sit several hundred miles to the south along the fault.

The majority of mature trees survived the conflagration though the scars will tell the story for decades to come.

Parking at Monrovia Canyon Park is limited both in space and time. The area provides for a small number of vehicles and requires a fee. The gates are closed from 5 p.m. to 8 a.m. Therefore, if you are seeking a sunset or sunrise hike, it may be necessary to find parking in the residential area just outside the park entrance. Currently, there are a limited number of reservations per day to hike in the park. Visit the park's website to obtain a permit.

There is a nature center and restroom facilities in the parking area north of the trailhead. Begin on

▶ Safety Tip: When hiking with children, hold hands at steep, narrow, or difficult sections.

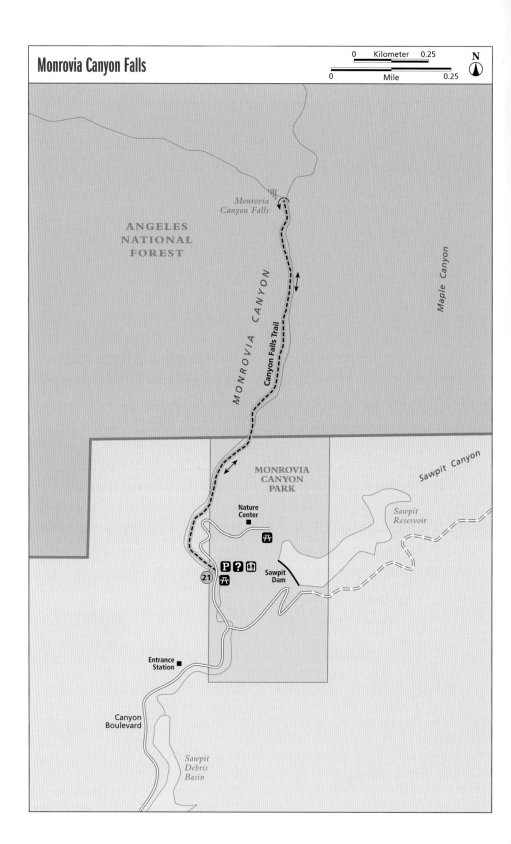

Monrovia Canyon Falls

0   Kilometer   0.25

0   Mile   0.25

N

Monrovia Canyon Falls

ANGELES NATIONAL FOREST

MONROVIA CANYON

Canyon Falls Trail

Maple Canyon

Sawpit Canyon

MONROVIA CANYON PARK

Nature Center

Sawpit Reservoir

P ? 🚻

21

Sawpit Dam

Entrance Station

Canyon Boulevard

Sawpit Debris Basin

the trail behind the nature center. The trail starts out as a narrow path following along a road but quickly twists off the pavement and into the mouth of the canyon. Plant life and animal life are abundant any time of year. The path is well maintained but may still have some protruding poison oak during the spring months, so be wary of straying off the dirt trail.

Continue following the natural curve of the trail up into the canyon along a burbling stream. The Los Angeles County water department has constructed a series of concrete weirs that provide added delight, with intermittent "waterfalls" along the route. At times, the trail widens and narrows along the canyon wall. The majority of the trail is canopied by overhanging trees of a variety of species, providing a good amount of shade from the sun, even after the 2020 Bobcat Fire.

Creek crossings can be fairly simple, like this one, though swift-moving and deep water should not be crossed. Photo by Allen Riedel.

At 0.75 mile, you will arrive at the aperture of Monrovia Falls. These 30-foot falls are dramatically set against large boulders and a canopy of trees. The boulders and rocks are plentiful and may be slippery or mossy, so caution is required when exploring the area around the falls. The pool at the base of the falls ranges from very shallow to moderate enough for wading. It is common to come upon fellow travelers wetting their feet in the pool or sitting on a rock dipping their toes in the cool mountain water. From the falls, return via the same trail, heading back down into the canyon and out to the trailhead by the parking area and nature center.

Miles and Directions

0.0 Begin your hike at the second parking lot, behind the nature center.

0.75 Arrive at Monrovia Canyon Falls. Return via the same route.

1.5 Arrive back at the trailhead and nature center.

Hike Information

Local information: Angeles National Forest, 701 N. Santa Anita Ave., Arcadia, CA, 91006; https://www.fs.usda.gov/angeles/; 747-322-6574 or 626-574-1613;

Monrovia Canyon Park, 1200 N. Canyon Blvd., Monrovia, CA, 91016; 415 South Ivy Avenue, Monrovia, CA, 91016; 626-932-5550; www.ci.monrovia.ca.us/community -life/parks/342-monrovia-canyon-park; 626-256-8282

Camping: Angeles National Forest campgrounds (first come, first served; 14-day stay maximum): Appletree, Bear, Bear Canyon, Big Rock, Blue Ridge, Chilao, Coldbrook, Crystal Lake, Gould Mesa, Guffy, Horse Flats, Idlehour Trail Camp, Little Jimmy Trail Camp, Los Alamos, Lupine, Manker, Messenger Flats, Millard Trail Camp, Monte Cristo, Mount Lowe Trail Camp, Oak Flat, Pacifico, Peavine, Sawmill, South, Sulphur Springs; https://www.fs.usda.gov/main/angeles/home

22 Mount Hawkins

This section of the Pacific Crest Trail (PCT) has been one of the most beautiful sections of trail for hiking in Southern California. The 2020 Bobcat Fire burned a large portion of Mount Islip up to Little Jimmy Campground altering the first 2 miles of this trail for our lifetimes at least. Though the trail has not yet officially reopened, it remains in the book due to its history, awe-inspiring views, and certain impending reopening. Fire may damage and change the landscape but much survives, and the natural ecology sports regrowth and rebirth. A large section of the Angeles National Forest was closed by the Bobcat Fire, and areas in the lower mountains remain off-limits. On April 1, 2022, most of the high country reopened, including the entire length of the PCT through the forest.

Start: Islip Saddle
Distance: 8.5 miles out and back
Hiking time: About 5 hours
Difficulty: Strenuous
Trail surface: Single-track dirt trail
Nearest town: Wrightwood
County: Los Angeles
Other trail users: None
Canine compatibility: Leashed dogs permitted
Trailhead facilities/amenities: Restrooms at trailhead and Little Jimmy Trail Camp, picnic area at camp, filterable water at Little Jimmy Spring

Land status: National forest
Fees and permits: Adventure Pass required for parking
Schedule: Open year-round, Highway 2 often closes at Islip Saddle during the winter
Maps: USGS Crystal Lake, CA; http://c027 8592.cdn.cloudfiles.rackspacecloud.com/ original/276832.jpg
Trail contact: Angeles National Forest, 701 N. Santa Anita Ave., Arcadia, CA, 91006; www.fs .fed.us/r5/angeles; 626-574-5200

Finding the trailhead: From Los Angeles, head north on I-5. Take Exit 139A for CA 2/Glendale Freeway, toward Glendale. Drive for 7.7 miles and take Exit 21A to merge onto CA 2/I-210, heading east toward Pasadena. Drive 1.2 miles. Take Exit 20 for CA 2/Angeles Crest Highway, heading toward La Canada Flintridge. Turn left onto CA 2 and drive 39.5 miles to Islip Saddle. Park on the left. CA 2 closes periodically due to storms, fire, fire danger, and rockslides, especially between Dawson Gap and Islip Saddle. GPS: 34°21'25.2"N 117°51'04.2"W

The Hike

From Islip Saddle, most hikers head to Mount Islip along the Pacific Crest Trail (PCT), and the trail is popular. Even after the 2020 Bobcat Fire, the hike to Islip will return to prominence, as the beautifully forested section from Little Jimmy Campground to the Windy Gap and beyond has survived unscathed. Some hikers take the route less traveled and trek on the desert side, heading toward Mount Williamson, a virtual twin hike and summit to Mount Islip, which was also closed and burned badly in the Bobcat Fire. Since Williamson is on the drier high-desert side of the Pacific Crest Ridge, it took the brunt of the fire, but pictures show regrowth with a partial mountainside and top filled with pine trees that survived. Only few take the trek to the top of Mount Hawkins. Overall, the distance for the entire trip adds 2 miles and the elevation gain is steeper and greater, but then again, so are the elements of freedom, the vestiges of solitude, and the vistas that pack a much more exceptional punch.

The Angeles Crest Highway follows much of the route, albeit several hundred feet below the trail, so when the highway is open all the way through the mountains, there is more noise on this trail—but mostly only when loud motorcyclists take to the mountains on Sunday. Midweek car noise will barely give off an audible peep.

The trail begins at Islip Saddle. Cross the highway from the large parking lot and restrooms and begin heading up into the mountains. The beginning section of the trail switchbacks and heads steeply up through manzanita, whitethorn, and mountain chaparral for the first 0.5 mile. This area all burned but is experiencing much regrowth and will continue to do so until the fire damage is unrecognizable. After the first bit, the route continues to gain elevation, but at a much slower pace, and the trail winds through a lovely forest of Jeffrey pine, sugar pine, and ponderosa pine trees. Here is where much of the Bobcat Fire did the most damage.

▶ **The fire lookout on South Mount Hawkins burned down in the 2002 Curve Fire.**

The trail crosses an old dirt access road several times, and there are signs along the way directing the hiker to Little Jimmy Camp, Little Jimmy Spring, and Mount Islip. Stay on the trail and not on the dirt road. Of course, the usual triangular-curved PCT trail sign can be seen on posts spaced consistently along the way. At times, the highway can be also seen below and sometimes heard. Just before Little Jimmy, the Bobcat Fire eased up and the forest here is lovely and primeval.

At 2 miles the trail enters Little Jimmy Trail Camp, named for "Little Jimmy" Swinnerton, a cartoonist who some say invented the comic strip. A favorite employee of William Randolph Hearst, he moved to the Southwest in 1906 after being diagnosed with tuberculosis. He frequented the campsite, drawing cartoons for guests and even carving a character on a tree there. He became such a regular that officials named the campsite after him.

Follow the trail through the lower section of the camp toward Little Jimmy Spring and Windy Gap. Restrooms are available in the campsite. In seasons with normal precipitation, Little Jimmy Spring flows throughout the year, though it dries up by the end of summer and in dry years may only be a trickle. Improvements were made to the spring so that the water drips from a pipe, though it is still suggested to boil or filter the water before drinking.

At 2.25 miles, hikers will come to Windy Gap, a great viewpoint and a trail junction for those heading up to Mount Islip, heading down to Crystal Lake, or continuing along the PCT. Turn left and follow the PCT as it winds and switchbacks up the slope of Mount Hawkins. The trail gains 1,200 feet in the next 2 miles, and though

The Pacific Crest Trail (PCT) winds up toward Mount Hawkins. Photo by Allen Riedel.

it isn't severely steep, there is enough of a gain to make this a strenuous hike. Some remnants of the 2002 Curve Fire will be visible on the higher reaches of the trail, and at 3.75 miles, the summit of Mount Hawkins sits 200 feet overhead as the trail passes it by.

At 4 miles, the trail gains the crest and hikers must veer sharply right to take the use trail to the top of Mount Hawkins. The trail gains a short 100 feet to the summit, and the views are decidedly amazing. There is a view of Mount Baldy that is straight on, and the high desert can be seen below as well as the other high peaks in this section of the national forest.

LITTLE JIMMY SWINNERTON

Little Jimmy Swinnerton (1875–1974), known by the names Little Jimmy, Swinny, and Swin, was a US cartoonist who was one of the first to develop newspaper cartoon strips. By some accounts, he was the first. His publication of *Little Bears and Tykes* in the *San Francisco Examiner* on June 1, 1892, predates the work of Richard F. Outcault, the man credited with the invention of the comic strip, by 2 years.

The illustrations he created used word bubbles, distinct panels, and recurring main characters. His work made use of animals, and he is credited with creating the first humorous anthropomorphic animal cartoon character, Mr. Jack, after relocating to New York and writing for Hearst's *New York Journal American*.

In 1904 Swinnerton created *Little Jimmy*, the comic for which he is most remembered. The character of Jimmy was a stereotypical young boy with a penchant for troublemaking. Little Jimmy earned his fair share of punishment by getting caught up in all sorts of shenanigans and forgetting the important things he needed to do. Little Jimmy appeared in nationwide daily syndication until the 1930s. Swinnerton continued to write a Sunday strip until he retired in 1958, when he suffered an accident which injured his hand.

Ironically, Swinnerton was told he had weeks to live when he contracted tuberculosis in 1906. He then moved West, alternating residences between Arizona and California, for the rest of his life. He disliked the heat of the desert summers and spent some time high in the San Gabriel Mountains at what is now known as Little Jimmy Trail Camp. It is reported that he carved a Little Jimmy character onto a tree there and delighted visitors with personalized drawings of Little Jimmy, who by that time was well known to newspaper readers across the country.

Swinnerton outlived his doctor and the prognosis he received, surviving in Palm Springs to the ripe old age of 98.

Mount Hawkins

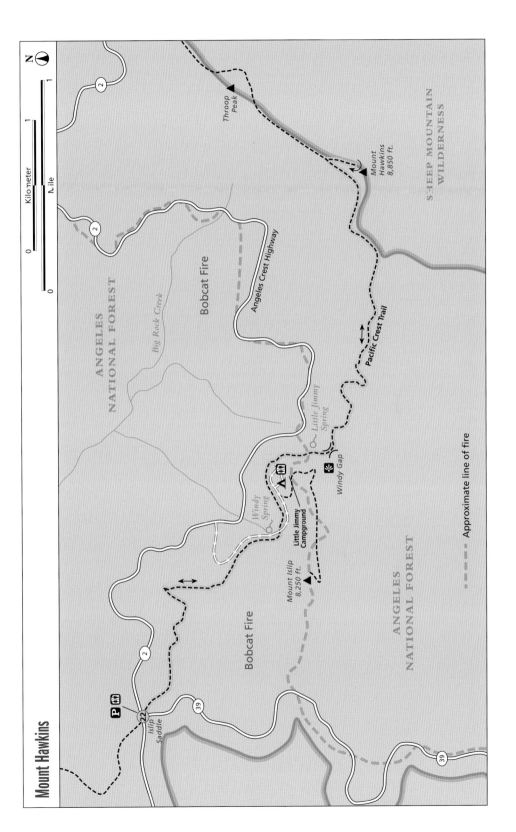

N

0 Kilometer 1

0 Mile 1

ANGELES
NATIONAL FOREST

Big Rock Creek

Bobcat Fire

Angeles Crest Highway

Throop Peak

Mount Hawkins
8,850 ft.

STEEP MOUNTAIN
WILDERNESS

Pacific Crest Trail

Little Jimmy
Spring

Windy Gap

Windy Spring

Little Jimmy
Campground

Mount Islip
8,250 ft.

Bobcat Fire

ANGELES
NATIONAL FOREST

Islip Saddle

Approximate line of fire

At 8,850 feet, Mount Hawkins is one of the tallest peaks in the forest, and it is a great place to take in the sights. The two peaks to the south, Middle Hawkins and South Mount Hawkins, also bear witness to the memory of a waitress, Nellie Hawkins, who worked at the Squirrel Inn at Crystal Lake early in the 20th century. Though information on her seems simply to point to her years serving customers, little else is known. One can only conjecture at her beauty and charm.

After enjoying the summit, return via the same route.

Miles and Directions

0.0 Start at Islip Saddle, cross the Angeles Crest Highway/CA 2, and hike along the Pacific Crest Trail (PCT).

0.75 Cross the fire road and continue along the PCT.

1.8 Cross the fire road again, then arrive at Little Jimmy Camp. Here, the fire damage from the 2020 Bobcat Fire gives way to lovely pine forest.

1.9 Arrive at the Little Jimmy Spring side trail. In another 250 feet, you'll meet the Little Jimmy Spring use trail. Both lead to the spring.

2.5 Arrive at Windy Gap. Turn left to stay on the PCT.

3.75 Pass below the summit of Mount Hawkins.

4.0 Turn sharply right to take the use trail back (south) to the summit of Mount Hawkins.

4.25 Arrive at the summit of Mount Hawkins. Return via the same route.

8.5 Arrive back at the trailhead and the Islip Saddle parking area.

Hike Information

Local information: Angeles National Forest, 701 N. Santa Anita Ave., Arcadia, CA, 91006; https://www.fs.usda.gov/angeles/; 747-322-6574 or 626-574-1613

Camping: Angeles National Forest campgrounds (first come, first served; 14-day stay maximum): Appletree, Bear, Bear Canyon, Big Rock, Blue Ridge, Chilao, Coldbrook, Crystal Lake, Gould Mesa, Guffy, Horse Flats, Idlehour Trail Camp, Little Jimmy Trail Camp, Los Alamos, Lupine, Manker, Messenger Flats, Millard Trail Camp, Monte Cristo, Mount Lowe Trail Camp, Oak Flat, Pacifico, Peavine, Sawmill, South, Sulphur Springs; https://www.fs.usda.gov/main/angeles/home

23 Mount Baden-Powell

On this no-nonsense hike to the top of one of Southern California's most prominent summits, take in jaw-dropping ridgeline and mountain views, walk past trees older than the English language itself, and get a great workout in the process.

Start: Vincent Gap
Distance: 8.2 miles out and back
Hiking time: About 4.5 hours
Difficulty: Strenuous
Trail surface: Single-track dirt trail
Nearest town: Wrightwood
County: Los Angeles
Other trail users: None
Canine compatibility: Leashed dogs permitted
Trailhead facilities/amenities: Restroom at trailhead, filterable water at spring
Land status: National forest

Fees and permits: Adventure Pass required for parking
Schedule: Open year-round, Highway 2 often closes between Wrightwood and Islip Saddle in winter
Maps: USGS Crystal Lake, CA; www.localhikes .com/HikeData.ASP?DispType=1&ActiveHike =0&GetHikesStateID=&ID=4031
Trail contact: Angeles National Forest, 701 N. Santa Anita Ave., Arcadia, CA, 91006; https:// www.fs.usda.gov/angeles/; 747-322-6574 or 626-574-1613

Finding the trailhead: From Los Angeles, head north on I-5 and take Exit 139A for CA 2/Glendale Freeway toward Glendale. Drive for 7.7 miles and take Exit 21A to merge onto CA 2/I-210, heading east toward Pasadena. Drive for 1.2 miles. Take Exit 20 for CA 2/Angeles Crest Highway toward La Canada Flintridge. Turn left onto CA 2 and drive 51 miles to the parking area for Vincent Gap on the right. CA 2 closes periodically due to storms, fire, fire danger, and rockslides, especially between Dawson Gap and Islip Saddle. When closures are in effect, use this alternate route: From Los Angeles, head east on I-10 and take Exit 58A for I-15 north. Drive for 21.8 miles and take Exit 131 for CA 138. Turn left onto CA 138 and drive west for 8.6 miles. Turn left onto CA 2 and drive for 13.9 miles to the Vincent Gap parking area. GPS: 34°22'24.6"N 117°45'08.4"W

The Hike

Mount Baden-Powell is an awesome mountain no matter which way you slice it. Sitting at 9,399 feet in elevation, it is the 16th-highest peak in Southern California. Because alternate routes to the top are longer in distance, this trip happens to be the most popular. The trail cuts back and forth, switchbacking 41 times before reaching the summit and gaining 2,800 feet of elevation in the process. Although not an easy distance or elevation gain, anyone with determination and a decent fitness level can make it to the summit.

The trail starts at the Vincent Gap parking area and is well marked. It is easy to follow as there is only one designated junction on the trail. Head southwest up the Pacific Crest Trail (PCT) toward the summit. For the first 3 miles, the trail is nicely

Views from the top of Mount Baden-Powell are expansive and broad. Photo by Allen Riedel.

shaded, passing through a mixed yellow pine forest of sugar, lodgepole, Jeffrey, and ponderosa pine with some white fir and incense cedar to boot.

Snow clings to this trail deep into summer due to its northern orientation, high elevation, and lack of direct sunlight. It is a favorite spot for novice glissading, with winter mountaineers practicing their craft with ice ax and crampons. The trail is also quite well used by Boy Scouts, casual hiking enthusiasts, backpackers, and tourists looking for a high mountain to climb just off the Angeles Crest Highway. There will be other people hiking along this trail every single day of the week, no matter what.

At about 1.8 miles, a short side trail leads left for around 100 yards to Lamel Spring. Water should be treated, filtered, or boiled before using. Trees along the route begin to thin out a little beyond 3.1 miles, and the mountain ridgeline becomes the most visible trait. The steepness of the mountain in front can be seen firsthand and the switchbacks become less lengthy as the trail turns into more of a straight-up-the-mountain venture.

There is a short-use trail that leads to a grove of limber pines at around 3.6 miles, but most people will want to bypass the trail and maybe visit on the way out. There are limber pines along the trail at this elevation anyway, and the largest one sits just ahead at the junction of the Baden-Powell Summit Trail and the PCT, which continues to the west just below the peak.

LORD BADEN-POWELL

Robert Stephenson Smyth Baden-Powell (1857–1941) was born the eighth of 10 children to a reverend father who was also a professor at Oxford University. His father passed on when Baden-Powell (or BP, as he was known for short) was only three years old. As a young boy, he spent his time hunting and exploring in the woods, avoiding his siblings and teachers by remaining out of sight.

He joined the military and embarked on campaigns in India and Africa. In Africa, he led reconnaissance missions deep into enemy territory, and this was the fundamental experience that led him to formulate his ideas on scouting. He first wrote of scouting in *Aids to Scouting*, from a military standpoint, to train young men entering into service in the army. His idea was to help young men understand and interpret their surroundings and others around them, equip them with the ability to survive, and use their powers of independent thought to solve problems. The manual became a bestseller and gave BP the idea to revise the work for all young men. Teachers across the country had begun to use the manual for instructing young boys.

Baden-Powell saw what he thought was a decline in the physical prowess of young boys, and he abhorred laziness. He wanted to instruct them in the ways of being a good citizen and helping others. The motto was to "be prepared," with an emphasis on being "good" and just to fellow citizens. Scouts were to value honor, duty, loyalty, helpfulness, courtesy, obedience, and thrift.

Baden-Powell was a gifted artist and musician; he was also known as an excellent storyteller. He died and was buried in Kenya in 1941.

In recent years, Baden-Powell has not escaped criticism from the controversies of his role in the past. He has been accused of racism and homophobia, prompting removal of statues and a reexamination of his career. Bear Gryllis, outdoor celebrity, and youngest Chief Scout ever when he was appointed at the age of 34, has remarked, "Baden-Powell may have taken the first step in creating Scouting, but the journey continues today without him. We know where we came from but we are not going back. . . . It's right we take time to listen, to educate ourselves and reflect on our movement's history. We need the humility to recognize there are times when the views and actions from our Scouting's past do not always match the values we live by today. We must learn, adapt and improve."

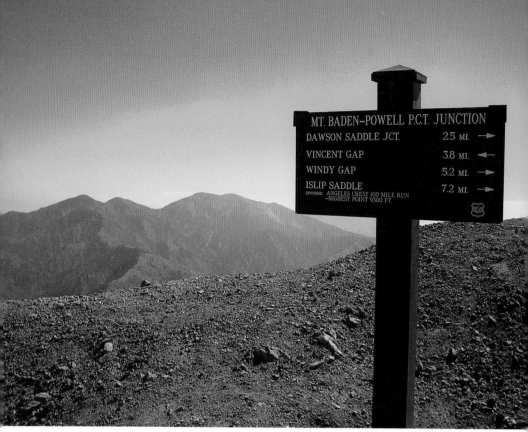

Trail sign showing the distances to popular trailheads and destinations within the Angeles National Forest. Photo by Allen Riedel.

After reaching the giant limber pine at about 3.9 miles—the Wally Waldron Tree, estimated to be between 1,500 and 2,000 years old—the vistas of the upper reaches of the San Gabriel Mountains and Mount San Antonio really open up. Turning around and looking north into the high-desert valleys is also breathtaking, provided there isn't any smog. From this point, it is a short jaunt to the top. Stay on the Baden-Powell Summit Trail, where a marker dedicated to Lord Baden-Powell, the founder of the Boy Scouts, was erected in 1957, listing some cardinal virtues and the dedication to service to others that all Scouts are supposed to stand for.

Once on top, those looking for a little isolation can continue hiking south along Baden-Powell's large hogback. Any elevation lost will have to be regained on the way out but getting as short a distance as 0.25 mile away from the summit will thin out any crowds and leave any hiker feeling like the summit belongs to them in its entirety.

Enjoy the views and return via the same route. The way down is just that—all downhill.

Miles and Directions

0.0 From the Vincent Gap parking area, head southwest up the Pacific Crest Trail.

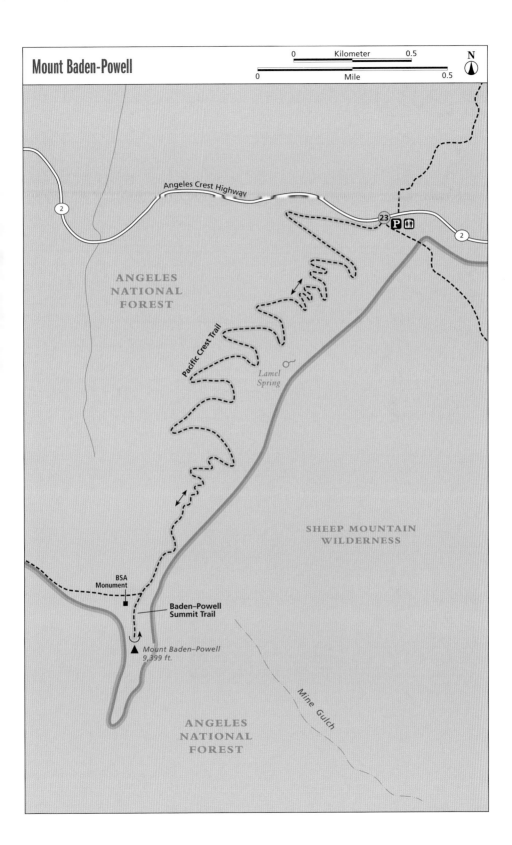

Mount Baden-Powell

Angeles Crest Highway

2

23 P 🚻

2

ANGELES
NATIONAL
FOREST

Pacific Crest Trail

Lamel
Spring

SHEEP MOUNTAIN
WILDERNESS

BSA
Monument

Baden–Powell
Summit Trail

▲ Mount Baden–Powell
9,399 ft.

ANGELES
NATIONAL
FOREST

Mine Gulch

0   Kilometer   0.5

0   Mile   0.5

N

1.8 Continue straight at the junction with the Lamel Spring Trail.

3.6 A small use trail leads to a grove of limber pines, the oldest trees in Southern California.

3.9 Continue up straight and left at the turnoff for Baden-Powell Summit Trail.

4.1 Arrive at the summit. Return via the same route.

8.2 Arrive back at the trailhead and parking area.

Hike Information

Local information: Angeles National Forest, 701 N. Santa Anita Ave., Arcadia, CA, 91006; 626-574-1613

Camping: Angeles National Forest campgrounds (first come, first served; 14-day stay maximum): Appletree, Bear, Big Rock, Blue Ridge, Cabin Flat Trail Camp, Chilao, Cooper Canyon Trail Camp, Cottonwood, Devore Trail Camp, Guffy, Horse Flats, Idlehour Trail Camp, Little Jimmy Trail Camp, Lupine, Manker Flats, Millard Trail Camp, Monte Cristo, Mountain Oak, Oak Flats, Peavine, Sawmill, South; www.fs.fed.us/r5/angeles

The monument atop Mount Baden-Powell to Lord Baden-Powell, founder of the Boy Scouts. Photo by Allen Riedel.

24 Big Horn Mine

A hardy 10-stamp mill stands intact on the stalwart slopes of Mount Baden–Powell. Follow an old wagon route to the mine and enjoy the scenery of Mount Baldy and the rugged East Fork of the San Gabriel River.

Start: Vincent Gap
Distance: 3.8 miles out and back
Hiking time: About 2 hours
Difficulty: Easy
Trail surface: Dirt and gravel trail
Nearest town: Wrightwood
County: Los Angeles
Other trail users: None
Canine compatibility: Leashed dogs permitted
Trailhead facilities/amenities: Restrooms available at trailhead
Land status: National forest

Fees and permits: Adventure Pass required for parking
Schedule: Open year-round; Highway 2 often closes between Wrightwood and Islip Saddle during the winter
Maps: USGS Crystal Lake, CA, and Mount San Antonio, CA; www.localhikes.com/HikeData .ASP?DispType=1&ActiveHike=0&GetHikes StateID=&ID=4677
Trail contact: Angeles National Forest, 701 N. Santa Anita Ave., Arcadia, CA, 91006; https://www.fs.usda.gov/angeles/; 747-322-6574 or 626-574-1613

Finding the trailhead: From Los Angeles, head north on I-5. Exit 139A for CA 2/Glendale Freeway toward Glendale. Drive for 7.7 miles and take Exit 21A to merge onto CA 2/I-210, heading east toward Pasadena. Drive for 1.2 miles. Take Exit 20 for CA 2/Angeles Crest Highway toward La Canada Flintridge. Turn left onto CA 2 and drive 51 miles to the parking area for Vincent Gap on the right. CA 2 closes periodically due to storms, fire, fire danger, and rockslides, especially between Dawson Gap and Islip Saddle. When closures are in effect, use this alternate route: From Los Angeles, head east on I-10 and take Exit 58A for I-15 north. Drive for 21.8 miles and take Exit 131 for CA 138. Turn left onto CA 138 and drive for 8.6 miles. Turn left onto CA 2 and drive west for 13.9 miles to the Vincent Gap parking area. GPS: 34°22'24.6"N 117°45'08.4"W

The Hike

The historic Big Horn Mine rests on the shoulder of mighty Mount Baden–Powell. The claim originally took shape in 1896, when old mountain man, prospector, hermit, and Civil War fighter Charles Vincent (Dougherty) found gold while hunting for bighorn sheep on the side of the mountain and discovered a vein. Vincent began to work the mine, digging tunnels, but had no way to transport the gold ore, so he ended up selling the claim in 1901. Then the stamp mill was erected, and the mine was enlarged to a massive endeavor. The mine became the largest in Los Angeles County. And, yes, Vincent Gap, Vincent Saddle, and Vincent Gulch are all named after the man who founded the mine.

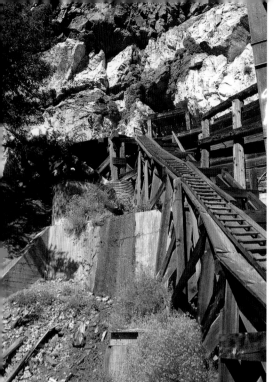

Rusted—but fascinating—machinery from the Big Horn Mine. Photo by Allen Riedel.

The mine was a towering complex, with six levels and miles of tunnel, though the exact extent is disputed. Spelunkers will no doubt scream with delight at the prospect of entering and exploring an old mine shaft, let alone an extensive network. The mine itself is inundated with water in many spots, and the old ladders are soggy and waterlogged. Deep shafts filled with water are everywhere, and the mine entrance has been closed off by the Forest Service and property owners on several occasions. It is unsafe to explore, although maps can be found online. Many of the tunnels lead in circles, and even the official maps of the mine make it look labyrinthine.

At one time, the mine was thought to have been the most lucrative in Southern California, but it did not end up as such. Still, the beauty of the mill sitting on the mountain slope is fascinating and will be of great interest to almost anyone who visits. It is fairly easy to reach and the hike is not difficult, but there are a few places where the old road has washed out, and getting to the stamp mill requires a leap over a small drainage area that may be difficult for young children.

The hike is straightforward for the most part. Look for the ROAD CLOSED sign and gate, and follow the old wagon road for the entire route. At just more than 0.1 mile there is a sign for the Sheep Mountain Wilderness, and the trail leading to Vincent Gulch follows on the left just beyond that. A little less than halfway into the hike, the main mineshaft entrance sits to the right. It is closed and welded shut, though water drips and seeps from the old mine. Stay on the old wagon road and continue the entire 1.9 miles to the stamp mill.

The views into the East Fork of the San Gabriel River and of the Devil's Backbone along the backside of Mount Baldy are fantastic; the high-mountain air is fresh and invigorating. It's a great place to ponder the history of the mountains, and what life must have been like for the lone mountain man who eked out his existence in his tiny cabin nearby. There is much to enjoy on this hike.

It is possible to visit old Vincent's cabin, a one-room shanty that still stands, by taking the spur trail with the Vincent Gulch Trail 0.4 mile from the start of the hike; the Vincent Gulch Trail veers off to the left, and in approximately 0.6 mile reaches the cabin. This adds 1.2 miles to the overall trip but is a worthwhile side exploit.

CHARLES TOM VINCENT

Charles Tom Vincent (1838–1926), a.k.a. Charles Vincent Dougherty, was an irascible old miner and mountain man who lived a solitary life on the steep slopes of what is now Mount Baden-Powell. Vincent was a man of extraordinary skill who was rumored to have killed three grizzly bears while they were in the process of attacking him.

What is known for sure is that Vincent established the claim for the Big Horn Mine, which sits just below the saddle and above the gulch that was named for him in the Angeles National Forest. It is purported that he found gold one day while out hunting for bighorn sheep. The mine became the biggest in Los Angeles County, spanning six levels and including several miles of tunnels, but it was hardly the most profitable mine. Vincent eked out the puny sum of $200,000, a small amount for gold mines in the heyday of mining. Vincent was unable to move the ore and sold his claim to the California Mining Company in 1901.

He lived in a solitary manner for the remainder of his days, befriending only Bob Pallett and Dr. Lee Nobel and his wife, Dorothy. Pallett delivered the mail to Vincent, and the trio would stop in from time to time to check on the old man. He regaled them with stories of his time in the forest, his days in the Union Army, and of the battle of Gettysburg, where he was wounded. Vincent was a member of the Eighth Ohio Infantry, F Company.

With his friends, Vincent shared the story of his life. Apparently, Vincent and a friend named Lockwood, who had registered for the army with him, set out West with ideas of making it rich prospecting for gold. Vincent and his friend found an Arizona claim, filed on it, and then, out of nowhere, left the claim behind and emigrated to California. Vincent would not reveal the details of why he left such a rich claim . . . until his deathbed, that is.

As Vincent lay dying, he pleaded with the doctor to have him buried in the Los Angeles National Cemetery with other soldiers. But to do that he had to release his real name, Charles Vincent Dougherty. Vincent had been hiding out in the Angeles National Forest since right after the Civil War. He and his friend, Lockwood, were about to become the victims of claim jumpers, who were planning to take the claim and kill the men who had staked it. Before the scoundrels could pull off their plot, Vincent and Lockwood snuck up on the three men and shot them dead. They were so worried about Western justice that they fled the scene without ever letting their side of the story be known. Vincent believed up until his dying days that he was a fugitive wanted for murder, so he changed his name and lived the life of a hermit. As it turned out, there was no connection to his name anywhere, no warrant for his arrest, and no search for justice of any kind.

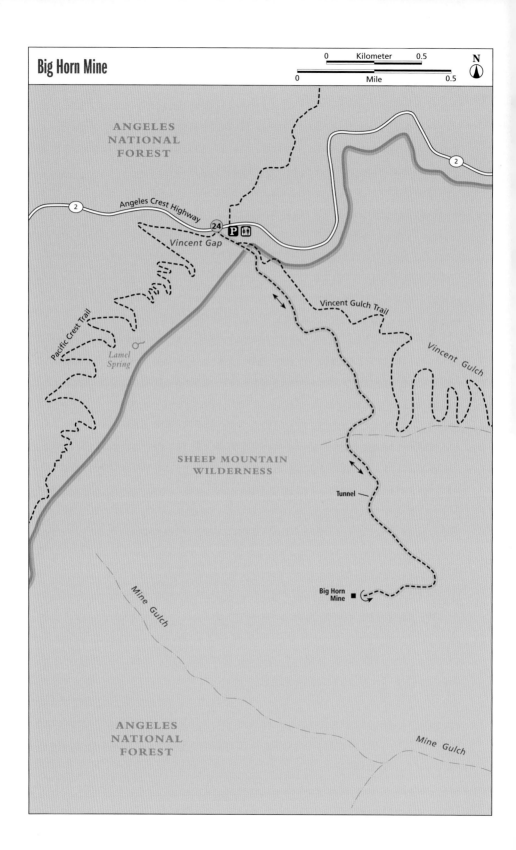

Big Horn Mine

ANGELES
NATIONAL
FOREST

Angeles Crest Highway

Vincent Gap

Pacific Crest Trail

Lamel
Spring

Vincent Gulch Trail

Vincent Gulch

SHEEP MOUNTAIN
WILDERNESS

Tunnel

Mine Gulch

Big Horn
Mine

ANGELES
NATIONAL
FOREST

Mine Gulch

Kilometer

Mile

N

A 10-stamp mill remains at the Big Horn Mine. Photo by Allen Riedel.

It was with hesitation this detail was added to the book because of the great possibility of vandalism and destruction, but web searches easily find videos and GPS coordinates for the cabin. Enjoy, but leave the cabin to history for future explorers.

Miles and Directions

0.0 Start on the old wagon road headed toward Vincent Gulch, past the gate with the ROAD CLOSED sign.

0.1 Reach the Sheep Mountain Wilderness boundary and the junction with Vincent Gulch Trail. Continue toward Big Horn Mine.

0.4 The Vincent Gulch Spur Trail leads to the left—an excellent diversion to Tom Vincent's cabin can be had here for those wishing to add an extra 1.2 miles to the overall trip. Continue straight for the mine.

0.6 Reach the main entrance to the mine (closed).

1.9 Arrive at the stamp mill. Return via the same route.

3.8 Arrive back at the trailhead and the Vincent Gap parking areas

Hike Information

Local information: Angeles National Forest, 701 N. Santa Anita Ave., Arcadia, CA, 91006; 747-322-6574 or 626-574-1613

Camping: Angeles National Forest campgrounds (first come, first served; 14-day stay maximum): Appletree, Bear, Bear Canyon, Big Rock, Blue Ridge, Chilao, Coldbrook, Crystal Lake, Gould Mesa, Guffy, Horse Flats, Idlehour Trail Camp, Little Jimmy Trail Camp, Los Alamos, Lupine, Manker, Messenger Flats, Millard Trail Camp, Monte Cristo, Mount Lowe Trail Camp, Oak Flat, Pacifico, Peavine, Sawmill, South, Sulphur Springs; https://www.fs.usda.gov/main/angeles/home

25 Dawson Peak

The Devil's Backbone is the colloquial moniker of the trail up the knifelike ridgeline to Mount San Antonio. The "other Devil's Backbone" follows a mountaineer use trail on the backside of Mount Baldy and traverses the second- and third-highest peaks in the Angeles National Forest. The way is steep, no-nonsense, not overused, and not for the timid or the acrophobic. Breathtaking views are the norm and scrambling over loose rock is guaranteed, as well as high-mountain adventure.

Start: Guffy Campground (if the gate is locked), or the pullout at the base of Pine Mountain

Distance: 8.3 miles out and back (if the road to the Pine Mountain trailhead is open, the hike can be 4.5 miles out and back)

Hiking time: 4 to 6 hours

Difficulty: Strenuous

Trail surface: Dirt road and dirt-use trail

Nearest town: Wrightwood

County: Los Angeles

Other trail users: None

Canine compatibility: Leashed dogs permitted

Trailhead facilities/amenities: Restroom and picnic facilities at Guffy, no water on trail

Land status: National forest

Fees and permits: Adventure Pass required for parking

Schedule: Open year-round; the road may be closed due to snow or dangerous fire conditions

Maps: USGS Mount San Antonio, CA

Trail contact: Angeles National Forest, 701 N. Santa Anita Ave., Arcadia, CA, 91006; https://www.fs.usda.gov/angeles/; 747-322-6574 or 626-574-1613

Finding the trailhead: From Los Angeles, head north. Take Exit 139A for CA 2/Glendale Freeway toward Glendale. Drive for 7.7 miles and take Exit 21A to merge onto CA 2/I-210, heading east toward Pasadena. Drive for 1.2 miles. Take Exit 20 for CA 2/Angeles Crest Highway toward La Canada Flintridge. Turn left onto CA 2, drive 54.3 miles, and turn right onto East Blue Ridge Truck Trail/FR 3N06. Drive for 5.1 miles to Guffy Campground, and follow the directions below to the trailhead. CA 2 closes periodically due to storms, fire, fire danger, and rockslides, especially between Dawson Gap and Islip Saddle. When closures are in effect, use this alternate route: From Los Angeles, head east on I-10 and take Exit 58A for I-15 north. Drive for 21.8 miles and take Exit 131 for CA 138. Turn left onto CA 138 and drive for 8.6 miles. Turn left onto CA 2 and drive for 10.6 miles. Turn left onto East Blue Ridge Truck Trail/FR 3N06 and drive for 5.1 miles to Guffy Campground. If the gate is locked, park alongside the road, but do not block the gate. If the gate is not locked, keep right and continue 0.5 mile. Veer left and continue on FR 3N06 for another 1.6 miles to the turnout on the left at the base of Pine Mountain. The trail heads down and then straight up the mountain from here. There is no trailhead sign, but a Sheep Mountain Wilderness sign sits just below the roadway along the use trail. GPS: 34°20'28.6"N 117°39'30.1"W

The Hike

At times, the road that leads to Pine Mountain is open, and at others it is closed. There hardly seems to be rhyme or reason for the closed or open nature of the road, but if

Views of Mount Baden-Powell in the distance. Photo by Allen Riedel.

hiking this trail, you must be prepared to find the gate closed (and be ready for an additional 3.8 miles round-trip of hiking for a total of 8.3) or be happily surprised if it is open for an out-and-back of 4.5. The description provided here and in the "Miles and Directions" begins from Guffy Campground and assumes the gate is locked.

The route out of Guffy Campground is pedestrian, a simple walk along FR 3N06 or along the Pacific Crest Trail (PCT). It is better to take the PCT, though the trail and road cross each other so frequently, either route is a viable option. Hike east from the small one-car pullout parking area next to the locked gate toward Guffy Campground. Head behind the restrooms and find the PCT just below the ridge. Follow it southeast. The trail intersects with the road multiple times. Follow the trail to the intersection with the Acorn Trail at 1.1 miles. Note that it is also possible to use the Acorn Trail starting from Wrightwood to access this trail. Just beyond this junction, the PCT enters the roadway again. Stay on the road and veer right at the fork at 1.5 miles, leaving the PCT. Take the lower section of roadway and follow it to the turnout parking area at 1.9 miles. The trailhead is easy to spot because Pine Mountain looms large in the foreground, and below the roadway there is a gray sign marker for Sheep Mountain Wilderness. The trail is also noticeable, heading straight up the edge of the ridgeline to the top of Pine Mountain at 9,648 feet—the second-tallest mountain in the Angeles National Forest. If the road is open, the route begins here, cutting off 3.8 miles from the entire trip.

From this point, hike downhill sharply for 0.1 mile. The unsigned use trail, also called the "other Devil's Backbone," heads up from here, gaining a whopping 1,500 feet of elevation in slightly more than 1 mile. The route is clearly defined and easy to follow, despite being simply a mountaineer's route. The views are spectacular, the scree is loose in spots, and the drops on either side of the ridge are heart-clenching and quite terrifying for anyone without a good sense of balance or a fear of heights.

After 1.2 miles of hiking from the road, reach the summit of Pine Mountain, which is wide open, rounded, and large. There is no good 360-degree viewpoint from the top, but there are several spots to rest and get at least a 290-degree view.

From atop Pine Mountain, the trail heads off toward the venerable Mount Baldy; the hump in the middle is Dawson Peak. Although this section of trail isn't nearly as frequented as the route up Pine Mountain, it is still easy to follow as it heads along the ridgeline, and it is the simplest route straight up the mountain.

The trail loses nearly 600 feet of elevation to the saddle between Pine Mountain and Dawson Peak in a little less than 0.5 mile. This elevation must be gained again on the way back, of course. An old logging road designated as Dawson Peak Trail (8W32) crosses the trail just above the saddle; continue straight up the mountain.

Abruptly, the path begins climbing again, gaining 500 feet in roughly 0.75 mile. The route is a bit gentler, but still tough after scrambling up Pine Mountain. And the view from on top of Dawson Peak, although at a lower elevation (9,575 feet), is better. From the summit block, it is possible to look 360 degrees, albeit with some trees blocking the way. Mount Baldy and Mount Harwood are up close and personal. It feels as if you could reach out and touch them. The Cajon Pass and the big mountains of the San Bernardino National Forest, San Jacinto and San Gorgonio, are also seemingly a stone's throw away. Enjoy the vantage point; there is none other like it in Southern California, and it should be yours and yours alone. If there does happen to be a like-minded individual hiking on the same day as you, it might be wise to strike up a conversation. You may just have found a friend for life.

▶ **Safety Tip: When hiking at high altitude (8,000–12,000 feet), be watchful for signs of altitude illness. If you or a member of your party suffers from headache, nausea, and fatigue, descend immediately.**

From the summit, the route up Mount Baldy can be discerned for the brutal butt-kicker it is. Some may want to continue, losing 700 feet to the next saddle and then gaining 1,300 feet to the top of Old Baldy, but most will be content sitting on top of out-of-the-way Dawson Peak. Head back along the same route to whichever parking area you started from.

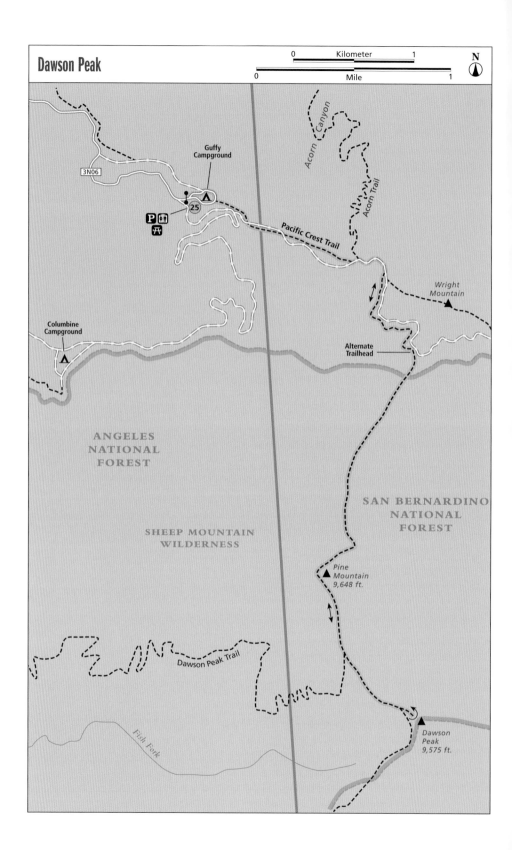

Miles and Directions

0.0 Start hiking eastward from the roadway toward the restrooms at Guffy Campground.

0.2 Below the restrooms along the ridgeline, meet up with the Pacific Crest Trail. Turn right and head east.

1.1 At the junction with Acorn Trail, stay straight and join FR 3N06.

1.2 Stay on the road as it turns right (south).

1.3 Stay right at the fork.

1.9 At the turnout and lower parking area, join the use trail as it leads toward the summit of Pine Mountain. A Sheep Mountain Wilderness sign is visible below the roadway.

3.2 Reach the summit of Pine Mountain. Continue south along the trail.

3.6 Continue straight up toward Dawson Peak at the junction with the old Dawson Peak Trail (8W32).

4.1 Reach the summit of Dawson Peak. Return via the same route.

8.3 Arrive back at the Guffy Campground trailhead and parking area.

Hike Information

Local information: Angeles National Forest, 701 N. Santa Anita Ave., Arcadia, CA, 91006; 747-322-6574 or 626-574-1613

Camping: Angeles National Forest campgrounds (first come, first served; 14-day stay maximum): Appletree, Bear, Bear Canyon, Big Rock, Blue Ridge, Chilao, Coldbrook, Crystal Lake, Gould Mesa, Guffy, Horse Flats, Idlehour Trail Camp, Little Jimmy Trail Camp, Los Alamos, Lupine, Manker, Messenger Flats, Millard Trail Camp, Monte Cristo, Mount Lowe Trail Camp, Oak Flat, Pacifico, Peavine, Sawmill, South, Sulphur Springs; https://www.fs.usda.gov/main/angeles/home

26 Mount Baldy

There is an "easy" route to climb Mount Baldy, a moderate way, and a straight-out difficult trek. This trail follows the Bear Canyon Trail from Mount Baldy Village, gaining 6,000 feet of elevation in 6 miles. It is one of the toughest hikes in the Angeles National Forest that doesn't require special skills. The views are magnificent, the traffic infrequent, and the workout unmatched.

Start: Mount Baldy Schoolhouse Visitor Center
Distance: 12 miles out and back
Hiking time: 8 to 12 hours
Difficulty: Extremely strenuous
Trail surface: Single-track dirt trail
Nearest town: Mount Baldy
County: Los Angeles
Other trail users: None
Canine compatibility: Leashed dogs permitted
Trailhead facilities/amenities: Restrooms and water at visitors' center

Land status: National forest
Fees and permits: Adventure Pass required for parking
Schedule: Open year-round; gate locked after 4 p.m., so do not park at visitors' center
Maps: USGS Mount San Antonio, CA
Trail contact: Angeles National Forest, 701 N. Santa Anita Ave., Arcadia, CA, 91006; https://www.fs.usda.gov/angeles/; 747-322-6574 or 626-574-1613

Finding the trailhead: From Los Angeles, take I-10 east. Take Exit 31B to merge onto I-605 north. Drive for 5.4 miles. Take Exit 27A to merge onto I-210 east. Drive for 15.5 miles. Take Exit 52 toward Baseline Road. Turn left onto Baseline Road and drive for 0.2 mile. Turn right onto Padua Avenue. Drive for 1.8 miles. Turn right onto Mount Baldy Road and drive for 7.4 miles to the Mount Baldy Visitor Center. Park just off Bear Canyon Drive in the parking lot 100 yards south of the visitors' center. GPS: 34°14'18.5"N 117°39'27.0"W

The Hike

From the parking area just south of the Mount Baldy Visitor Center, walk northwest up Bear Canyon Drive to where the Bear Canyon Trail begins at the signed trailhead. The first 2 miles along the trail gain 1,000 feet of elevation. This is a steep trail—usually 1,000 feet gained in a mile is about as tough as trails maintained by the Forest Service get. But after the second full mile, the trail gets even steeper and heads straight up the mountain, gaining a monstrous 1,600 feet in the next mile, even with switchbacks. From there it levels off some, but make no mistake, this trail is a workout, a true leg-burner.

The trail follows lovely Bear Canyon, which is shaded for a good portion of the early hike by old oaks and scattered pines. There are quite a few forest cabins along the trail, like on some other routes in the Angeles National Forest. Most of the owners seem to take pride in their uniqueness and most seem well cared for. The last cabin sits just about 1 mile up the trail; at the last cabin, stay to the right on Bear Canyon

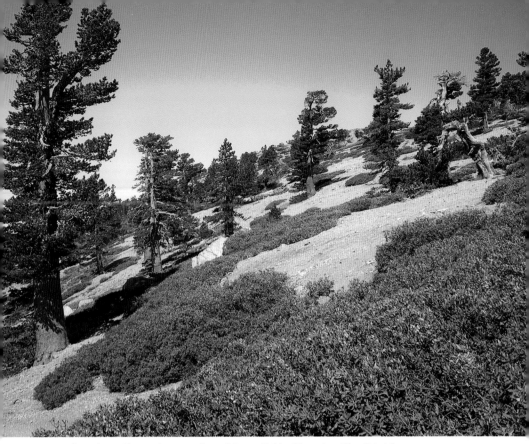

View from the trail near the summit on Mount Baldy. Photo by Allen Riedel.

Trail and follow it the rest of the way up the mountain. There aren't any confusing junctions or unsigned trails beyond this point.

After 1.75 miles, the marshy fern-lined meadow area known as Bear Flat comes into view. A sign with a goofy bear marks the location. From here, the trail takes on a whole different level of intensity. First the trail exits the shady confines of the canyon and begins to climb and switchback up the mountain. There is less tree cover, and if the sun is shining directly on the south-facing slope, it can get hot. A fire in 2008 burned off some of the ground cover here, but spared the canyon, most of the pines, and the upper reaches of the mountain. Evidence of the fire is nearly erased, and the recovery of the mountain chaparral and manzanita hardly shows any signs at all. Views into Icehouse Canyon open up and soon so will views into the entire Southern California basin.

The trail works its way back under pines, which are mostly tall and isolated to begin with, but eventually become evenly spaced along the trail, providing shade intermittently with ample spots for respite from the sun.

At 2.5 miles, the trail hits the West Baldy ridgeline, near the prominence marked 7,451 feet on the topo map. Views open up into Cattle Canyon below and across to Big Horn Ridge, which meets the trail and West Baldy Ridge 2 miles and 2,000 feet ahead and above. The route follows the steep ridgeline for the remaining 2,500 feet to the top.

The trail seems to climb incessantly, but the views get continually better and better. From the notch above Big Horn Ridge, the summit of Mount Baldy and the closer West Baldy can be seen. The route traverses a few hundred feet below the summit of West Baldy and eventually meets the saddle between the two peaks. Turn left and take the small 0.2-mile use trail to the summit of West Baldy. Hardly anyone does; most people only go for the gusto of Mount Baldy itself. But the peak is way less crowded, and the views are nearly as remarkable. Take a short break, head back to the main trail, and continue the remaining 0.4 mile to the summit of Mount Baldy.

Mount Baldy was so named due to its lack of tree cover and hence its "bald" appearance, especially in winter when snow caps the peak for a good portion of the darker months. Its true name is Mount San Antonio, but hardly anyone calls it that; others, including the USGS topo map of the region, refer to it as "Old Baldy."

> **Mount Baldy, also known as Mount San Antonio, is the highest point in Los Angeles County at 10,046 feet.**

There will more than likely be other hikers atop the peak; it is a popular destination with many trails leading to the summit. If you planned your trip on a weekend, some hikers will have even taken a ski lift to a point a mere 2,000 feet below the top to begin hiking to the same destination. While still not an easy trip up, these hikers likely won't be as tired as you and your party, but they have earned it just as well. Relish the knowledge that your trip has followed the truly intrepid route. From the summit, take the trail back to Mount Baldy Village.

Caution: The summit of Mount Baldy is quite large and open. Many visitors have lost their bearings on top and taken the wrong trail back to the bottom. Pay attention to your surroundings, look back frequently to remember your route, and be wary that temperatures and weather patterns can shift rapidly at such high altitudes. Do not continue climbing in storms unless you are prepared for them and knowledgeable in methods of route finding/winter mountaineering. Mount Baldy's proximity to the sunny beaches of Los Angeles doesn't make it safer than other high-altitude mountains. Paradoxically, it only makes it more dangerous because people underestimate its potential for tragedy. Many have paid for this hubris with their lives. If weather conditions turn bad, turn back. Don't overestimate your abilities or of those in your party.

Miles and Directions

0.0 Start up Bear Canyon Drive 100 yards south of Mount Baldy Visitor Center.

1.0 Reach the last cabin and take the right fork in the trail.

1.75 Reach Bear Flat.

5.6 Turn left onto the West Baldy use trail.

5.8 Arrive on the summit of West Baldy. Return to the main trail.

6.0 Turn left onto the main trail and head for the summit of Mount Baldy.

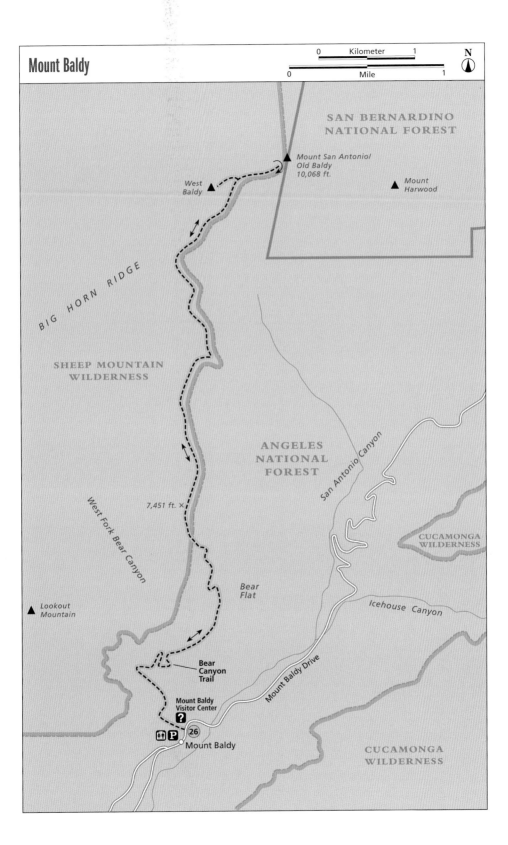

Mount Baldy

SAN BERNARDINO
NATIONAL FOREST

▲ Mount San Antoniol
Old Baldy
10,068 ft.

West
Baldy ▲

▲ Mount
Harwood

BIG HORN RIDGE

SHEEP MOUNTAIN
WILDERNESS

ANGELES
NATIONAL
FOREST

San Antonio Canyon

CUCAMONGA
WILDERNESS

West Fork Bear Canyon

7,451 ft. ×

Bear
Flat

Icehouse Canyon

▲ Lookout
Mountain

Bear
Canyon
Trail

Mount Baldy Drive

Mount Baldy
Visitor Center

26

Mount Baldy

CUCAMONGA
WILDERNESS

0   Kilometer   1

0   Mile   1

N

6.4 Arrive at the summit of Mount Baldy. Follow the main trail back.

12.0 Arrive back at the trailhead and parking area.

Hike Information

Local information: Angeles National Forest, 701 N. Santa Anita Ave., Arcadia, CA, 91006; 747-322-6574 or 626-574-1613

Camping: Angeles National Forest campgrounds (first come, first served; 14-day stay maximum): Appletree, Bear, Bear Canyon, Big Rock, Blue Ridge, Chilao, Coldbrook, Crystal Lake, Gould Mesa, Guffy, Horse Flats, Idlehour Trail Camp, Little Jimmy Trail Camp, Los Alamos, Lupine, Manker, Messenger Flats, Millard Trail Camp, Monte Cristo, Mount Lowe Trail Camp, Oak Flat, Pacifico, Peavine, Sawmill, South, Sulphur Springs; https://www.fs.usda.gov/main/angeles/home

27 Timber Mountain

Icehouse Canyon is a lovely sylvan glen that leads into the rugged Cucamonga Wilderness. Hikers of all ages will enjoy the splendor of the mixed oak and pine forest, the cabins in the woods, the flowing creek, and the towering summits that reach high above the confines of the canyon. Timber Mountain is the first in a line of mountains called the Three-T's: Timber, Telegraph, and Thunder. Timber Mountain is the closest peak to Icehouse Saddle.

Start: Icehouse Canyon Trailhead
Distance: 9 miles out and back
Hiking time: About 5 hours
Difficulty: Strenuous
Trail surface: Single-track dirt trail
Nearest town: Mount Baldy
County: San Bernardino
Other trail users: None
Canine compatibility: Leashed dogs permitted
Trailhead facilities/amenities: Restrooms at trailhead, filterable water at Columbine Spring
Land status: National forest

Fees and permits: Wilderness permit required; Adventure Pass required for parking. Wilderness permits can be acquired at the Mount Baldy Visitor Center, Mount Baldy Road, Mount Baldy, CA, 91759; 909-982-2829
Schedule: Open year-round
Maps: USGS Cucamonga Peak, CA, and Mount San Antonio, CA
Trail contact: Angeles National Forest, 701 N. Santa Anita Ave., Arcadia, CA, 91006; https://www.fs.usda.gov/angeles/; 747-322-6574 or 626-574-1613

Finding the trailhead: From Los Angeles, take I-10 east. Take Exit 31B to merge onto I-605 north. Drive for 5.4 miles. Take Exit 27A to merge onto I-210 east. Drive for 15.5 miles. Take Exit 52 toward Baseline Road. Turn left onto Baseline Road and drive for 0.2 mile. Turn right onto Padua Avenue. Drive for 1.8 miles. Turn right onto Mount Baldy Road and drive for 8.9 miles. Turn right onto Ice House Canyon Road. Drive for 0.1 mile and park in the lot. GPS: 34°15'00.4"N 117°38'11.7"W

The Hike

Icehouse Canyon is a lovely slice of the Southern California mountains, and it is an incredibly popular region as well. In fact, the canyon is one of the most popular hiking destinations in all of the Angeles National Forest. Even though there are a lot of visitors, the area still seems remote. It is a large enough region to accommodate everyone, but this is not the hike to take if you are looking for solitude.

The Icehouse Canyon Trail begins up a gated road, which eventually turns into a dirt road that narrows until it simply becomes a dirt path. Forest cabins line the road and eventually dot the trail as well. This is a common occurrence in the Angeles National Forest as there are quite a few cabin-lined trails and canyons. Most of the woodland homes are well taken care of and some are absolutely beautiful.

The trail winds up Icehouse Canyon toward Timber Mountain. Photo by Allen Riedel.

The route follows the powerful unnamed stream that flows through Icehouse Canyon and floods the spillway at the San Antonio Dam, just north of the community of Upland. At high runoff, the creek can be a raging torrent, making crossings dangerous, but normally its flow is strong, and the area is lush year-round, which gives the canyon its genuine appeal. The trail gains a steady 700 feet per mile, which isn't necessarily an easy hike, but it is manageable for most people, and a lot of parents bring their children along to play in the forest and the stream when it is gently flowing. The route is luxuriant, and those who come here generally return repeatedly.

At 1 mile, the trail junctions with the Chapman Trail, though it is not marked on the USGS topo map. The Chapman Trail is a semicircle loop that ascends and rejoins the Icehouse Canyon Trail, gaining elevation less rapidly but also covering more distance. (**Option:** Taking the Chapman Trail one way will add an additional 1.7 miles to the total hike distance.)

After the junction, the hike leaves the mountain cabins behind, though some large ruins still exist farther up the canyon, and the trail continues to follow the lovely sylvan stream. Some reworking of the trail has been completed over the past few years, and improvements have been made to curb erosion along the trail.

As the trail ascends, the surrounding woods become a pine forest and the trail wanders away from the stream, even though the creek is never more than a hundred or so yards lower in the canyon. At 1.8 miles, the trail enters the Cucamonga Wilderness, and there is a sign to mark this boundary, along with an interpretative informational kiosk. The next trail junction occurs at Columbine Spring, an ice-cold freshwater source that pours from out of the rock year-round. A short spur trail of less than 0.1 mile leads to the spring and back.

> **Hiking Tip:** To avoid rattlesnakes, don't put your hands into places into which you can't see. Back away and give a wide berth to rattlesnakes on the trail. At best, rattlesnakes can strike between one-half and two-thirds their total body length.

Mile markers indicate distance along the Icehouse Canyon Trail; the Chapman Trail rejoins the main route just before the 3-mile marker. The saddle is another 0.5 mile beyond. The saddle is a cool spot for a rest—taking in the fresh mountain air, looking over the various canyons that drop off below—complete with a four-way trail junction.

Trails lead to all parts of the wilderness from the saddle. Follow the route that is labeled the Three-T's Trail. The summit of Timber Mountain is listed as being another 0.9 mile. There will be foot traffic at the saddle, but there is a good chance that taking a step onto the Three-T's Trail will lead to solitude. At the very least, there will no longer be the mass of people found lower in Icehouse Canyon.

From the junction, the trail to Timber Mountain climbs steeply up the slope. It drops just to the west of the summit, and a use trail departs to the right at 4.25 miles, leading to the summit. In another 0.25 mile, the trail reaches the summit of Timber Mountain.

At 8,308 feet, Timber Mountain is tall enough to command outstanding views of the surrounding countryside, mountains, and wilderness. There are trees on top, so hikers have to move around to get in all the differing views. An illegible sign marks the summit, along with a metal sign featuring Mount Chapman.

After taking in the views, return via the same route, or take the Chapman loop back to the parking area for Icehouse Canyon.

Miles and Directions

0.0 Start by hiking east along the road from the Icehouse Canyon parking lot.

0.1 The road becomes a dirt road and then a trail.

1.0 At the junction with the Chapman Trail, continue straight.

1.8 Enter the Cucamonga Wilderness.

2.5 Continue straight at the spur trail to Columbine Spring.

2.8 Continue right at the second junction with the Chapman Trail.

3.5 Arrive at Icehouse Saddle. Turn left and take the Three-Tee's Trail.

4.25 Turn right onto the Timber Mountain use trail.

4.5 Arrive on top of Timber Mountain. Return via the same route.

9.0 Arrive back at the trailhead.

Timber Mountain

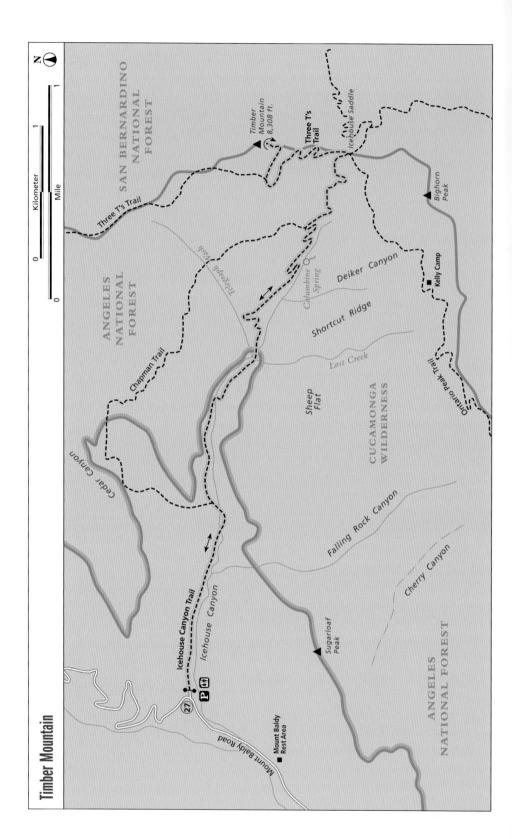

Hike Information

Local information: Angeles National Forest, 701 N. Santa Anita Ave., Arcadia, CA, 91006; 747-322-6574 or 626-574-1613

Camping: Angeles National Forest campgrounds (first come, first served; 14-day stay maximum): Appletree, Bear, Bear Canyon, Big Rock, Blue Ridge, Chilao, Coldbrook, Crystal Lake, Gould Mesa, Guffy, Horse Flats, Idlehour Trail Camp, Little Jimmy Trail Camp, Los Alamos, Lupine, Manker, Messenger Flats, Millard Trail Camp, Monte Cristo, Mount Lowe Trail Camp, Oak Flat, Pacifico, Peavine, Sawmill, South, Sulphur Springs; https://www.fs.usda.gov/main/angeles/home

28 Etiwanda Peak

The hike to Etiwanda Peak combines a trek up the Middle Fork of Lytle Creek and an epic adventure from Icehouse Saddle deep into the Cucamonga Wilderness to Cucamonga Peak—and ultimately to remote Etiwanda Peak, where views into the Southern California basin are incredible and the serenity is sublime.

Start: Middle Fork Lytle Creek trailhead
Distance: 16.5 miles out and back
Hiking time: 8 to 12 hours
Difficulty: Extremely strenuous
Trail surface: Single-track dirt trail
Nearest town: Lytle Creek
County: San Bernardino
Other trail users: None
Canine compatibility: Leashed dogs permitted
Trailhead facilities/amenities: None
Land status: National forest
Fees and permits: Wilderness permit required; Adventure Pass required for parking. Obtain your wilderness permit at Lytle Creek Ranger Station, 1209 Lytle Creek Rd., Lytle Creek, CA, 92358; 909-382-2851
Schedule: Open year-round; the road closes during inclement weather
Maps: USGS Cucamonga Peak, CA, and Devore, CA; http://c0278592.cdn.cloudfiles .rackspacecloud.com/original/405624.jpg
Trail contact: Angeles National Forest, 701 N. Santa Anita Ave., Arcadia, CA, 91006; https:// www.fs.usda.gov/angeles/; 747-322-6574 or 626-574-1613. San Bernardino National Forest, 602 S. Tippecanoe Ave., San Bernardino, CA, 92408; https://www.fs.usda.gov/sbnf; 909-382-2682

Finding the trailhead: From Los Angeles, take I-10 east. Take Exit 58A to merge onto I-15 North/Ontario Freeway, and continue for 10.7 miles. Take Exit 119 for Sierra Avenue and turn left. Drive for 6.5 miles on Sierra Avenue/Lytle Creek Road. Turn left onto Middle Fork Road. Drive for 2.8 miles. Park in the lot at the end of the road. GPS: 34°15'13.5"N 117°32'23.6"W

The Hike

Lytle Creek marks the eastern boundary of the San Gabriel Mountains; its waters flow from the highest peaks in the range, draining down the steep eastern slopes through lovely, wooded canyons. All forks of Lytle Creek are lovely, but the Middle Fork is the standout. In fall the foliage displays some of the best autumn color in all of Southern California. In spring, the wildflowers bloom in abundance. The canyon also happens to be one of the best places to see some of the remaining bighorn sheep in the range, as well as other wildlife. Backcountry camping options exist in several spots along the trail, and the hiking is some of the best anywhere—no doubt about it.

This hike is an epic journey and not for the faint of heart, beginners, or the uninitiated. The trail begins in a portion of the canyon that was severely burned during the devastating 2003 Old Fire, and it climbs over 1 mile in elevation to two spectacular summits. At the lower elevations though, it seems to be little more than a dry, dusty

On top of Etiwanda Peak you can see for miles and then some. Photo by Allen Riedel.

wash filled with yucca and other desert shrubs. Although some of the canyon's beauty was destroyed in the fire, most of the upper reaches of the canyon survived unscathed.

The trail comes to a junction at 0.6 mile. Both trails meet up and cover about the same amount of distance, so take the one on the left, which dips down into Middle Fork of Lytle Creek and passes the Stone House Crossing campsite. Here, the forest starts off as a mixed pine and deciduous forest and quickly elevates into an alpine wonderland.

The trail meets up with the spur trail again at 1.4 miles. Continue straight up into the canyon. At 2 miles, a small use trail leads into a steep and obviously spectacular drainage. (**Option:** Many people will want to scramble the short 0.15 mile over rocks up into the side canyon. The scramble is a bit challenging but definitely worth the extra effort. A lovely 30-foot waterfall plunges over a cliff into a deep pool, and there are more waterfalls up the dramatic gorge, but those without mountaineering experience will want to return to the main trail after visiting the first fall and continue up the mountain.)

At the Third Stream Crossing campsite, the trail makes a 90-degree turn to the left (southwest) and begins to climb more steeply and enter the pine wonderland. Continue up the mountain along the trail and pass the Comanche campsite at 3.7 miles.

The trail continues to climb sharply until it levels off at Icehouse Saddle at 5.2 miles. The saddle is the major intersection for five trails in the Cucamonga Wilderness. It has plenty of signs and is easy to follow. Turn left and follow the Cucamonga Peak Trail as it drops 200 feet before beginning to climb again at a rate of 1,500 feet in 1.5 miles to the top of Cucamonga Peak. The narrow route follows along the side of the slope of the mountain.

At 7 miles, turn right on the Cucamonga Peak use trail. It is a small mountaineer's trail marked with an old wooden sign that is barely hanging on. In another steep 0.25 mile, the trail tops out on the apex of Cucamonga Peak. The views down into Los Angeles and beyond are breathtaking.

Take a rest. Those who are exhausted may want to stop for the day, but for those wanting to reach a peak that is rarely visited, along a trail that is traversed more by bighorn sheep and Bigfoot than homo sapiens, head back down to the main trail and turn right along one of the least-traveled paths, the Cucamonga Peak Trail as it leads to San Sevaine Flats in the Angeles National Forest. It is another 0.8 mile to the use trail to the summit of Etiwanda Peak. The trail loses another 600 feet before it begins climbing up to Etiwanda. The small use trail veers off the main trail to the right and quickly gains the summit block of Etiwanda Peak. Atop the mountain, the views are fairly similar to those on Cucamonga, but the summit block is much smaller and more intimate. A summit register has only a few entries in it, and there is solitude and serenity on the top.

The trail back leads 300 feet up to Cucamonga Peak Trail, and from there the route is mostly downhill all the way back to the Middle Fork of Lytle Creek.

Miles and Directions

0.0 Begin by hiking west up the Middle Fork of Lytle Creek.

0.6 Continue straight at the junction with the spur trail, heading into the creek bed.

1.0 Arrive at Stone House Crossing campsite. Continue straight.

1.4 Continue straight at the second junction with the spur trail.

2.0 A use trail leads to spectacular falls on the left. Continue straight.

2.1 Reach the Third Stream Crossing campsite. The trail turns south, heading up to Icehouse Saddle.

3.7 Reach Comanche campsite.

5.2 Arrive at Icehouse Saddle. Turn left and follow the Cucamonga Peak Trail.

7.0 Turn right onto the Cucamonga Peak use trail.

7.25 Arrive atop Cucamonga Peak. Return to the main trail.

7.5 Turn right onto the Cucamonga Peak Trail, heading east toward Etiwanda Peak.

8.3 Veer right and continue straight onto the use trail for Etiwanda Peak.

8.5 Arrive atop Etiwanda Peak. Return via the same route.

16.5 Arrive back at the trailhead and parking area.

Etiwanda Peak

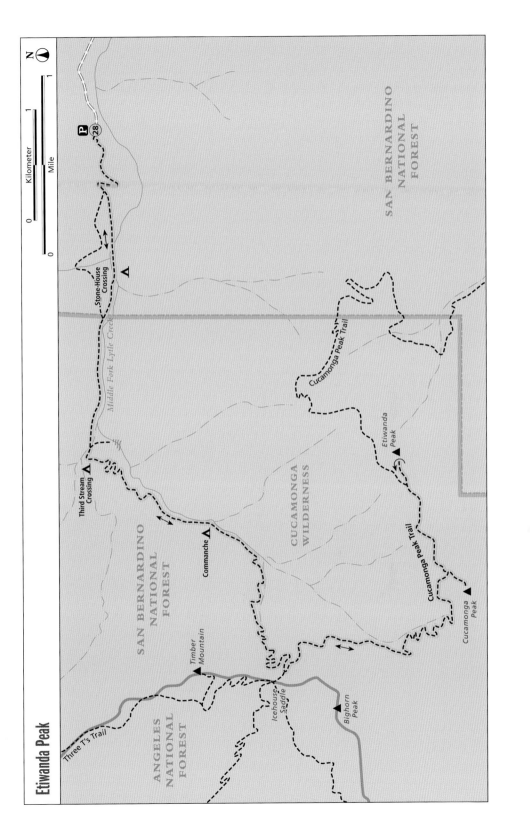

Three T's Trail

ANGELES NATIONAL FOREST

Timber Mountain

Icehouse Saddle

Bighorn Peak

Commanche

SAN BERNARDINO NATIONAL FOREST

Third Stream Crossing

Middle Fork Lytle Creek

Stone-House Crossing

P 28

CUCAMONGA WILDERNESS

Cucamonga Peak Trail

Cucamonga Peak

Cucamonga Peak Trail

Etiwanda Peak

SAN BERNARDINO NATIONAL FOREST

N

Kilometer

Mile

0   1   1

0   1

Hike Information

Local information: Angeles National Forest, 701 N. Santa Anita Ave., Arcadia, CA, 91006; https://www.fs.usda.gov/angeles/; 747-322-6574 or 626-574-1613. San Bernardino National Forest, 602 S. Tippecanoe Ave., San Bernardino, CA, 92408; https://www.fs.usda.gov/sbnf; 909-382-2682

Camping: Angeles National Forest campgrounds (first come, first served; 14-day stay maximum): Appletree, Bear, Bear Canyon, Big Rock, Blue Ridge, Chilao, Coldbrook, Crystal Lake, Gould Mesa, Guffy, Horse Flats, Idlehour Trail Camp, Little Jimmy Trail Camp, Los Alamos, Lupine, Manker, Messenger Flats, Millard Trail Camp, Monte Cristo, Mount Lowe Trail Camp, Oak Flat, Pacifico, Peavine, Sawmill, South, Sulphur Springs; https://www.fs.usda.gov/main/angeles/home

Honorable Mentions

B Mount Islip

Damaged in the 2020 Bobcat Fire, the trail to Mount Islip finally reopened on April 1, 2022. Mount Islip is a great high peak, rising to 8,250 feet near the eastern end of the San Gabriel Mountains. The trail begins at Islip Saddle, a parking area and trail junction for the Pacific Crest Trail (PCT) in the Angeles National Forest. The trail climbs gently around the base of the mountain through desertlike chaparral to the Little Jimmy Camp and Little Jimmy Spring, following the PCT along the same route as the trip to Mount Hawkins. Hikers can take two trails up to the summit. One starts from the back end of the camp, or hikers can simply follow the trail to Windy Gap, another fantastic trail junction of the high Angeles forest. The route then steeply climbs up the side of the mountain through remnants of the 2002 Curve Fire, which burned a good portion of the eastern edge of the San Gabriel range. The views are outstanding along the way for the entire route. Once on top, the rocky summit of Mount Baldy is visible, and the walls of an old stone lookout structure from the 1920s remain on the summit. Climbing on mostly north-facing slopes, the trail ascends through a nice yellow pine forest with a round-trip total mileage of 6 miles.

C Mount Williamson

Mount Williamson was badly damaged by the 2020 Bobcat Fire. Mount Williamson is the twin summit to Mount Islip, on the north across Islip Saddle. Both peaks sit high above the Angeles Crest Highway at almost the same elevation, with Williamson being only 6 feet shorter at 8,244 feet above sea level. Although the two summits start from the same trailhead, they could hardly be any more different. Both are obviously arid Southern California peaks, but Mount Williamson is slightly north and much closer to the dry Mojave Desert and the Victor Valley; the vegetation clearly shows this distinction and bore a much heavier brunt of the fire. The Pacific Crest Trail (PCT) climbs along its south-facing slopes, and although there are tall pines along this route, the vegetation is much sparser and the trail seems quite a bit rockier.

The summit is one of the strangest of all of the Southern California peaks. All three bumps along the summit ridge seem higher, giving a grass-is-greener effect when on top. The middle bump is actually the tallest, even though it is hard to tell when standing atop it. The summit was named for a lieutenant, Robert S. Williamson, in the US Army Corps of Engineers. Williamson was sent with his men to find a feasible site for a railroad to enter Southern California. Their Pacific Railroad Survey of

1853, on the backside of the San Gabriel and San Bernardino Mountains, led to the modern-day Cajon Pass and the railroad tracks that run through there, which are also clearly visible from the top. The round-trip total mileage is 6 miles.

San Bernardino National Forest

The San Bernardino National Forest has the distinction of being the most heavily populated forest region in the US. Its borders stretch from Mount Baldy in the west to the Coachella Valley in the east and the Salton Sink in the south. The highest mountain in Southern California, San Gorgonio, resides at 11,499 feet within the boundaries

The San Gorgonio Wilderness, once the premier unspoiled forest in Southern California, has been badly damaged by the recent Lake, Apple, El Dorado, and Valley Fires, but the forest along much of the Vivian Creek Trail is mostly unchanged. Alpine shooting star. Photo by Allen Riedel.

of the forest. The area provides several popular skiing destinations for all of Southern California, and the forest has been home to many memorable scenes from both the small screen and the silver screen. A recreation mecca, the forest offers climbing, hiking, mountain biking, skiing, boating, fishing, camping, winter mountaineering, and more.

The ecology of the forest is varied, ranging from high desert in the far north to foothills and alpine forests. There is also a broad variety of scenery, flora, and fauna. The mountaintops are some of the highest in the US, and the wilderness areas were once without a doubt some of the most magnificent, lush forests in the world, but climate change and forest fires have rapidly and systematically damaged once pristine timberlands. The forest has creeks, hot springs, towering peaks, alpine lakes, and world-class resorts. Many species of animals reside within the forest, including endangered desert bighorn sheep and black bear. Wildflowers are amazing in the spring, and the region is also home to Southern California's only stand of quaking aspen. Although most of the aspens burned in the 2015 Lake Fire, baby aspens have returned, and the area is growing green once more.

The San Bernardino Mountains were created by the uplift of the San Andreas Fault and the pressure between the Pacific and North American tectonic plates and are young and still growing. The range is known as a transverse range for its east–west orientation, and because of this, the area has fallen victim to a rash of wildfires in the recent decades. Due to the position of Earth, the sun shines on the southern-facing mountains all day long, even in winter, melting away snow at a tremendous rate and leaving the mountains exposed to extreme dryness. Coupled with the non-native grasses that have invaded the continent since the arrival of the Spanish, the dryer areas react like a tinderbox, and conflagrations are likely during the dry season and droughts.

Due to the effects of fire suppression as a means of forest management for the past century, plus decades of drought conditions, the forest has grown unhealthy, with more trees living in areas without the proper nutrients to survive. A bark beetle infestation has weakened and killed many trees in the forest, leaving the region further susceptible to fire, and the forest's survival has even been called into question by the US Congress.

Recently, fire has been incredibly destructive, especially in the San Gorgonio Wilderness with the Lake, Apple, El Dorado, and Valley Fires burning nearly 80 percent of the wilderness in less than a decade. The lower reaches outside the wilderness area have been spared thus far, and it is hopeful that remains. The San Jacinto Wilderness has also fallen victim to the Mountain, Cranston, and Snow Fires, but most of the beloved areas have remained well forested with the exception being the area surrounding Laws Camp and its environs. Though the wilderness has changed, its greatness remains, and rebirth continues out of the old.

Despite that, the region is exquisitely beautiful, overflowing with glorious scenery, wonderful history, and wildlands filled with woodland creatures. Streams, lakes, peaks, and even wondrous waterfalls grace the mountains. The area is so captivating that most visitors will feel a pull to remain and wish that they could call the region home.

29 Heart Rock Falls

The hike to Heart Rock Falls follows lovely Seeley Creek through wooded pine and cedar. An overlook provides the best views of the heart formation, and both the top and bottom of the falls can be visited. Several pools below the falls can be used for wading and swimming.

Start: At the end of FR 2N03
Distance: 2 miles out and back
Hiking time: About 2 hours
Difficulty: Easy
Trail surface: Single-track dirt trail
Nearest town: Crestline
County: San Bernardino
Other trail users: None
Canine compatibility: Leashed dogs permitted
Trailhead facilities/amenities: None

Land status: National forest
Fees and permits: Adventure Pass required for parking
Schedule: Open year-round
Maps: Silverwood Lake, CA, and Devore, CA
Trail contact: San Bernardino National Forest, 602 S. Tippecanoe Ave., San Bernardino, CA, 92408; https://www.fs.usda.gov/sbnf; 909-382-2682

Finding the trailhead: From Los Angeles, take I-10 east. Take Exit 31B to merge onto I-605 north. Drive for 5.4 miles. Take Exit 27A to merge onto I-210 east. Drive for 31.5 miles. Take Exit 76 for CA 18/Waterman Avenue. Turn left and drive for 12.3 miles to the junction with CA 138. Turn north on CA 138 toward Crestline and drive for 1.8 miles to the left turn for Camp Seeley. Don't enter the camp but take a left onto paved FR 2N03 as it crosses Seeley Creek, which can be forded by passenger vehicles. Look for the signed trail (4W07) and roadside parking on the right. GPS: 34°15'16.0"N 117°18'12.3"W

The Hike

At the dirt parking area next to the swimming pool at the end of FR 2N03, head north along the road/trail marked 4W07. After a short distance, the road narrows into a single-track trail. At that point, the trail begins to descend, steeply in spots, along the sides and narrows of the canyon carved out by Seeley Creek. The trees are tall, and the route is forested and shaded for the entire trip to the falls. It is easy to miss the overlook, so keep a watch out for an unmarked use trail leading off to the right at 0.7 mile. The main trail leads to the left, but an obvious path leads down to the right and over a large rocky outcropping. Scramble down and around the rock a bit to find the obvious viewpoint.

At the overlook, a less obvious and more difficult scramble leads to the top of the falls, or hikers can return to the main trail and continue down below the 25-foot cascade. It is possible to hop across the creek and meander down among the pools below the

> ▶ **Hiking Tip: To increase safety, hike in groups. Join an outdoor club or find like-minded individuals online.**

Erosion has led to a perfectly formed heart-shaped basin. Photo by Allen Riedel.

falls for those who are so inclined. The trail sits off to the west of the creek and is easy to pick back up from the bottom. Hiking down the trail, it is simple to overlook the falls. The trail leads to two large pools below the falls, with gentle cascades dropping over into them. There are often people wading in the pools and many hikers like to bring children along on this trip. If you reach this area, you will know that you are below the falls.

Caution: If children do come along, it is important to keep an eye on them: Some parts of the route are steep and there are roots along the trail, along with drop-offs. The rocky outcrop from which you view the falls could also prove problematic for young children.

But anyone visiting is sure to love the wonderfully wooded surroundings and the peaceful atmosphere. The falls are quite enchanting, and it goes without saying that the hiking is easy enough to bring a date. The heart shape is fascinating, caused by years of erosion into the perfect formation. If the water is running well, after rains and a good season of precipitation, with the flowing water pouring over or through the heart, the falls are quite magical.

The return route does climb steeply in spots, but it is such a short distance that anyone can make the trip. For those who need to take it slowly, just relax and enjoy the beautiful surroundings.

Miles and Directions

0.0 From the parking area, hike north along the trail/road marked by the pole labeled 4W07.

0.7 Turn right for an overlook of Heart Rock and the falls.

1.0 Take a fork to the creek and pools below the falls for an upward view. Return via the same route.

2.0 Arrive back at the parking area.

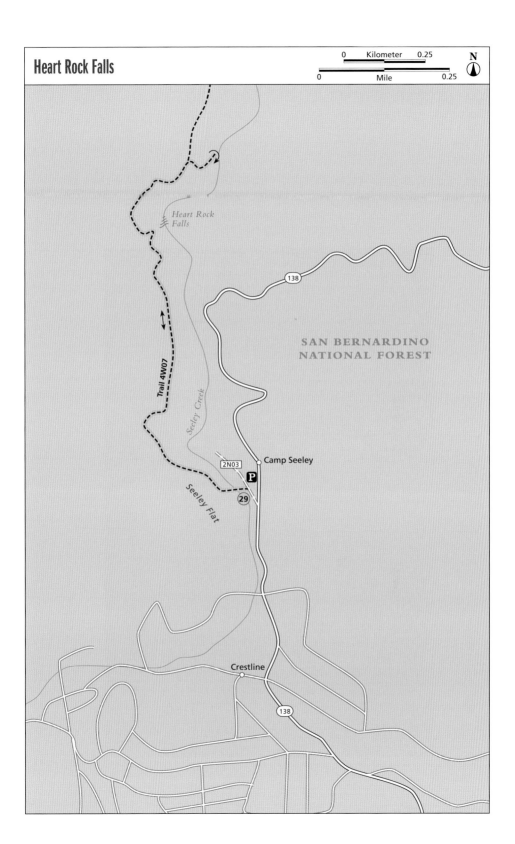

Heart Rock Falls

0   Kilometer   0.25

0   Mile   0.25

N

Heart Rock
Falls

Trail 4W07

Seeley Creek

138

SAN BERNARDINO
NATIONAL FOREST

2N03   Camp Seeley

P

29

Seeley Flat

Crestline

138

Hike Information

Local information: San Bernardino National Forest, 602 S. Tippecanoe Ave., San Bernardino, CA, 92408; https://www.fs.usda.gov/sbnf; 909-382-2682

Camping: San Bernardino National Forest campgrounds (www.recreation.gov and some first come, first served sites, many close seasonally): Applewhite, Barton Flats, Big Pine Flats, Crab Flats, Dogwood, Fisherman's, Green Valley, Hanna Flat, Heart Bar, Holcomb Valley, Horse Springs, Mission Springs, North Shore, Pineknot, San Gorgonio, Serrano, South Fork; www.fs.fed.us/r5/sanbernardino/

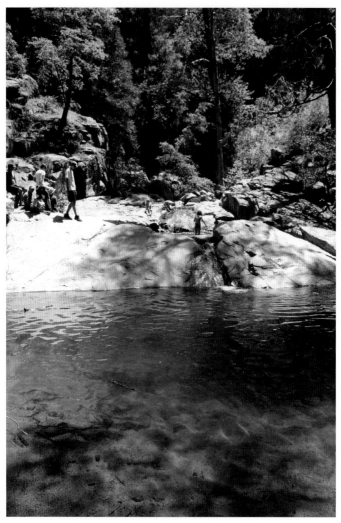

Pools below Heart Rock Falls offer a cool respite for those looking for a swim. Photo by Allen Riedel.

30 Castle Rock

Hike along a watershed to an easy climb, even for small children, to a rock promontory overlooking Big Bear Lake.

Start: At the Castle Rock Trail Head on Hwy. 18, just west of the town of Big Bear Lake in Boulder Bay

Distance: 5.1 miles out and back (1.5 miles to Castle Rock and back)

Hiking time: 2 to 3 hours

Difficulty: Easy to moderate

Trail surface: Single-track dirt trail

Nearest town: Big Bear Lake

County: San Bernardino

Other trail users: Equestrians

Canine compatibility: Leashed dogs permitted

Trailhead facilities/amenities: None

Land status: National forest

Fees and permits: Adventure Pass required for parking

Schedule: Open year-round

Maps: USGS Big Bear Lake, CA; www.parks.ca .gov/pages/636/files/MtSanJacintoSPmap.pdf

Trail contacts: San Bernardino National Forest, 602 S. Tippecanoe Ave., San Bernardino, CA, 92408; www.fs.fed.us/r5/sanbernardino/; 909-382-2600 or 909-382-2921

Finding the trailhead: From the intersection of Highway 18 and Highway 38 at the Big Bear Dam, follow Highway 18 for 1.2 miles east toward the town of Big Bear Lake. Park in the dirt pullouts by the trailhead sign. GPS: 34°14'12.0"N 116°57'42.2"W

The Hike

Castle Rock is a popular destination for hikers of all experience levels and with good reason. Relative to effort, it is quite possibly the best hike in the region for views of the lake, attainable for almost anyone of any skill level. The surrounding white fir, Jeffrey, and ponderosa pine forest is quite lovely.

The trail also presents many great options on completion, and the ability to wander on the roads and trails for hours afterward if one desires is a nice diversion. This hike heads to Castle Rock from Highway 18 and then on to a view of Bluff Lake Reserve (a reservation with the Wildlands Conservancy is required for admittance) and the Champion Lodgepole Pine. Parking can be crowded even early in the day, and the highway is a bit dangerous and curvy, so if you have to turn around while driving, do so cautiously. Be careful when bringing young children as the road is not the only danger. Drops and falls can and do occur on the rocks when the trail isn't followed. There are much steeper and dangerous rock-climbing routes that may look easy but are quite precarious. Before climbing a rock, remember that it is often easier to scramble up than it is to come down.

The trail begins at the highway and climbs steeply up and north through the forest along the creek bed. Since lots of people take this hike, many people also get lost and create spur trails; try to remain on the path through the rocky outcroppings,

The wall and face of Castle Rock is aptly named. Photo by Allen Riedel.

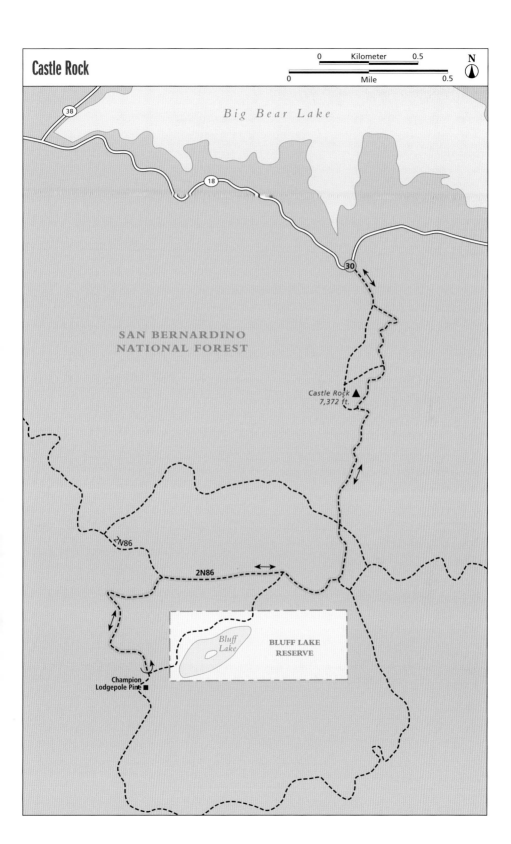

though this can be difficult. If you feel like you are lost, trace your way back to the trail, and keep forging upward and north. The trail opens up along the watershed and travels to the east of the large outcropping known as Castle Rock. Follow the trail all the way past the rocks and around the backside for the easiest access to the top. Once you reach the top, you are rewarded with a panoramic view of the lake and surrounding mountains. It is certainly a good place to while away the time, though it isn't likely you will have it all to yourself, even on a weekday.

Descend from the rock and continue north along the trail until you reach Road 2N86, turn right and follow the road for 0.2 mile. Turn left down the road to the Bluff Lake Reserve. A picturesque ruin sits at the entrance to the lake. Please do not enter the reserve without permission. Contact the Wildlands Conservancy at 909-790-3698 or mountainpreserves@twc-ca.org for more information. Once you've caught a glimpse of the reserve, return to 2N86 and turn left, follow it for 0.7 mile to the intersection with a use road. Turn left and follow it for 0.4 mile to the Champion Lodgepole Pine.

Retrace your steps back to the parking area, or if you want, explore some more along 2N10 as it intersects with many other trails.

Miles and Directions

0.0 Start north up the Castle Rock Trail from Highway 18.

0.75 Reach the top of Castle Rock.

0.8 Turn right and continue north along the trail. Follow it to road 2N86.

1.5 Turn right onto Road 2N86.

1.7 Turn left onto the old road to Bluff Lake.

1.8 Stop and admire the lake from afar. Return to Road 2N86.

1.9 Turn left onto Road 2N86.

2.65 Turn left onto the use trail/road.

3.1 Arrive at the Champion Lodgepole Pine. Follow the trail back to Road 2N86.

3.85 Turn right onto Road 2N886.

4.8 Turn left onto the Castle Rock Trail.

6.7 Return to the Parking Area.

Hike Information

Local information: San Bernardino National Forest, 602 S. Tippecanoe Ave., San Bernardino, CA, 92408; https://www.fs.usda.gov/sbnf; 909-382-2682

Camping: San Bernardino National Forest campgrounds (www.recreation.gov and some first come, first served sites, many close seasonally): Applewhite, Barton Flats, Big Pine Flats, Crab Flats, Dogwood, Fisherman's, Green Valley, Hanna Flat, Heart Bar, Holcomb Valley, Horse Springs, Mission Springs, North Shore, Pineknot, San Gorgonio, Serrano, South Fork; www.fs.fed.us/r5/sanbernardino/

31 Cougar Crest–Bertha Peak

Hike up to the Pacific Crest Trail on a gentle slope and then head to the most prominent summit on the north side of Big Bear.

Start: At the Cougar Crest Trail parking lot on Hwy. 38, just west of the town, near the Big Bear Discovery Center
Distance: 7.5 miles out and back
Hiking time: 3 to 4 hours
Difficulty: Easy to moderate
Trail surface: Single-track dirt trail, dirt road
Nearest town: Big Bear Lake
County: San Bernardino
Other trail users: Equestrians
Canine compatibility: Leashed dogs permitted

Trailhead facilities/amenities: Restrooms at trailhead parking
Land status: National forest
Fees and permits: Adventure Pass required for parking
Schedule: Open year-round
Maps: USGS Big Bear Lake, CA; www.parks.ca .gov/pages/636/files/MtSanJacintoSPmap.pdf
Trail contacts: San Bernardino National Forest, 602 S. Tippecanoe Ave., San Bernardino, CA, 92408; www.fs.fed.us/r5/sanbernardino/; 909-382-2600 or 909-382-2921

Finding the trailhead: From the intersection of Highway 18 and Highway 38 at the Big Bear Dam, follow Highway 38 for 6 miles east toward the town of Fawnskin. Turn left into the parking area. GPS: 34°15'49.4"N 116°54'39.5"W

The Hike

The Cougar Crest Trail is one of the most popular in the Big Bear region. The large parking lot located near the Big Bear Discovery Center makes it an easy destination for Big Bear travelers and those looking for something to do. The wide trail, which used to be an old dirt road, is so broad that four people could easily walk hand in hand for at least the first mile, which is an easy walk. After that, the path becomes a trail, though it is still fairly wide for the remainder of the trip. The route climbs up to the ridgeline and meets the Pacific Crest Trail (PCT) in 2.5 miles. What is truly spectacular about this trip are the expansive views of Big Bear Lake that open up shortly after the trail narrows. Jaw-dropping vistas of the San Gorgonio Wilderness sit behind the beautiful placid blue of the lake. The PCT can and will be a destination for some, but the views from the Bertha Peak region beckon as they do in another 1.25 miles with a minimal amount of climbing.

The PCT heads left (north) toward the Angeles National Forest and Canada, and right (south) toward the San Jacinto Wilderness and Mexico. Take the right fork and head to the summit of Bertha Peak. The views from Bertha Peak are well worth the effort, even though the service road leading to the top is steep. There are radio towers on top of the summit; they are gated off, so it is impossible to get a 360-degree

SAN GORGONIO WILDERNESS

The San Gorgonio Wilderness has been the preeminent wilderness area in Southern California. A recent spate of wildfires has left the area scarred and a shell of its former self. The Lake, Apple, El Dorado, and Valley Fires burned nearly 80 percent of the forest in the wilderness. However, new growth is everywhere, the trails have mostly reopened, and the forest hasn't gone away; it is simply changed from the ideal many might have once had of its primeval forests. With nearly 60,000 acres of wildland, much of it above 7,000 feet in elevation, the wilderness contains the six highest summits between the Sierra Nevada to the north and Picacho Del Diablo 300 miles to the south in Baja California. The San Bernardino Peak Divide Trail traverses the highest reaches of the wilderness, traveling 18 miles across the ridgeline of the wilderness to the summit of San Gorgonio Mountain, with more than 10 miles of trail above 10,000 feet.

Home to lakes, waterfalls, meadows, streams, hundreds of miles of trails, historic cabins, plane crashes, and the baseline from which all of the Southern California basin was surveyed and mapped, the area is a beautiful, forested paradise. By the 1920s, thousands of visitors attracted by the natural beauty of the area had begun to make their way into the San Bernardino Mountains and the San Gorgonio Wilderness. An outdoor group appealed to the Angeles National Forest to set aside the San Gorgonio region as a wilderness area, but developers and planners had decided on using the region as the best place for skiing and winter recreation in Southern California.

A ski resort was planned for South Fork Meadows, and ski lifts were going to go straight up to the summit of Jepson Peak and San Gorgonio Mountain itself. Ski organizations and developers fought to have the area transformed, hoping to prevent it from being included in the Wilderness Act of 1964, but with the help of the Sierra Club, Defenders of Wilderness (now the San Gorgonio Wilderness Association), and conservationists, the region was preserved as a natural habitat for posterity—even though development interests attempted to develop the area again in 1971.

view of the area, but it is still magnificent. There will be lots of other travelers along the route, some walking, some jogging, and maybe even some with strollers. Enjoy.

Miles and Directions

0.0 From the parking area, hike north along the Cougar Crest Trail.

1.0 The trail narrows and continues north.

2.5 Turn right at the junction with the Pacific Crest Trail.

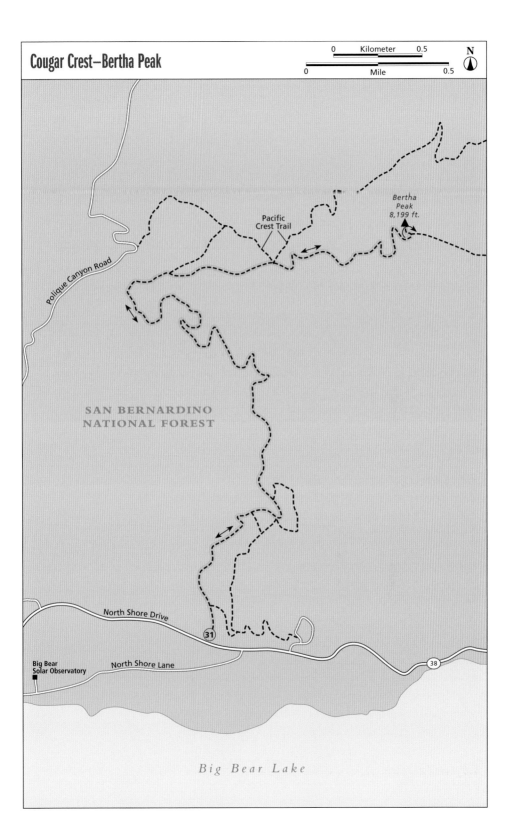

0   Kilometer   0.5

0   Mile   0.5

N

Bertha
Peak
8,199 ft.

Pacific
Crest Trail

Polique Canyon Road

SAN BERNARDINO
NATIONAL FOREST

North Shore Drive

31

Big Bear
Solar Observatory

North Shore Lane

38

Big Bear Lake

Western wallflower graces the trail with views of Big Bear Lake and the San Gorgonio Wilderness. Photo by Allen Riedel.

2.9 Turn right onto Bertha Peak Road.

3.4 Turn left onto the service road to the top of Bertha Peak.

3.5 Reach the peak. Return via the same route.

7.0 Return to the parking area.

Hike Information

Local information: San Bernardino National Forest, 602 S. Tippecanoe Ave., San Bernardino, CA, 92408; https://www.fs.usda.gov/sbnf; 909-382-2682

Camping: San Bernardino National Forest campgrounds (www.recreation.gov and some first come, first served sites, many close seasonally): Applewhite, Barton Flats, Big Pine Flats, Crab Flats, Dogwood, Fisherman's, Green Valley, Hanna Flat, Heart Bar, Holcomb Valley, Horse Springs, Mission Springs, North Shore, Pineknot, San Gorgonio, Serrano, South Fork; www.fs.fed.us/r5/sanbernardino/

32 Jepson Peak

The hike to Jepson Peak is a demanding one. Beginning in a dusty wash and ending on an alpine summit ridge, the trail leads to a short cross-country traverse up to the second-highest summit in Southern California. The views are stellar and wide.

Start: Parking lot at the end of Valley of the Falls Drive/Falls Road
Distance: 16 miles out and back
Hiking time: 10 to 12 hours
Difficulty: Extremely strenuous
Trail surface: Single-track dirt trail, use trail, and cross-country
Nearest town: Forest Falls
County: San Bernardino
Other trail users: None
Canine compatibility: Leashed dogs permitted
Trailhead facilities/amenities: All facilities available at trailhead
Land status: National forest

Fees and permits: Wilderness permit required; Adventure Pass required for parking. Wilderness permits are available at the San Gorgonio Ranger Station, 34701 Mill Creek Rd., Mentone, CA, 92359; 909-382-2882
Schedule: Open year-round; winter mountaineering skills necessary in winter
Maps: USGS Forest Falls, CA, and San Gorgonio Mountain, CA
Trail contact: San Bernardino National Forest, 602 S. Tippecanoe Ave., San Bernardino, CA, 92408; https://www.fs.usda.gov/sbnf; 909-382-2682

Finding the trailhead: From Los Angeles, take I-10 east. Take Exit 79 toward Orange Street/CA 38/Downtown Redlands. Turn left onto Pearl Avenue. Drive for 0.2 mile. Turn left onto Orange Street and drive for 0.6 mile. Turn right onto CA 38 East/Lugonia Avenue and drive for 13.9 miles. Make a slight right onto Valley of the Falls Drive and drive for 4 miles. Continue onto Falls Road and drive for 0.4 mile to the parking lot at the end. GPS: 34°04'55.0"N 116°53'36.6"W

The Hike

Most people who hike to the summit of Jepson Peak do so as a side trip to acquiring the popular zenith of San Gorgonio Mountain. Sitting merely 1 mile apart, the 11,205-foot summit of Jepson Peak is barely a few hundred feet shy of claiming the mantle of tallest peak in Southern California. The views from on high are similar—360 degrees in nature—but on just about any given day of the week, the summit of Jepson will be quiet and full of calm serenity, whereas the summit of San Gorgonio will be anything but. Since San G (as it is colloquially called) is the highest summit, many people make the trek to its apex without a thought to its only slightly diminutive neighbor.

Even on a weekend, it is unlikely to find another visitor atop the summit of Jepson Peak. There is good reason for this. There isn't an established trail to the summits of San Gorgonio or Jepson that doesn't include at least 3,500 feet of elevation gain and between 16 and 25 miles of hiking. Simply put, most people who summit San

Gorgonio are pooped, and they aren't looking to top out on another peak. There will always be those who are super gung ho (I will neither confirm nor deny if that means me), but it isn't that normal to run into them.

This route follows the popular Vivian Creek Trail, which is the shortest maintained route to either summit. Be sure to get permits ahead of time, especially if traveling on a weekend or popular holiday. The route is all uphill, and steeper in the first mile and in the last notch up to the saddle between the two summits than the rest of the trail, but hikers should expect a steady climb all the way to the top. It does not get easier around any corner. In fact, it is this author's opinion that the climb to San Gorgonio is tougher than the ascent to the summit of Mount Whitney, making this a fine training hike for that trip as well.

At the outset of the hike, follow the dirt road east beyond the gate for 0.5 mile, to where the trail drops down into the Mill Creek wash. Cross the rocky wash bottom and find the trail sign on the north side of the drainage. Here, the trail begins a brutal climb of almost 1,000 feet in just 0.5 mile. Ascending through oak and scattered desert brush, the trail seems dusty, rough, and not scenic. Actually, the trail does ease up for a moment, just a little after the rise. The biggest change is in the flora of the area once Vivian Creek comes into view. A lovely verdant forested meadow of pine, cedar, and fern welcomes visitors to the San Gorgonio Wilderness. Shortly thereafter, the trail begins climbing sharply upward again and follows Vivian Creek toward its source.

At 3 miles, the trail passes Halfway Camp—halfway to what nobody is sure, but that is the name of the lovely little forested campsite. The trail continues to climb and climb, but the forest is quite charming and the views of the Yucaipa Ridge to the south are vivid and stunning. The sawtooth crest is reminiscent of high Sierra summits, and it is almost hard to imagine that the ultimate destination of this hike will end up more than 2,000 feet higher than the tallest peak along that ridge. The 2020 Apple Fire burned that entire summit crest; the fire was started by a diesel vehicle's exhaust in the hottest and driest of Southern California conditions. It along with the El Dorado Fire, which burned an entirely different section of the wilderness and was started by a gender reveal party, are the clearest demonstrations of the damage careless humans can cause.

At 5 miles, the trail reaches High Creek Camp, complete with resident waterfall. Sitting at 9,500 feet, the air is certainly thinner here, and nights can be a might chilly.

After the camp, the trail switchbacks up to a high knob just over 10,000 feet. It is from this point that hikers catch their first glimpse of the other monumental Southern California summit, Mount San Jacinto, to the south. From the viewpoint, it nearly seems possible to toss a stone and hit the other side. By this time, the Yucaipa Ridge is well beneath you and not blocking any of the views. Looking to the north can be daunting for many because the summits of Jepson and San Gorgonio loom overhead, nearly 1,500 vertical feet above. Here, a section of the Apple Fire crossed over the trail and burned among the thin strands of high-altitude limber pines. One of the most

Take the trail to the left and head for the highest peak along the way. Photo by Allen Riedel.

sun exposed sections of the trail before the summit is now more exposed than ever and the next half mile is an eerie landscape stretching up to the sky.

The trail begins to exit the forest and ascends a barren alpine slope until it climbs above tree line. What pines do exist are mostly little shrubs, battered by wind, storms, and snow. At around 11,000 feet though, even those disappear.

At 7.1 miles, the trail junctions with the San Bernardino Peak Divide Trail. Turn left at the signed junction toward Dollar Lake Saddle. Follow the trail along the awesome ridgeline for 0.5 mile as it loses a couple of hundred feet before finding the use trail up the ridge to cone-shaped Jepson Peak.

The use trail ascends the slope for another 0.4 mile and reaches the summit of Jepson. Enjoy the views and the blissful emptiness, sign the register, and if you have enough energy, head to the summit of San Gorgonio Mountain, adding 1.2 miles to your hike, before returning via the same route to the trailhead.

Miles and Directions

0.0   Begin by hiking east beyond the parking lot up the gated Valley of the Falls Boulevard.

0.5   Turn left and cross the Mill Creek wash to find the signed trailhead for Vivian Creek Trail.

1.1   Enter the San Gorgonio Wilderness.

Jepson Peak

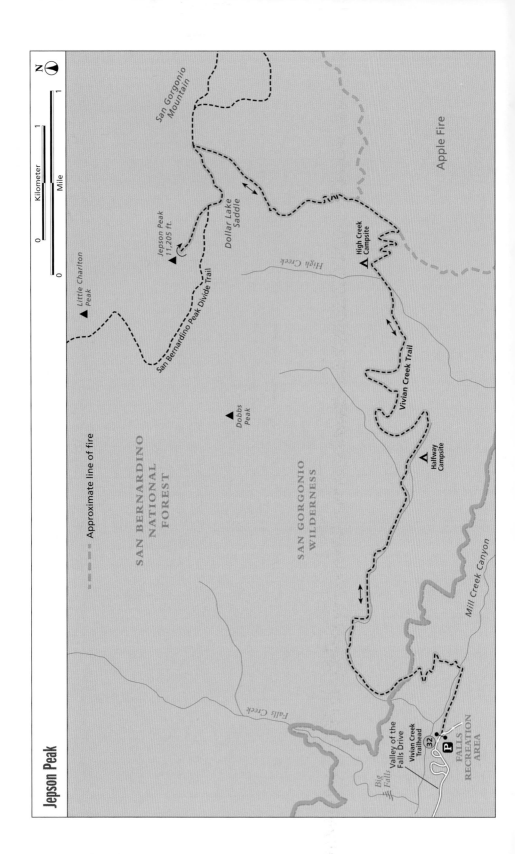

N

Kilometer

Mile

Little Charlton Peak

San Bernardino Peak Divide Trail

Jepson Peak
11,205 ft.

Dollar Lake Saddle

San Gorgonio Mountain

SAN BERNARDINO NATIONAL FOREST

Dobbs Peak

High Creek

SAN GORGONIO WILDERNESS

High Creek Campsite

Vivian Creek Trail

Apple Fire

Falls Creek

Halfway Campsite

Mill Creek Canyon

Big Falls

Valley of the Falls Drive

Vivian Creek Trailhead

32

P

FALLS RECREATION AREA

--- Approximate line of fire

1.3	Meet up with lush Vivian Creek.
3.0	Pass Halfway Camp.
5.0	Pass High Creek Camp. Cross through the burn scar of the Apple Fire.
7.1	Turn left at the junction onto the San Bernardino Peak Divide Trail.
7.6	Turn right onto the Jepson Peak use trail.
8.0	Arrive atop Jepson Peak. Return via the same route.
16.0	Arrive back at the Forest Falls parking area and the trailhead.

Hike Information

Local information: San Bernardino National Forest, 602 S. Tippecanoe Ave., San Bernardino, CA, 92408; https://www.fs.usda.gov/sbnf; 909-382-2682

Camping: San Bernardino National Forest campgrounds (www.recreation.gov and some first come, first served sites, many close seasonally): Applewhite, Barton Flats, Big Pine Flats, Crab Flats, Dogwood, Fisherman's, Green Valley, Hanna Flat, Heart Bar, Holcomb Valley, Horse Springs, Mission Springs, North Shore, Pineknot, San Gorgonio, Serrano, South Fork; www.fs.fed.us/r5/sanbernardino/

33 San Jacinto Peak

San Jacinto is one of the most majestic peaks in Southern California. It is also one of the most heavily visited. The surrounding forest is supremely beautiful, and you'll get a great view of this forest as this hike begins by ascending via the magnificent Palm Springs Aerial Tramway. The summit block is one of the most picturesque in Southern California. John Muir once called the view from the top sublime.

Start: Palm Springs Aerial Tramway
Distance: 11.6 miles out and back
Hiking time: 6 to 9 hours
Difficulty: Very strenuous
Trail surface: Single-track dirt trail
Nearest town: Palm Springs
County: Riverside
Other trail users: None
Canine compatibility: No dogs permitted
Trailhead facilities/amenities: All facilities at tram debarkation
Land status: National forest, California state park
Fees and permits: You must purchase a Palm Springs Aerial Tramway ticket; also, get the required wilderness permit at the Long Valley Ranger Station; pick up your permit at the bottom of the hill in Long Valley after leaving the tram debarkation station

Schedule: Open year-round; tram closes mid-Sept. for 2 weeks for maintenance; Mon.–Fri. first tram up 10 a.m.; Sat., Sun., holidays first tram up 8 a.m.; last tram up 8 p.m. and last tram down 9:45 p.m. Expect snow and mountaineering conditions in winter
Maps: USGS Palm Springs, CA, and San Jacinto Peak, CA; www.parks.ca.gov/pages/636/files/MtSanJacWebPDF2009.pdf
Trail contacts: Mount San Jacinto State Wilderness, P.O. Box 308/25905 CA 243, Idyllwild, CA, 92349; www.parks.ca.gov/?page_id=636; 951-659-2607. San Bernardino National Forest, 602 S. Tippecanoe Ave., San Bernardino, CA, 92408. San Jacinto Ranger District, 54270 Pine Crest Ave., P.O. Box 518, Idyllwild, CA, 92549; https://www.fs.usda.gov/sbnf; 909-382-2682, 909-382-2682, or 909-382-2921. Palm Springs Aerial Tramway, www.pstramway.com; 888-515-TRAM

Finding the trailhead: From Los Angeles, take CA 60 east to Beaumont. Merge onto I-10 east and continue for 18.3 miles. Take Exit 112 to merge onto CA 111 south, heading toward Palm Springs, for 8.6 miles. Turn right onto Tram Way and drive for 3.9 miles to the parking lot. GPS: 33°50'34.4"N 116°36'27.8"W

The Hike

This adventure begins in the parking lot for the Palm Springs Aerial Tramway. Purchase tickets or get them ahead of time online (suggested for weekends), get in line, and ride the world's largest rotating tram from the desert elevation of 2,600 feet up to the cool alpine forest at 8,500 feet. At the top, the trail begins right outside the back doors. Start down the concrete path. There will be throngs of people at first but follow the path to the ranger station at the bottom of the hill and get a wilderness

Marion and Jean Mountains were named for the two loves of topographer Edmund Taylor Perkins. Photo by Allen Riedel.

permit. This is important because rangers will turn a party back even from near the summit if they do not have one in their possession. Follow the Low Trail through blissful pine forest and meadows toward Round Valley. At 1.75 miles, intersect with the High Trail, which turns eastward to the left; continue straight on the Low Trail toward the campground. At 2 miles, a trail on the right leads north to Tamarack Valley; continue straight.

In the next mile, the trail gains 800 feet to Wellman Divide. Turn right onto the San Jacinto Peak Trail. Here a nice window of viewpoints begins to open up of the lower peaks of the San Jacinto Mountains to the south. The high-mountain air is crisp and invigorating. The trail circles beneath the contours of Jean Peak and winds through granite, prickly whitethorn, ceanothus, and manzanita. The outstanding views get better and better as the trail climbs gently toward the summit. When the trail reaches a saddle between the summit of San Jacinto and Miller Peaks, at just over 5.2 miles, it hairpins abruptly south and begins ascending sharply to the top of the mountain.

The San Jacinto Peak Trail junctions with the summit trail at 5.5 miles. Continue upward toward the right, and soon the stone summit hut, built by the California Conservation Corps in 1935, comes into view. Visitors can enter and write in some

Clouds covering the Southern California basin sometimes have no effect on the higher elevations, but their effect can also be multiplied by factors of 10 on other occasions. Photo by Allen Riedel.

of the various summit registers. From there, continue 0.3 mile to the summit, which requires scrambling over large boulders to the rocky top of the peak.

The views are some of the best anywhere due to the mountain's prominence and height. On a clear day, all of Southern California can be seen. It is reported that John Muir climbed to the summit in 1887 and said that the view at sunrise was the "most sublime spectacle on the earth." The quote does not come directly from Muir's writings, however, but from a text written in 1927 that credits the sentiment to him. Even if those words did not escape his lips, one can only imagine what the view must have been like at that time, without any smog or modernity. Most people will want to spend a good deal of time on the summit.

Return via the same route.

GREEN TIP
Support environmental organizations and parks
by donating time, energy, and money.

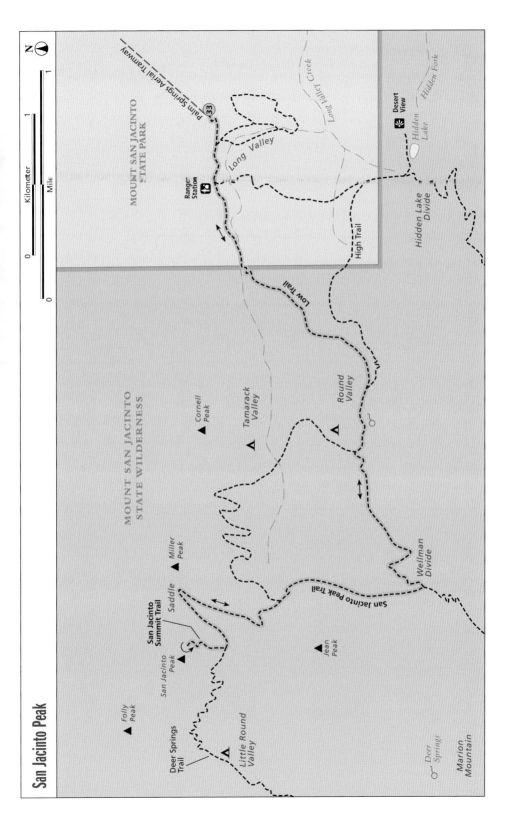

San Jacinto Peak

N

Kilometer

0   1

Mile

0   1

MOUNT SAN JACINTO
STATE PARK

Palm Springs Aerial Tramway

33

Long Valley

Long Valley Creek

Range
Station

High Trail

Hidden Lake
Divide

Desert
View

Hidden
Lake

Hidden Fork

Low Trail

Round
Valley

Tamarack
Valley

Cornell
Peak

Wellman
Divide

San Jacinto Peak Trail

MOUNT SAN JACINTO
STATE WILDERNESS

Miller
Peak

Saddle

San Jacinto
Summit Trail

San Jacinto Peak

Folly
Peak

Deer Springs
Trail

Little Round
Valley

Jean
Peak

Deer
Springs

Marion
Mountain

Miles and Directions

0.0 Start hiking from the southern exit of the Palm Springs Aerial Tramway's Upper Terminal.

0.3 Get a wilderness permit at the ranger station. Continue hiking on the Low Trail.

1.7 Stay to the right and continue straight ahead at the junction with the High Trail, toward Round Valley.

2.0 Continue straight and toward the left (west) at the campsite, heading toward Wellman Divide.

3.0 Turn right (north) onto the San Jacinto Peak Trail at Wellman Divide.

5.5 Turn right onto the summit trail.

5.8 Arrive atop San Jacinto Peak. Return via the same route.

11.6 Arrive back at the trailhead at the Upper Terminal.

Hike Information

Local information: San Bernardino National Forest, 602 S. Tippecanoe Ave., San Bernardino, CA, 92408; https://www.fs.usda.gov/sbnf; 909-382-2682

Camping: San Bernardino National Forest campgrounds (www.recreation.gov, some first come, first served; 14-day stay maximum; and seasonal closures): Boulder Basin, Dark Canyon, Fern Basin, Marion Mountain, Pinyon Flat, Santa Rosa Springs, Tool Box Springs, www.fs.fed.us/r5/sanbernardino/; Hurkey Creek, www.riverside countyparks.org/locations/regional-parks/hurkey-creek/; Idyllwild Campground, 25905 CA 243, Idyllwild–Pine Cove, CA, 92549; 951-659-2607

34 Suicide Rock

Take the Deer Springs Trail through lovely pine forests to an outcropping rife with local lore.

Start: On Highway 243 north of Idyllwild at the Deer Springs Trail parking lot
Distance: 6.9 miles out and back
Hiking time: 3 to 4 hours
Difficulty: Moderate
Trail surface: Single-track dirt trail
Nearest town: Idyllwild
County: Riverside
Other trail users: Equestrians
Canine compatibility: Not permitted in state park
Trailhead facilities/amenities: None
Land status: National forest
Fees and permits: Adventure Pass required for parking; wilderness permit, also required, available at San Jacinto Ranger District, P.O.

Box 518/54270 Pine Crest Ave., Idyllwild, CA, 92349; 909-382-2921
Schedule: Open year-round
Maps: USGS San Jacinto Peak, CA; www.parks .ca.gov/pages/636/files/MtSanJacintoSPmap .pdf
Trail contacts: Mount San Jacinto State Wilderness, P.O. Box 308/25905 CA 243, Idyll-wild, CA, 92349; www.parks.ca.gov/?page_id =636; 951-659-2607. San Bernardino National Forest, 602 S. Tippecanoe Ave., San Bernardino, CA, 92408; San Jacinto Ranger District, 54270 Pine Crest Ave., P.O. Box 518, Idyllwild, CA, 92549; https://www.fs.usda .gov/sbnf; 909-382-2682, 909-382-2682, or 909-382-2921

Finding the trailhead: From the intersection of I-5, US 101, I-10, and CA 60, take CA 60 east for 52.3 miles to I-215. Continue on I-215 south for 19.1 miles. Take Exit 15 for CA 74, heading east toward Hemet. Take CA 74 for 31.9 miles. Turn right onto CA 243 north and drive for 5.3 miles. Park in the large dirt pullout lot by the trailhead sign. GPS: 33°45'10.9"N 116°43'21.5"W

The Hike

Hiking to Suicide Rock sounds more dangerous than it really is. Some people say the rock received its name due to a Romeo-and-Juliet–like story, in which two Native American lovers who were refused permission to marry leaped to their deaths from the rock, but there is no corroboration for such a story anywhere in the local Native American mythos. Apparently, the story has been told for quite some time and is interesting in that regard since it seems to be an urban legend about a proposed legend. The rock has been so named, at least colloquially, since the late 1800s, but it is unknown as to why it was given such a moniker because there aren't any known occurrences of suicide at the rock. Perhaps due to its vertical drop-off from the face— it is impossible not to look up and imagine someone teetering dangerously close to the edge—it may have been the stuff of nightmares for old-timers in Idyllwild.

The route starts among a confusing confluence of trails and dirt roads at the parking lot, and it can be difficult for anyone new to the trail to find the actual entrance.

Views into the high country are magnificent. Photo by Allen Riedel.

Hike up the hill to the dirt road, turn left/north and follow the dirt road until it turns into the signed Deer Springs Trail. The route travels through a mostly pine forest of Jeffrey and ponderosa pine, with a few scattered Coulter pines and their notoriously spiked and heavy cones, dubbed colloquially as "widow-makers." The route follows the Deer Springs Trail for 2.3 miles through granite and forest, crossing a seasonal watershed before the junction with the Suicide Rock Trail. The open forest in this area is a lesser known snow play area until late in the season and the most wonderful place in Idyllwild to head to after a fresh snow. Note, it is not advisable after a fresh snowfall to continue onto Suicide Rock Trail, unless one is a seasoned winter explorer as the next mile encounters a few drops before crossing Marion Creek, and the trail can become icy and treacherous.

From the junction, continue for 1 mile past Marion Creek, which in normal years flows year-round. From there, the trail climbs steeply around Suicide Rock to a precipitous drop where the slab faces Lily Rock and the Devil's Slide Trail. If you pay careful attention, you can spot hikers headed to Saddle Junction and beyond. A short 0.1 mile scramble up and north leads to the "top" of Suicide Rock where there isn't much of a view, but there is likely still a trail register hidden among the rocks that young and old can sign after "bagging" the summit.

Enjoy the views and follow the same route back to the parking area.

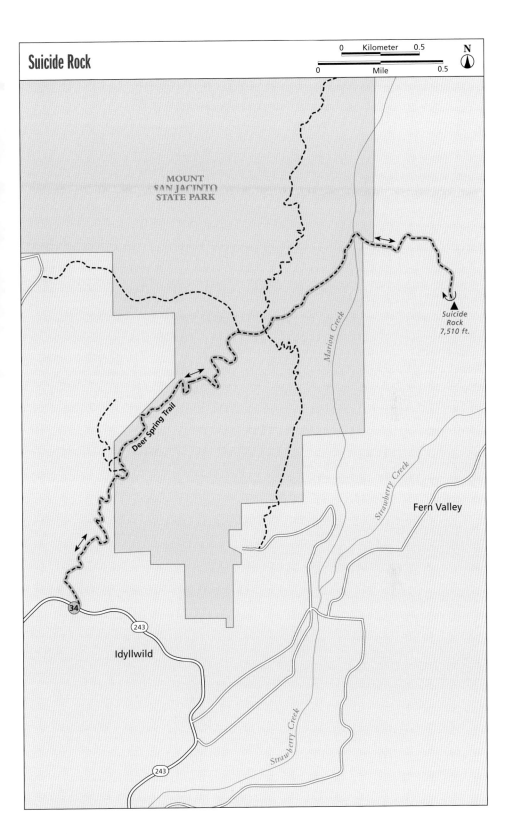

Suicide Rock

Miles and Directions

0.0 Hike up the trails to the dirt road, turn left and follow it for 0.1 mile to the trail sign.

0.1 Follow the Deer Springs Trail to the junction of the Suicide Rock Trail.

0.6 Enter Mount San Jacinto State Park.

2.1 Cross a seasonal watershed.

2.3 Reach the junction with the Suicide Rock Trail, follow it straight toward Suicide Rock.

2.8 Reach Marion Creek.

3.3 Arrive at Suicide Rock overlook.

3.4 Scramble 0.1 mile to the summit of Suicide Rock.

3.6 Return on the Suicide Rock Trail.

4.6 Stay straight to remain on the Deer Springs Trail.

6.9 Return to the parking area.

Hike Information

Local information: Mount San Jacinto State Wilderness, P.O. Box 308/25905 CA 243, Idyllwild, CA, 92349; www.parks.ca.gov/?page_id=636; 951-659-2607. San Bernardino National Forest, 602 S. Tippecanoe Ave., San Bernardino, CA, 92408; San Jacinto Ranger District, 54270 Pine Crest Ave., P.O. Box 518, Idyllwild, CA, 92549; https://www.fs.usda.gov/sbnf; 909-382-2682, 909-382-2682, or 909-382-2921

Camping: San Bernardino National Forest campgrounds (www.recreation.gov, some first come, first served; 14-day stay maximum; and seasonal closures): Boulder Basin, Dark Canyon, Fern Basin, Marion Mountain, Pinyon Flat, Santa Rosa Springs, Tool Box Springs, www.fs.fed.us/r5/sanbernardino/; Hurkey Creek, www.riverside countyparks.org/locations/regional-parks/hurkey-creek/; Idyllwild Campground, 25905 CA 243, Idyllwild–Pine Cove, CA, 92549; 951-659-2607

35 Ernie Maxwell Scenic Trail

The Ernie Maxwell Scenic Trail is a great introduction to Idyllwild hiking and the San Jacinto Mountains. Children and hikers of all ages will enjoy the views, the shady forest, and the gentle trip to Humber Park and back.

Start: Trailhead on Tahquitz View Drive
Distance: 5 miles out and back
Hiking time: About 2.5 hours
Difficulty: Easy
Trail surface: Single-track dirt trail
Nearest town: Idyllwild
County: Riverside
Other trail users: Equestrians and bicyclists
Canine compatibility: Leashed dogs permitted
Trailhead facilities/amenities: Restroom and picnic facilities at Humber Park
Land status: National forest
Fees and permits: Adventure Pass required for parking

Schedule: Open year-round
Maps: USGS San Jacinto Peak, CA; www.parks
.ca.gov/pages/636/files/MtSanJacintoSPmap
.pdf
Trail contacts: Mount San Jacinto State Wilderness, P.O. Box 308/25905 CA 243, Idyllwild, CA, 92349; www.parks.ca.gov/?page_id
=636; 951-659-2607. San Bernardino National Forest, 602 S. Tippecanoe Ave., San Bernardino, CA, 92408; San Jacinto Ranger District, 54270 Pine Crest Ave., P.O. Box 518, Idyllwild, CA, 92549; https://www.fs.usda.gov/
sbnf; 909-382-2682 or 909-382-2921

Finding the trailhead: From Los Angeles, take CA 60 east to I-215. Continue on I-215 south for 19.1 miles. Take Exit 15 for CA 74 east, heading toward Hemet. Follow CA 74 for 31.9 miles. Turn right onto CA 243 north and drive for 3.8 miles. Turn right onto Saunders Meadow Road and drive for 0.2 mile. Continue right to stay on Saunders Meadow Road and drive for 0.4 mile. Continue left to stay on Saunders Meadow Road and drive for 0.3 mile. Turn left onto Pine Avenue and drive for 0.1 mile. Turn right onto Tahquitz View Drive and drive for 0.6 mile. Park in the roadside turnout for the Ernie Maxwell Scenic Trail. GPS: 33°45'53.0"N 116°41'13.9"W

The Hike

The Ernie Maxwell Scenic Trail is just that, scenic. It is a great place to bring children, though not very small ones because the overall distance is a bit far to travel for really little ones. This easy trail works its way through a lovely forest canopy of pine on a fairly gentle incline, gaining about 300 feet or less per mile. The trail wraps just behind the town of Idyllwild and is quite close to houses, but they are unseen and the route feels remote and secluded.

The trail was created late in the 1950s so that equestrian users of the wilderness could avoid confrontations with motorists on the way to Humber Park. The late Ernie Maxwell, founder of Idyllwild's *Town Crier* newspaper, led the charge in getting the trail established and was a frequent visitor on the trail up until his death in 1994.

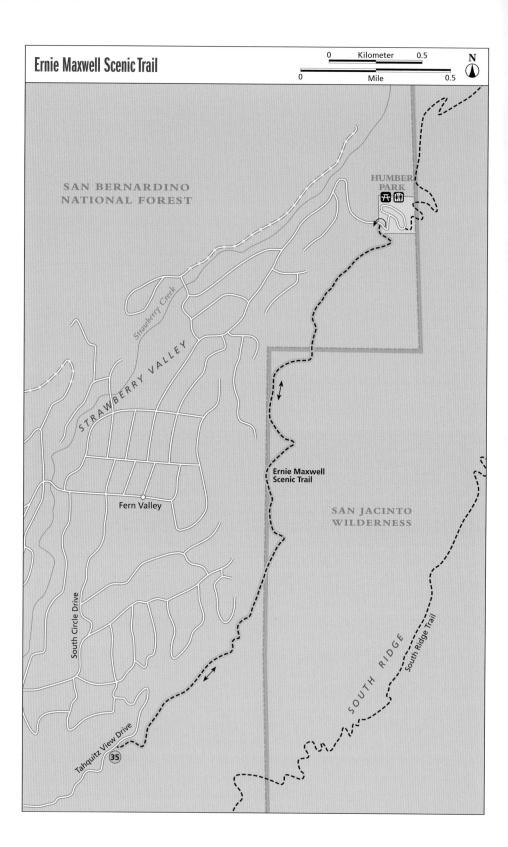

0   Kilometer   0.5

0   Mile   0.5

N

SAN BERNARDINO
NATIONAL FOREST

HUMBER
PARK

Strawberry Creek

STRAWBERRY VALLEY

Fern Valley

Ernie Maxwell
Scenic Trail

SAN JACINTO
WILDERNESS

South Circle Drive

SOUTH RIDGE

South Ridge Trail

Tahquitz View Drive

35

The trail is a great hike for beginners and anyone looking to find a pretty spot in nature. And while there isn't a spectacular destination at the end of this hike, the Ernie Maxwell Trail is one of those places where doing something for the sake of doing it is all that matters. The hike itself is the pleasure. It is gentle, but not so easy that there isn't some workout involved. There is mountain scenery galore, but the trail is wonderfully shaded, so the sun never becomes burdensome. Newcomers to hiking, children, and older adults alike can get out and enjoy the beauty of nature and the outdoors. The trail has a feel-good quality to it from the outset.

From the trailhead, hike north along the trail. For most of the route there are great views of Suicide Rock, and farther along, Lily Rock can be seen towering above. The trail parallels a nice creek for a short way just before reaching the turn-around at Humber Park, where there are picnic tables and restrooms.

Corn Lilies grow along almost any wetland at higher elevations. Photo by Makaila Riedel.

Turn around and return via the same route, enjoying the scenery from the reverse perspective.

Miles and Directions

0.0 From the trailhead, hike north along the Ernie Maxwell Scenic Trail.

2.5 Reach Humber Park, return via the same route.

5.0 Arrive back at the trailhead.

Hike Information

Local information: San Bernardino National Forest, 602 S. Tippecanoe Ave., San Bernardino, CA, 92408; https://www.fs.usda.gov/sbnf; 909-382-2682

Camping: San Bernardino National Forest campgrounds (www.recreation.gov, some first come, first served; 14-day stay maximum; and seasonal closures): Boulder Basin, Dark Canyon, Fern Basin, Marion Mountain, Pinyon Flat, Santa Rosa Springs, Tool Box Springs, www.fs.fed.us/r5/sanbernardino/; Hurkey Creek, www.riverside countyparks.org/locations/regional-parks/hurkey-creek/; Idyllwild Campground, 25905 CA 243, Idyllwild–Pine Cove, CA, 92549; 951-659-2607

36 Red Tahquitz

Travel up the invigorating South Ridge Trail, through tall pine forests, to the top of Tahquitz Peak, then drop into lush and lovely meadows and travel to the panoramic summit of a rarely visited peak in the lower San Jacinto Mountains.

Start: At the end of FR 5S11/South Ridge Road
Distance: 11.7 miles out and back
Hiking time: 6 to 9 hours
Difficulty: Very strenuous
Trail surface: Single-track dirt trail
Nearest town: Idyllwild
County: Riverside
Other trail users: Equestrians
Canine compatibility: Leashed dogs permitted
Trailhead facilities/amenities: None
Land status: National forest
Fees and permits: Adventure Pass required for parking; wilderness permit, also required, available at San Jacinto Ranger District, P.O. Box 518/54270 Pine Crest Ave., Idyllwild, CA, 92349; 909-382-2921
Schedule: Open year-round
Maps: USGS San Jacinto Peak, CA; www.parks .ca.gov/pages/636/files/MtSanJacintoSPmap .pdf
Trail contacts: San Bernardino National Forest, 602 S. Tippecanoe Ave., San Bernardino, CA, 92408; San Jacinto Ranger District, P.O. Box 518/54270 Pine Crest Ave., Idyllwild, CA, 92349; www.fs.fed.us/r5/sanbernardino/; 909-382-2600 or 909-382-2921

Finding the trailhead: From Los Angeles, take CA 60 east to I-215. Continue on I-215 south for 19.1 miles. Take Exit 15 for CA 74, heading east toward Hemet. Take CA 74 for 31.9 miles. Turn right onto CA 243 north and drive for 3.8 miles. Turn right onto Saunders Meadow Road and drive for 0.2 mile. Continue right to stay on Saunders Meadow Road and drive for 0.4 mile. Continue left to stay on Saunders Meadow Road and drive for 0.3 mile. Turn left onto Pine Avenue and drive for 0.1 mile. Turn right onto Tahquitz View Drive and drive for 0.3 mile. Turn right onto FR 5S11/ South Ridge Road and drive to its end. High-clearance vehicles are recommended. Park in the large dirt pullout lot by the trailhead sign. GPS: 33°44'07.8"N 116°41'45.6"W

The Hike

The hike up the South Ridge Trail begins in a mixed pine and oak forest. Fewer people take this route up to the popular lookout on top of Tahquitz Peak because of the dirt road driving required to get to the trailhead. The Devil's Slide Trail, which leads from Humber Park, is the more fashionable path, but it is also more heavily traveled. However, on weekends, it is still quite possible to see between 50 and 100 people along this route, so the trail does get a fair share of use. Even so, it feels more remote.

It is tricky to get a solid and steady GPS reading along this trail, which makes measuring distances a little difficult, and there are many estimates out there, even on published maps. Trip estimates vary in distance as much as 1 mile from the trailhead to the first summit. In my experience, it seems closer to the shorter distance than the

The damage from the 2018 Cranston and 2021 Mountain Fires is readily evident on top of Red Tahquitz, but regrowth is everywhere. Photo by Allen Riedel.

longer one, but because of the elevation gained, it is easy to understand why others would rate this trip as longer. It can be a tough and long climb for some, especially in the sun.

From the trailhead, the trail starts climbing immediately and enters the wilderness in slightly less than 0.5 mile. The 300 feet in elevation gain is fairly standard for 0.5-mile distances along this route, making it steep. It does get steeper in parts, sometimes gaining 500 feet per 0.5 mile. There are only a few places along the way where it eases up until after summiting Tahquitz Peak. One of those places is a tranquil open plateau at the halfway point, where the views open up and granite boulders line the trail through what is a lovely pine forest.

After the plateau, the trail begins climbing again among manzanita, whitethorn, and mountain chaparral. The route ascends along the western slope and is completely exposed in the midday sun. At the junction, turn right onto the short Tahquitz Peak Trail to Tahquitz Peak. Enjoy the lookout; it is a historic building and has been staffed exclusively by volunteers since 1998. On weekends and many summer days, friendly volunteers are available to talk and answer questions. The views are magnificent.

After spending some time at the lookout, head back to the junction and turn right at the sign marked for Saddle Junction.

TAHQUITZ

The name *Tahquitz* was derived from the name of a Native American god/demon called Tachuish or Dawkwish. Legend has it that the powerful spirit made his home high on the mountain summits of the San Jacintos, where he resided in a cave and a canyon. His anger and wrath were felt through earthquakes, lightning, and thunder, the sound of which was his horrible howling as he prowled the landscape looking for humans to devour, especially young girls. In the tales, he would not only eat their flesh but also devour their souls.

The large piles of rocks spread across the valleys of the Inland Empire were said to have been hurled down from the mountains by mighty Tahquitz when he was enraged. He was feared to have the powers of the storm and the earthquake, and to this day, strange, unexplained "booming" noises sometimes creep from within the bowels of the San Jacinto Mountains. These are said to be the screams or the voices of the demon's victims as he devours them whole.

In some stories, Tahquitz is a Cahuilla chieftain who begins to capture young maidens and kill them; in others, he is a shaman that begins to play cruel tricks on children, eventually culminating in murder; and in yet others, he is the creation of Mukat and Temayawet, the Cahuilla creator and ruler of the dead, respectively. In all the stories, however, Tahquitz shares a penchant for disguises and has the ability to morph into the physical features of other humans, beasts, or fantastical creatures.

A hero chief named Algoot is often connected with Tahquitz. It is said that a great battle occurred, with the giant boulders of Lily Rock and Suicide Rock being thrown by the chief and the demon and lodging in their present-day locations. Tahquitz was always killed in the legends, but not before his tail carved out what is now Lake Elsinore. As his body burned on a funeral pyre, his spirit is said to have left his body in a puff of smoke and returned to the high mountaintops, wreaking havoc unto this day.

The South Ridge Trail meets up with the Pacific Crest Trail (PCT) in 0.5 mile. Stay to the right and continue straight on the PCT, heading east as it skirts along the edge of lovely Tahquitz Meadow and Little Tahquitz Valley. Continue straight along the PCT for 1.4 miles, and watch for telltale signs on the right of the use trail leading to Red Tahquitz. Sometimes the trail is marked with a pile of rocks, known as a cairn, but people have been known to knock them down for various reasons. If there is no cairn, the trail looks like a little use path leading up to the south and eventually up to the summit of Red Tahquitz.

The summit of Red Tahquitz is wide open and rocky. There is a 360-degree view and the lookout atop Tahquitz seems near enough to touch. The summits of South

Red Tahquitz

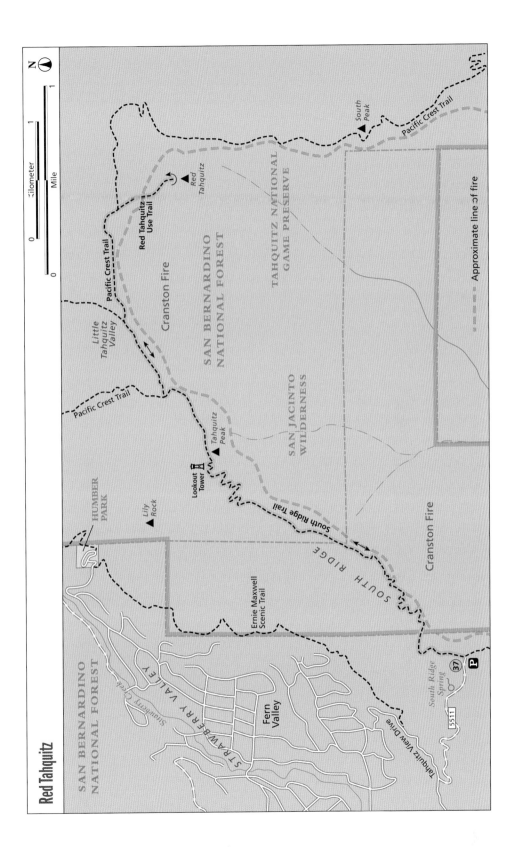

N

0   1 Kilometer
0   1 Mile

SAN BERNARDINO NATIONAL FOREST

HUMBER PARK

Lily Rock ▲

Lookout Tower 🗼

Little Tahquitz Valley

Pacific Crest Trail

Pacific Crest Trail

Cranston Fire

Red Tahquitz Use Trail

Red Tahquitz ▲

South Peak ▲

Pacific Crest Trail

TAHQUITZ NATIONAL GAME PRESERVE

SAN BERNARDINO NATIONAL FOREST

Tahquitz Peak ▲

SAN JACINTO WILDERNESS

South Ridge Trail

Cranston Fire

- - - Approximate line of fire

SOUTH RIDGE

Ernie Maxwell Scenic Trail

SAN BERNARDINO NATIONAL FOREST

STRAWBERRY VALLEY

Strawberry Creek

Fern Valley

Tahquitz View Drive

South Ridge Spring

5S11

🅿 37

Peak and some of the lower San Jacinto peaks drop away to the south. It is not likely that there will be anyone else on the top of Red Tahquitz as this peak is quite remote and there isn't a designated signed trail leading to the top. However, those with a sense of adventure will love this destination.

If you aren't in the mood for peak bagging, and would like to get similar views, it is also possible to stay along the PCT as it wraps around the backside of Red Tahquitz for a wonderful desert and peak panorama along the Desert Divide.

Follow the same route back to the parking area.

Miles and Directions

0.0 Start north up the South Ridge Trail from the sign in the parking area.

0.5 Reach the San Jacinto Wilderness boundary.

1.7 Reach a level plateau about halfway to the top of Tahquitz Peak.

3.3 Reach the junction with the Tahquitz Peak Trail; turn right toward the summit.

3.4 Arrive at the summit of Tahquitz Peak. Return to the junction.

3.5 Turn right (northeast) and take the trail toward the junction with the Pacific Crest Trail (PCT).

4.0 At the PCT intersection, stay straight and to the right on the PCT.

4.5 Stay straight on the PCT at the trail junction.

5.4 Look for the use trail on the right and follow it up to Red Tahquitz.

5.9 Arrive on top of Red Tahquitz. Return via the use trail to the PCT.

6.4 Turn left on the PCT to return via the same route.

7.8 Stay straight and left at the junction.

8.3 Take the South Ridge Trail toward Idyllwild.

11.7 Arrive back at the trailhead and parking area.

Hike Information

Local information: San Bernardino National Forest, 602 S. Tippecanoe Ave., San Bernardino, CA, 92408; https://www.fs.usda.gov/sbnf; 909-382-2682

Camping: San Bernardino National Forest campgrounds (www.recreation.gov, some first come, first served; 14-day stay maximum; and seasonal closures): Boulder Basin, Dark Canyon, Fern Basin, Marion Mountain, Pinyon Flat, Santa Rosa Springs, Tool Box Springs, www.fs.fed.us/r5/sanbernardino/; Hurkey Creek, www.riverside countyparks.org/locations/regional-parks/hurkey-creek/; Idyllwild Campground, 25905 CA 243, Idyllwild–Pine Cove, CA, 92549; 951-659-2607

37 Spitler Peak

Take an excellent cardio hike up and through a transitional forest to the ridgeline, and then along a secluded section of the Pacific Crest Trail (PCT). Enjoy panoramic 360-degree views of all of Southern California from the summit block of Spitler Peak.

Start: At the Spitler Peak trailhead parking area along Apple Canyon Road
Distance: 12 miles out and back
Hiking time: 6 to 9 hours
Difficulty: Very strenuous
Trail surface: Single-track dirt trail
Nearest town: Idyllwild
County: Riverside
Other trail users: Bicyclists (not allowed on the PCT) and equestrians
Canine compatibility: Leashed dogs permitted
Trailhead facilities/amenities: None

Land status: National forest
Fees and permits: Adventure Pass required for parking
Schedule: Open year-round
Maps: USGS Idyllwild, CA, and Palm View Peak, CA; https://caltopo.com/m/3J0G
Trail contacts: San Bernardino National Forest, 602 S. Tippecanoe Ave., San Bernardino, CA, 92408; San Jacinto Ranger District, 54270 Pine Crest Ave., P.O. Box 518, Idyllwild, CA, 92549; https://www.fs.usda.gov/sbnf; 909-382-2682 or 909-382-2921

Finding the trailhead: From the intersection of I-5, US 101, I-10, and CA 60, take CA 60 east for 52.3 miles to I-215. Continue on I-215 south for 19.1 miles. Take Exit 15 for CA 74, heading east toward Hemet. Follow CA 74 for 35.4 miles. Turn left onto Apple Canyon Road and drive for 2.6 miles. Park in the turnout parking area for the Spitler Peak Trail. GPS: 33°41'51.7"N 116°39'09.3"W

The Hike

According to thru-hikers, the first "real" chain of mountains the Pacific Crest Trail (PCT) runs through on its way north from Mexico to Canada is the San Jacinto range. The "Desert Divide" is the appellation given to the trail's passage through the lower section of the range. Along the way, the route skirts no less than 10 named peaks, eight of which are higher than 7,000 feet, before entering Tahquitz Valley. Most of the summits provide spectacular clear-day views of the entire Southern California region. On clear days, it is possible to see the Channel Islands, Mexico, and Arizona. The best thing about the Desert Divide is that it is much less frequented than the higher reaches of the San Jacinto Mountains and the state park that includes the namesake summit.

Hiking the Desert Divide is great in the late fall through early spring. Hot days are not pleasant due to the lower elevations of the trailheads, the lack of trees and shade in certain areas, and the steep, brutal climbs needed to ascend to the PCT. The Spitler Peak Trail is no exception. Starting at just under 5,000 feet, the trail gains 2,500 feet

Apache Peak, Antsell Rock, Red Tahquitz, Tahquitz Peak, and Mount San Jacinto. Photo by Allen Riedel.

of elevation in 6 miles, beginning its climb in a high-desert ecosystem complete with yucca, chaparral, and cacti. The path quickly enters a once mixed forest of maple and oak, which burned completely in 2013, though a few trees survived. The area is recovering though much of the forested area was wiped out and dead husks line the trail in an otherworldly landscape. Due to the lack of heavy use, parts of the trail can be overgrown in areas, making this an ideal hiking spot for wearing pants (no bare legs).

The trail is easy to follow as it leads to the base of the mountain. In slightly less than 1 mile, the trail begins its climb, snaking its way up the contours of the mountain. Spitler Peak sits high overhead, and its conical summit is unmistakable.

The trail gains elevation steadily until the 3.5-mile mark. At that point a series of switchbacks take over for the next 1.5 miles, until you reach the ridgeline. The switchbacks gain elevation more rapidly than the previous section of trail, making this an excellent route for exercise and or trail running.

▶ **Hiking Tip: Share your experience with others. Find special places and invite others to go along the next time.**

Once atop the crest, an old wooden sign illegibly marks the trail and gives mileage marks for several prominent trail features. Turn right (south) and head

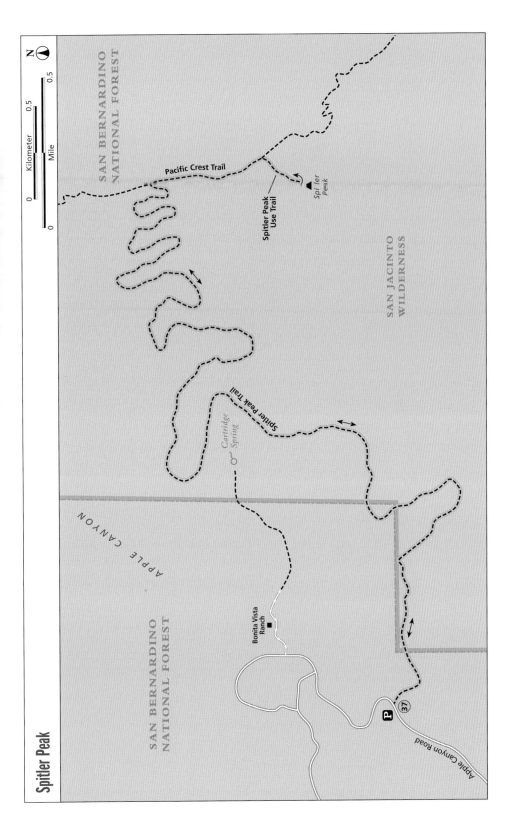

Spitler Peak

Pacific Crest Trail

Spitler Peak Use Trail

Spitler Peak

Spitler Peak Trail

Cartridge Spring

SAN BERNARDINO NATIONAL FOREST

SAN BERNARDINO NATIONAL FOREST

SAN JACINTO WILDERNESS

APPLE CANYON

Bonita Vista Ranch

Apple Canyon Road

N

Kilometer

0   0.5

0   0.5

Mile

Clouds can dazzle on cool wintry mornings, but so can the summits in the Lower San Jacinto range. Photo by Allen Riedel.

along the PCT toward Cedar Spring. Hike a short 0.3 mile south along the PCT to the obvious use trail up to the summit of Spitler Peak.

The route is no longer forested as it clambers up to the top. Once on top, the clear, boulder-marked summit block makes the perfect spot for a rest and an even better perch to take in the panoramic views. The best part about this hike is that most hikers hike in the summer and not the fall, spring, or winter when it's much more secluded. There is an excellent chance of being the only person on the summit and possibly even the trail, especially if hiking on a weekday.

Return via the same route.

Miles and Directions

0.0   Hike east through desert shrubs toward the mountains along the Spitler Peak Trail.

5.5   Reach the Pacific Crest Trail (PCT). Turn right onto the PCT.

5.8   Veer right up the use trail toward Spitler Peak.

6.0   Arrive at the summit of Spitler Peak. Return via the same route.

12.0   Arrive back at the trailhead.

Hike Information

Local information: San Bernardino National Forest, 602 S. Tippecanoe Ave., San Bernardino, CA, 92408; https://www.fs.usda.gov/sbnf; 909-382-2682

Camping: San Bernardino National Forest campgrounds (www.recreation.gov, some first come, first served; 14-day stay maximum; and seasonal closures): Boulder Basin, Dark Canyon, Fern Basin, Marion Mountain, Pinyon Flat, Santa Rosa Springs, Tool Box Springs, www.fs.fed.us/r5/sanbernardino/; Hurkey Creek, www.riverside countyparks.org/locations/regional-parks/hurkey-creek/; Idyllwild Campground, 25905 CA 243, Idyllwild–Pine Cove, CA, 92549; 951-659-2607

38 Lion Peak

Traverse along the Pacific Crest Trail along the Desert Divide. Enjoy expansive views into Palm Desert, Joshua Tree National Park, the Salton Sea, the Santa Rosas, and the high country of the San Jacinto massif. Exceptional 360-degree views abound along a large portion of the route.

Start: At the Cedar Springs Trail, on the dirt road behind the gate on Morris Ranch Road
Distance: 10 miles out and back
Hiking time: 5 to 7 hours
Difficulty: Very strenuous
Trail surface: Dirt road for the first quarter of a mile, single-track dirt trail
Nearest town: Idyllwild
County: Riverside
Other trail users: Equestrians
Canine compatibility: Leashed dogs permitted
Trailhead facilities/amenities: None
Land status: National forest

Fees and permits: Adventure Pass required for parking.
Schedule: Open year-round, best season fall through spring
Maps: USGS Palm View Peak, CA; https://cal-topo.com/m/3JOG
Trail contacts: San Bernardino National Forest, 602 S. Tippecanoe Ave., San Bernardino, CA, 92408; San Jacinto Ranger District, P.O. Box 518/54270 Pine Crest Ave., Idyllwild, CA, 92349; www.fs.fed.us/r5/sanbernardino/; 909-382-2600 or 909-382-2921

Finding the trailhead: From the intersection of I-5, US 101, I-10, and CA 60, take CA 60 east for 52.3 miles to I-215. Continue on I-215 south for 19.1 miles. Take Exit 15 for CA 74, heading east toward Hemet. Take CA 74 for 40.2 miles. Turn left onto Morris Ranch Road. Follow it for 3.7 miles to the roadside parking turnouts. Do not block the gate. Park in the large dirt pullout lot by the trailhead sign. GPS: 33°39'14.7"N 116°35'22.8"W

The Hike

The Cedar Springs Trail begins unceremoniously along a dirt road. There is a pedestrian gate beside the road gate, go through it and walk down the dirt road. Close all gates on the trail after going through them, as there are several. The first portion of the hike traverses the road and trail through private property along an easement. At 0.1 mile, you'll pass a water tank on the left and continue along the roadway. At 0.3 mile, the trail begins on the left, go through the gate and close it behind you. Here, you enter a forest of live oak; follow the trail along the creek bed, which is often dry and filled with acorns. The trail begins to climb gently for the first mile and stays mostly in the shade. At 0.9 mile, there is another gate, which leads to a national forest picnic ground with a couple of old tables and some downed signs warning of the rough trail ahead. Occasionally, cattle may be present here. If they are, keep moving slowly along the trail and try not to bother them; they will likely not bother you and will happily, or at least lazily, get out of your way. Be careful not to spook a herd.

To the north of the Desert Divide lies the high peaks surrounding Mount San Jacinto. Photo by Allen Riedel.

At the 1-mile mark, the trail leaves the shade of the oaken valley and begins to traverse 10 long switchbacks up the dry and rocky mountainside. After this, there is little to no shade, except for a few trees at the trail junction, along the crest and on the top of Lion Peak. One more gate awaits in another half mile, after which the way to the top is unimpeded. The desert chaparral, dotted with spiky *yucca whipplei*, also known as Our Lord's Candle, spouts a tall green stem pointed skyward filled with lovely white blossoms when in bloom.

It is best to climb the next 1.3 miles to the Pacific Crest Trail (PCT) in the shade of the dawn, no matter what time of year you are hiking. Early winter mornings can be quite brisk, windy, and cold. It is inadvisable to take this trail in the heat of summertime because it can be incredibly hot once the sun lifts over the mountains. Even the return trip down can be a punishing one in the heat.

At 2.3 miles, the trail meets up with the north/south junction of the PCT, with the route also continuing east and straight to Cedar Springs as a possible side option for another mile. Take the route to the right and travel south. Here, the views begin to open up in all directions. Breathtaking is the best way to describe them because a nearly 360-degree view graces every step. The higher San Jacinto Mountains in the north descend into Palm Desert and the Coachella Valley down to the Salton Sea, which remains in view under the shoulder of Martinez Mountain. The southern view takes in Santa Rosa Peak and the long sloping hogback of Thomas Mountain, which sits above Garner Valley and Lake Hemet. To the west, on clear days, the Pacific Ocean and the sprawling metropolises of Los Angeles and Orange County can be clearly seen as well as the Santa Monica Mountains and the high peaks of the Angeles National Forest.

A side summit can be had in Pyramid Peak, and it is well worth the trip. Travel south along the PCT for 1.1 miles to the use trail that leads to Pyramid Peak. It is marked with a small cairn that leads off to the right and upward. It is easy to miss the trail junction, and the cairns that mark the way upward, as is evidenced by the large number of side routes through the thorny manzanita and whitethorn, so carefully find your way to the top of the rocky summit in about 0.2 mile. The best way down is to return the same way, though a route along the ridge can be tracked down to the PCT continuing south toward Lion Peak. This side trip adds 0.6 mile to the overall hike.

From the Pyramid Peak use trail, continue for another 1.3 miles past the summit of Pine Mountain off to your left and around a slope on your right to the Lion Peak use trail. The trail is marked again with a cairn and leads straight up the forested peak in 0.25 mile. It is fairly easy to spot and to stay on the use trail. There is shade at the top of the summit, some great views, a USGS summit marker, and a trail register. Return the way you came heading north along the PCT and left at the junction with the Cedar Springs Trail.

Miles and Directions

0.0 Start down the dirt road through the pedestrian gate.

0.1 Pass the water tank on your left.

0.3 Turn left onto the trail and go through the gate.

0.9 Go through another gate and arrive at the picnic area.

1.0 Leave the oak valley and begin traversing up the western slope of the mountain.

1.5 Reach the final gate and go through it.

2.3 Turn right (south) and take the Pacific Crest Trail (PCT) toward Hwy 74.

3.4 Reach the Pyramid Peak use trail. Taking a side trip to the summit adds 0.6 mile to the overall hike.

4.7 Reach the Lion Peak use trail. Veer right and straight to take the trail to the summit.

5.0 Reach the summit of Lion Peak.

5.2 Return to the PCT, veer left, and head north.

7.6 Arrive at the Cedar Springs Junction. Turn left and take the Cedar Springs Trail to the trailhead.

10.0 Return to the trailhead.

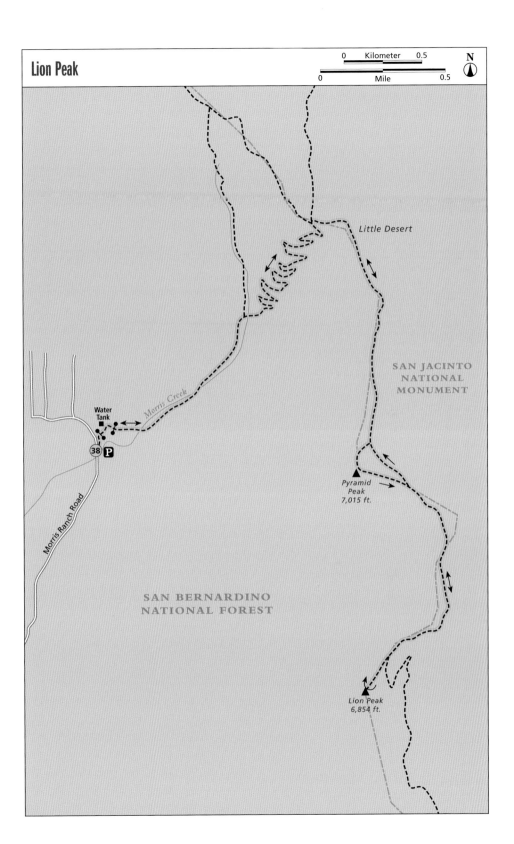

Lion Peak

Little Desert

SAN JACINTO
NATIONAL
MONUMENT

Water
Tank

Morris Creek

38 P

Pyramid
Peak
7,015 ft.

Morris Ranch Road

SAN BERNARDINO
NATIONAL FOREST

Lion Peak
6,854 ft.

N

0   Kilometer   0.5

0   Mile   0.5

Santa Rosa Peak to the south is a massive summit in its own right. Photo by Allen Riedel.

Hike Information

Local information: San Bernardino National Forest, 602 S. Tippecanoe Ave., San Bernardino, CA, 92408; https://www.fs.usda.gov/sbnf; 909-382-2682

Camping: San Bernardino National Forest campgrounds (www.recreation.gov, some first come, first served; 14-day stay maximum; and seasonal closures): Boulder Basin, Dark Canyon, Fern Basin, Marion Mountain, Pinyon Flat, Santa Rosa Springs, Tool Box Springs, www.fs.fed.us/r5/sanbernardino/; Hurkey Creek, www.riverside countyparks.org/locations/regional-parks/hurkey-creek/; Idyllwild Campground, 25905 CA 243, Idyllwild–Pine Cove, CA, 92549; 951-659-2607

Honorable Mentions

D Grays Peak

Grays Peak is an enjoyable climb that travels around the back of the southern slopes of the mountains just north of Big Bear, surrounding the Fawnskin and Holcomb Valleys. The trail traverses up around the mountain, climbing evenly for 3.5 miles before nearing the summit of Grays Peak. The views are more than worth it, but the outstanding vistas occur mostly to the north side of the trail, looking down into the valleys below. Giant boulders line the route, part of which travels up an old dirt road and some rocky trail surfaces.

Looking out into the old northern valleys of the Big Bear region is like looking into history. Difficult-to-spot campgrounds sporadically line the valley now, where mining settlements once crowded the land and grizzly bears roamed, bestowing the region with its namesake. More than 10,000 people lived in the Holcomb Valley boomtown of Belleville, making it the largest town in San Bernardino County during its heyday. At the time, its population was even larger than the population of Los Angeles. It was a rough-and-tumble place; murder and lynching were commonplace. It's hard to believe such activities took place here little more than 100 years ago.

The mines are mostly gone now, though some of the remnants can still be seen from near the summit, and some prospectors still work claims in their spare time. The grizzlies are all gone now; the last one was killed in the mountains in 1906. However, bald eagles have returned, and they roost on Grays Peak. Because this is a sensitive habitat for them, the trail is closed from November 1 to April 1. The views of Big Bear Lake are fleeting, and unfortunately, there are no sweeping viewpoints from the peak, but this is definitely a trail worth taking. The trail begins from Grout's Bay Picnic Area just east of the town of Fawnskin on CA 38. The round-trip to the summit is 7 miles.

E Pine Knot Trail to Grand View Point

Grand View Point is a wonderful lookout spot close to FR 2N10, and hikers, drivers, and mountain bikers can actually cheat, making the hike into a mere 0.2 mile to the top. But that would be a mistake because all the fun is getting there. The trail leaves the Aspen Glen Picnic Area and heads up into the high mountains. The area is heavily wooded and carpeted with manzanita and whitethorn. During spring, the area is filled with wildflowers, and although it is popular with mountain bikers, it is a fantastic trail that gently climbs to nearly 7,800 feet above sea level, with incredible views of the San Gorgonio Wilderness and the Santa Ana River valley below. The trail passes directly through Deer Group Camp and intersects with several roads. Viewpoints of the lake begin to open up almost immediately on the trail, but you have to turn around to view them. Better to wait until you reach the turnaround point on the trip and then simply enjoy the opposing views on the way down. Clouds often float by right in front of the viewpoint, but the beauty lies in the simplicity of an open valley and a high mountain range that appears almost close enough to touch. The Aspen Glen Picnic Area is located near the junction of Mill Creek Road and Tulip Lane on the south side of Big Bear Lake. The trip to Grand View is 6 miles round-trip.

F Fuller Ridge-Marion Mountain-Devil's Slide-Cactus to Clouds Trails to Mount San Jacinto

The Fuller Ridge, Marion Mountain, Devil's Slide, and Cactus to Clouds Trails are all alternate routes that lead to the top of Mount San Jacinto. For the most part, the standard trip to the top is via the Palm Springs Aerial Tramway, which is a fantastic way to travel, and then hiking through Round Valley as described in this guide. Most people do the hike this way; some people describe this route as the "easy" way. Although the hike to the top of Mount San Jacinto from the tram is not really an easy hike, it certainly is easier than any of these four routes.

Fuller Ridge travels 7.3 miles, the first 5 of which follow the Pacific Crest Trail (PCT) from Black Mountain Road and Fuller Ridge Campground. Traveling along the awesome northeastern arm of the San Jacinto massif, loaded with trees and boulders, the 14.6-mile round-trip is quite an adventure. The route passes through Little Round Valley Campground and then heads up to the boulder-blocked summit. Take CA 243 from either Banning or Idyllwild, and drive until you reach Black Mountain Road. Turn east onto the dirt road. It is rutted and rough, but you should be able to make it with even a low-clearance vehicle. Follow the road for 8 miles to the turnoff for the Fuller Ridge Trail Road (signed). Drive to the parking area, and the posts for the PCT are easy to pick up.

The Marion Mountain Trail runs 5.3 miles from the trailhead to the summit, making this the shortest trip to the top, but the trail starts a full 2,000 feet below the upper terminal of the tramway, gaining nearly a mile of elevation in the process. The first 2.5 miles, which climb to the PCT, are a serious workout and are sure to stop some from making it to the summit; alternatively, the way down can be brutal on the knees and feet. It certainly qualifies as a toe-jammer. This trail works well for those ready to do some serious mountain training or for the seriously masochistic. Its beauty cannot be understated though, and it is likely to have far fewer people on it than any of the other routes, with the exception of Cactus to Clouds. Drive north on CA 243 from Idyllwild a few miles to the Mount San Jacinto State Park entrance. Turn right and follow the signs for Marion Mountain Campground. Or drive south on CA 243 from Banning 19 miles to the turnout for Mount San Jacinto State Park. Turn left and follow the signs for Marion Mountain Campground.

The Devil's Slide Trail is a popular route up into the wilderness and to the Tahquitz Peak Fire Lookout on the southern side of Mount San Jacinto State Park. A few people use it to gain access to the higher areas by connecting with the PCT at Saddle Junction and then taking the trip to Wellman Divide and on to the summit from there. The one-way distance is an 8-mile trek. This is a fairly tough route to take, starting at 6,500 feet at Humber Park, but again, the views are unmatched, and for those looking to explore all around the mountain, why not take all the different paths to the top? From Idyllwild, turn east on North Circle Drive. Proceed north for more than a mile until you reach South Circle Drive. Turn right and then take your first left onto Fern Valley Road. Take Fern Valley Road to Humber Park.

Cactus to Clouds is an insane route for serious endurance hikers only. It begins on the desert floor near Palm Springs and gains 10,400 feet (nearly 2 miles) in elevation over 17.5 miles, the first 12 of which are spent hiking through dry, arid, and often brutally hot conditions. The trail starts out climbing and keeps climbing . . . and then climbs some more. After 1 mile of hiking, a sign warns hikers that there is no water on the trail for 8 miles and 10 hours, and the sign errs on the side of the trail—the actual distance is 12 brutal miles to Round Valley and the Palm Springs Aerial Tramway's Upper Terminal. From there, the distance is a mere 5.5 miles to the top. Most people take the tram back down, making the whole adventure into a 23-mile round-trip, but for the ultraserious, taking the trail up and down is a 35-mile all-day epic. From I-10, take CA 111 into Palm Springs. Turn right in Ramon Road and park at the end of the street. The trail leads up the mountain to the right.

Cleveland National Forest

The northern portion of the Cleveland National Forest is primarily made up of the Santa Ana Mountains and surrounding foothills. The Santa Ana Mountains run roughly north from the Santa Ana River to the Santa Margarita and San Luis Rey

The Tenaja Falls trail follows a riparian canyon for part of the route. Photo by Allen Riedel.

Rivers in the south, dividing Orange and Riverside Counties; foothills ebb off into the Pacific Ocean in the west and taper into the Inland Valley in the east. Primarily a coastal range, the mountains are sparsely forested, vegetated mostly by coastal chaparral and sage scrub grasslands. Non-native flora and grasses have changed the ecology of the region since the arrival of the Spanish, and frequent wildfires have altered the landscape, which little more than 100 years ago was heavily forested.

Today, even the tops of the mountains are mostly without trees, and remaining stands of pine trees are few and far between. The hotter seasons and lower elevations, coupled with invasive species, have taken a toll on the native woodlands. Canyons and arroyos, along with many isolated pockets, still retain their arboreal splendor under the shade of cottonwood, laurel, sycamore, walnut, ash, willow, alder, and oak. The intermittent streams and canyons in the Santa Ana Mountains are some of the most beautiful in all of California; often magnificent, the riparian habitats sparkle, as do the clear views from on high.

Because the mountain chain is low in elevation—all peaks sit below 6,000 feet— summer temperatures are often scorching. Ocean breezes do not make it far inland, which makes the Santa Anas perfect for late fall, winter, and early spring exploration. Because most people hike solely in the summertime, there are miles upon miles of trails in the forest that go largely unvisited and are underexplored. It should be noted that poison oak is abundant, and ticks often come out after rains.

The mountain range is bordered by CA 91 in the north, CA 76 in the south, and divided by CA 74 almost directly through the heart of the range. National forest campgrounds and visitors' centers are located in the most popular areas, and an Adventure Pass is required for parking in most spots throughout the region.

39 Tenaja Falls

Cascades of water plummet over four tiers, making this 150-foot waterfall one of the highest in Southern California. A short hike to the falls can be accomplished by almost anyone, and children will love the simple yet elegant fall.

Start: At the parking lot on Tenaja Truck Trail Road

Distance: 1.5 miles out and back

Hiking time: About 1 hour

Difficulty: Easy, with a knee-deep water crossing

Trail surface: Dirt road

Nearest town: Wildomar

County: Riverside

Other trail users: Equestrians and bicyclists

Canine compatibility: Leashed dogs permitted

Trailhead facilities/amenities: None

Land status: National forest

Fees and permits: Adventure Pass required for parking

Schedule: Open year-round

Maps: USGS Sitton Peak, CA; www.goodtime .net/mvi/lomvi091.htm

Trail contacts: Cleveland National Forest, 10845 Rancho Bernardo Rd., Suite 200, San Diego, CA, 92127; www.fs.fed.us/r5/cleve land; 858-673-6180. Trabuco Ranger District, 1147 East Sixth St., Corona, CA, 92879; 951-736-1811

Finding the trailhead: From Los Angeles, take CA 60 east. Take Exit 29A to merge onto CA 71, heading south toward Corona. Drive for 13 miles. Merge onto CA 91 east for 4.2 miles. Take Exit 51 to merge onto I-15 south, toward San Diego, and drive for 27.9 miles. Take Exit 68 for Clinton Keith Road; turn right and drive for 5.1 miles. Make a slight right to veer onto Tenaja Road and drive for 1.7 miles. Turn right to stay on Tenaja Road and drive for 4.2 miles. Turn right onto FR 7501/Tenaja Truck Trail and drive for 5.2 miles. Park in the pullout parking area. GPS: 33°32'56.8"N 117°23'40.0"W

The Hike

The hike to Tenaja Falls is short and simple. From the parking area, the trail drops down into a surprisingly wet arroyo. Here, the tributary of San Mateo Creek that feeds the falls farther upstream crosses the pavement and pools, making the first steps of the hike into a water crossing. If the falls are flowing, the water will be at least ankle deep, and in heavy flow nearly knee-deep. It is possible to hop rocks farther upstream and avoid the water, but it is also possible to walk through poison oak and brush heavy with ticks while doing so. In light of this, there are a few possibilities: One, hike through the water, socks, boots, and all; two, remove socks and boots and ford the crossing barefoot, being aware that sharp rocks and slippery stones abound; and three, purchase some water shoes and walk across in those. If you do walk across, you will have wet feet, but it is a short hike, and isn't that just part of a nice adventure?

After the crossing, the trail/road becomes pedestrian, climbing somewhat sharply for the next 0.4 mile to the top of the rise. Halfway along the upward path, the trees

Tenaja Falls are the most dependable and spectacular waterfall in the Santa Ana Mountains.
Photo by Allen Riedel.

and brush diminish slightly, allowing the canyon to open up in spots. These clearings provide wonderful access to views of the falls. All four tiers can be clearly seen across the chasm. Water flowing down smooth time-worn rock stands in contrast to the blocky boulders and chunks of rocks near the falls.

Trees and shrubs block the view farther on and soon after, the trail nears the top of the falls. From the top the falls can be explored, but extreme caution should be taken. The rocks are worn and slippery near the edge. Years of erosion from the flowing creek have left the rocks smooth, and several drops can make climbing back upward difficult and dangerous without ropes and climbing gear. Hikers should descend to the pools at their own risk, and children are better off simply observing nature's beauty. A sign marks the route leading farther north along the Tenaja Trail into the San Mateo Wilderness toward the Morgan Trail.

If visiting after a heavy rain, the falls will be quite magnificent. Conversely, if there hasn't been much rain for quite some time, expect little water at all. Return via the same route.

Miles and Directions

0.0   From the parking area along FR 7501, walk east down into the arroyo.

0.4   Look across the canyon for wide views of the entire falls.

0.75   Reach the top of the falls. Return via the same route.

1.5   Arrive back at the trailhead and parking area.

Hike Information

Local information: Cleveland National Forest, 10845 Rancho Bernardo Rd., Suite 200, San Diego, CA, 92127; 858-673-6180

Camping: Cleveland National Forest campgrounds (www.recreation.gov, some first come, first served; 14-day stay maximum; and seasonal closures): Lower San Juan Campground, Upper San Juan Campground, Falcon Campground, Blue Jay Campground, El Cariso Campground, www.fs.fed.us/r5/124leveland/; Caspers Regional Park, www.ocparks.com/caspers/

40 Chiquito Trail

The Chiquito Trail is a secluded wonder known mostly to mountain bikers and those with the verve to explore out-of-the-way territory in one of California's more ignored mountain chains and national forests. The hike passes through a sylvan canyon, making parts of the trail well shaded, and traverses near a splendid seasonal waterfall. The downhill point-to-point nature of the hike makes it fairly easy for anyone wanting to attempt a longer hike.

Start: Parking area for Chiquito/San Juan Trail just before the turnoff for Blue Jay and Falcon Campgrounds
Distance: 8 miles point to point (shuttle)
Hiking time: About 4 hours
Difficulty: Moderate
Trail surface: Single-track dirt trail
Nearest towns: San Juan Capistrano and Lake Elsinore
Counties: Orange and Riverside
Other trail users: Equestrians and bicyclists
Canine compatibility: Leashed dogs permitted

Trailhead facilities/amenities: All facilities available
Land status: National forest
Fees and permits: Adventure Pass required for parking
Schedule: Open year-round
Maps: Sitton Peak, CA, and Alberhill, CA
Trail contacts: Cleveland National Forest, 10845 Rancho Bernardo Rd., Suite 200, San Diego, CA, 92127; www.fs.fed.us/r5/cleveland; 858-673-6180. Trabuco Ranger District, 1147 E. Sixth St., Corona, CA, 92879; 951-736-1811

Finding the trailhead: From Los Angeles, take I-5 south. Take Exit 82 for CA 74/Ortega Highway. Turn left onto CA 74/Ortega Highway and drive 19.4 miles east to the large parking area on the west side of the highway. Drop off one car at the parking area, turn left and head north on CA 74 for 2.4 miles to FR 6S05/Main Divide Truck Trail. Turn left and drive for 0.6 mile. Veer left onto Long Canyon Road and drive for 2.4 miles to the turnout on the left for the Chiquito Trail. GPS: 33°39'08.3"N 117°26'54.7"W

The Hike

The Chiquito Trail is not widely known in the hiking community. Most hikers take trips to the Angeles or San Bernardino National Forests to go for seemingly more glorious and esteem-worthy adventures. That is a shame because there are some downright amazing places to hike that are not that far off the beaten path for those who live in Orange County and the southern sections of Riverside County. The region is better known to mountain bikers, and this is a premier destination for outdoorsy types looking for a little more adrenaline than that provided by just walking through the woods. There is a good possibility of running into mountain bikers on this route, so always be aware and on the lookout for those coming down the hill at a rapid pace.

The trail winds through San Juan Canyon. Photo by Allen Riedel.

The hike begins at the Blue Jay Campground along the San Juan Trail. Some of the route crossings are confusing because newer trail work is not reflected on any map of the region, and some of the intersections are not that well marked. Just veer left at every trail junction, and the route will lead to the parking area for the San Juan Trail across from the Ortega Country Cottage Candy Store on CA 74/Ortega Highway. The lower elevations in the Santa Ana Mountains do not make for good summer hiking, and this trip is no exception: Take this one from late fall to early spring for maximum enjoyment and safety.

The trail begins by wandering through the large Blue Jay Campground; it meanders for the first mile, losing and gaining only nominal elevation. The oak forest provides decent shade for most of this section, and at times, views into the surrounding valley are quite exceptional.

Here, after the first mile, the trail begins to descend much more rapidly. The trail has been reworked in this area, so follow the signs pointing to the Chiquito Trail and stay left wherever there is a junction.

At 1.8 miles, veer left at the fork to take the Chiquito Trail and leave the San Juan Trail. At 2 miles, turn left to avoid the Viejo Tie Loop, which connects again at 2.2 miles. Again, stay left and continue along the Chiquito Trail as it begins its descent through beautiful Lion Canyon. Water is present here, specifically during

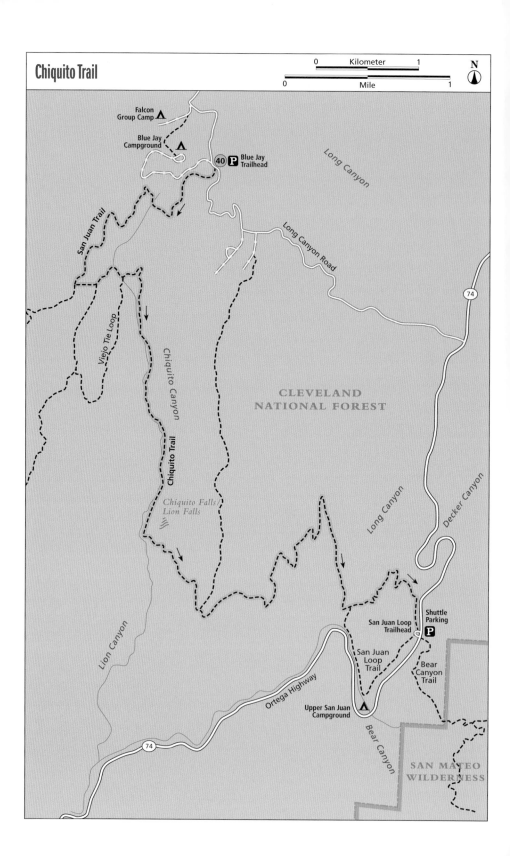

Chiquito Trail

0 — Kilometer — 1

0 — Mile — 1

N

Falcon Group Camp

Blue Jay Campground

40 P Blue Jay Trailhead

Long Canyon

Long Canyon Road

74

San Juan Trail

Viejo Tie Loop

Chiquito Canyon

Chiquito Trail

CLEVELAND
NATIONAL FOREST

*Chiquito Falls /
Lion Falls*

Lion Canyon

Long Canyon

Decker Canyon

Shuttle Parking

San Juan Loop Trailhead

P

San Juan Loop Trail

Bear Canyon Trail

Ortega Highway

Upper San Juan Campground

Bear Canyon

74

SAN MATEO
WILDERNESS

wetter months, but the creek dries up as the summer progresses. Early in spring, the canyons are especially lovely, filled when blooming with wildflowers.

Oak trees and sycamores line the trail in most places, making this part of the trip particularly idyllic. Lovely Chiquito Falls/Lion Falls are rarely visited and sometimes not even noticed because they are truly intermittent due to the lack of water found in the region. But when they are flowing heavily (mostly just after a rainfall), the 15-foot drop makes them one of the loveliest cascades around.

After the falls, the trail leaves the canyon behind and begins climbing around the contours of a higher unnamed summit to the east. The trail loses its shade here and winds around the southern edge of the summit block. At 5.2 miles, a trail intersects on the left, heading up to the prominent unnamed peak. This is the only junction where you stay right; continue around the base of the summit and down toward a branch of San Juan Canyon.

The trail turns south into San Juan Canyon and connects with the San Juan Loop Trail at 7 miles. Turn left onto the San Juan Loop to take the shorter path to the parking area, where the shuttle awaits. At this point, noises from CA 74 will be apparent, making the ending feel all that much closer.

Miles and Directions

0.0 Start at the San Juan Trail just south of the entrance to Blue Jay Campground.

1.8 Turn left onto the Chiquito Trail.

2.0 Stay left at the junction with the Viejo Tie Loop.

2.2 Stay left again at the second junction with the Viejo Tie Loop.

4.2 Chiquito Falls/Lion Falls sits just off the edge of the trail before it begins climbing.

5.2 Continue straight and to the right avoiding the trail heading north, up the slope.

7.0 Turn left at the junction of the San Juan Loop Trail.

8.0 Arrive at the shuttle parking area on the Ortega Highway.

Hike Information

Local information: Cleveland National Forest, 10845 Rancho Bernardo Rd., Suite 200, San Diego, CA, 92127; 858-673-6180

Camping: Cleveland National Forest campgrounds (www.recreation.gov, first come, first served; 14-day stay maximum; and some seasonal closures): Lower San Juan Campground, Upper San Juan Campground, Falcon Campground, Blue Jay Campground, El Cariso Campground, www.fs.fed.us/r5/cleveland/; Caspers Regional Park, www.ocparks.com/caspers/

Honorable Mentions

G San Juan Loop Trail

The San Juan Loop is an enormously popular trail. It sits right off the Ortega Highway, across from the Ortega Country Cottage Candy Store at nearly the midpoint of the trip from Lake Elsinore to San Juan Capistrano. It is a nice little trip with some worthwhile scenery, trickling brooks, and cascading waterfalls—not large ones, but if rainfall has been heavy, there are some quite lovely spots. A short hike, at 2.2 miles, it is a good one for families and people looking for a small breather to get out into nature. The oak canyons are lovely, and for being right off the beaten path, it is quaint, peaceful, and fairly secluded. There is definite car noise on parts of the route, but it is easy to ignore, especially when entranced by a wildflower display or an idling stream that floats by like a dream. Not for summer hiking, the lower elevations are positively desiccating in any sort of heat, but in winter and spring it is a near paradise. If traveling with young children, be mindful of poison oak and ticks. Take CA 74 east for 19.5 miles from the I-5 freeway in Orange County, or west from I-15 in Riverside County for 13 miles. Park in the large lot on the west side of the highway. The trailhead is directly across the road and next to the legendary Ortega Country Cottage Candy Store.

H Sitton Peak

The trail to Sitton Peak is located just next to the Ortega Country Cottage Candy Store, across from the large parking lot for the San Juan Trail. This route up Bear Canyon is not as popular as the San Juan Loop across the street and with good reason. There is not as much shade; no, there is not much shade at all. On hotter days, the trip is an accident waiting to happen, but hiking in the wintertime on a foggy or drizzly day can be a wonderful adventure. When the sun is out, it is best to get started early or on a cold day to avoid any kind of heat at all. The views from the summit are amazing. There is a nice 360-degree panorama, and since the mountain is the highest peak around for at least 5 miles in any direction, there isn't much in the way to block the view, especially looking down toward Orange County and the Pacific Ocean. The round-trip is 10 miles. Take CA 74 east for 19.5 miles from the I-5 freeway in Orange County, or west from I-15 in Riverside County for 13 miles. Park in the large lot on the west side of the highway. The trailhead is directly across the road and next to the legendary Ortega Country Cottage Candy Store.

Palos Verdes Peninsula

Palos Verdes means "green sticks" in Spanish and the name is probably derivative from the native palo verde tree common to the area. There are many open spaces left on the peninsula and access is relatively free to most of them.

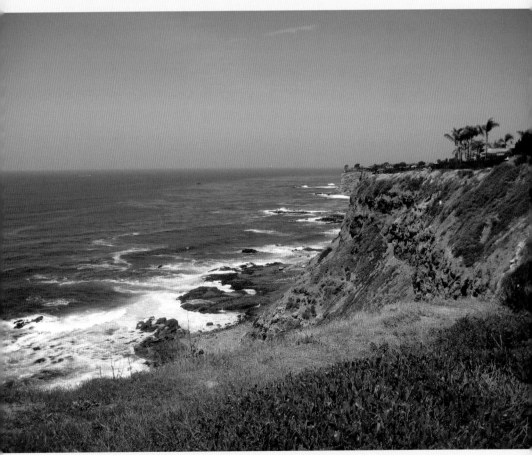

Coastal views along the Palos Verdes Peninsula are spectacular. Photo by Monique Riedel.

Coastal views are the stock and currency of trails along the Palos Verdes Peninsula. Photo by Monique Riedel.

Luxurious homes dominate much of the region, and equestrian trails abound. Tremendous views of the coast and coastal regions can be had at many different opportunities, and an escape to a seminatural setting is only minutes away almost anywhere in the area. Although the truly wild may be out of grasp, and you will be sharing these "trails" with many other outdoor seekers and those out for exercise, most of these open spaces and parks will leave you satisfied with your ability to enjoy some time in the great outdoors.

The Palos Verdes Land Conservancy has purchased quite a bit of land over the past three and a half decades. These preserves are dedicated to restoring the land's original native ecosystems, those in place before the arrival of the Spanish. The conservancy has done a fantastic job of opening these lands to hiking and keeping them beautiful. Conservancy members have also been highly successful in restoring native habitat critical for the survival of certain endangered species.

▶ Hiking Tip: Set a turnaround time and stick to it, no matter what.

41 White Point

Take a leisurely walk through a nature preserve that offers a glimpse of the native flora and fauna of the Palos Verdes Peninsula and a historical overview of this wondrous geologic structure. Conclude your stroll among the tide pools of historic Palm Beach, site of a grandiose hot spring resort of the Roaring Twenties.

Start: At the parking lot of White Point Nature Preserve

Distance: 2.6-mile lollipop

Hiking time: About 1.5 hours

Difficulty: Easy

Trail surface: Dirt road, single-track trail, and pavement

Nearest town: Rancho Palos Verdes

County: Los Angeles

Other trail users: None

Canine compatibility: Leashed dogs permitted; no dogs allowed on the beach

Trailhead facilities/amenities: All facilities available

Land status: Los Angeles city park

Fees and permits: None

Schedule: Open year-round, sunrise to sunset

Maps: USGS San Pedro, CA; www.pvplc.org/land/white_point/Whitepointsmall.pdf

Trail contacts: Palos Verdes Peninsula Land Conservancy, 916 Silver Spur Rd., Suite 207, Rolling Hills Estates, CA, 90274; 310-541-7613; www.pvplc.org. Los Angeles Department of Recreation and Parks, 221 N. Figueroa St., Suite 350, Los Angeles, CA, 90012; 213-202-2700; www.laparks.org

Finding the trailhead: From Los Angeles, take I-110 south to its terminus. Turn left onto North Gaffey Street and drive for 0.2 mile. Turn right onto West 1st Street and drive for 1 mile. Turn left onto South Western Avenue and drive for 2.3 miles. Veer left and continue onto West Paseo Del Mar for 0.4 mile. Turn left into the parking area for White Point Nature Preserve. The trail begins next to the visitors' center. GPS: 33°42'56.7"N 118°18'53.9"W

The Hike

There has been some speculation as to how White Point received its name. One legend claims it was named for a sailor who jumped ship and landed in the cove at White Point. However, the Palos Verdes Historical Society confirms that White Point is named for the prominent white shale visible along the cliff walls.

White Point is located at the summit of the bluffs overlooking Palm Beach. A nature preserve provides a fabulous embarkation to this excursion. As you walk around the White Point Nature Preserve and Visitor Center, you'll see charming gardens brimming with native flora, as interpretive signs strategically placed throughout the gardens guide you through this enchanting little gem. Aside from information about indigenous plants, there are also interesting and fascinating postings featuring wildlife unique to the Palos Verdes Peninsula, such as the Allen's hummingbird, which is native only to the California coast and a diminutive section of the Oregon coast.

The ocean puts on a spectacle at White Point. Photo by Monique Riedel.

From the nature preserve, cross Paseo Del Mar. It's a busy roadway, so use extreme caution when making this traverse. Once on the other side of Paseo Del Mar, you will find yourself at White Point Beach Park. There are bathroom facilities, park benches, picnic tables, and a web of small trails overlooking the bluffs down to Palms Beach Park. The park offers magnificent views of Santa Catalina Island and the Pacific Ocean.

From White Point Beach Park, follow the road west down the canyon for 1 mile. The trail is a paved road that provides beach access to Palms Beach Park and the tide pools. Traffic can be heavy, make sure to exercise caution while making your descent to the beach area.

At the bottom of the road, turn left into the parking area for Palms Beach Park and follow the beach side to the rock formations just a few hundred feet up the beach. This is a popular destination for anglers, artists, sun seekers, historians, and explorers of the tide pools, so be prepared to share your experience with a variety of other travelers. This cove was once home to the majestic Royal Palm Beach resort, which boasted a natural hot spring, a palm grove, and ambrosial gardens. All that remains today of the resort are fragments of the original concrete foundation and

▶ **The Palos Verdes Peninsula is home to many an open space park thanks to the Palos Verdes Land Conservancy Project.**

scattered palm groves. The hot spring was covered by an earthquake and is no longer accessible.

The tide pools are unbelievably easy to access. From the beach, large volcanic boulders have settled at the nape of the cove, creating the perfect environment for an intricate maze of tide pools. Be prepared to hop some rocks and traverse slippery rocks as waves crash tantalizingly close, dousing anyone seeking to explore the pools with a bit of sea foam. For optimal viewing of marine life in the pools, it is best to plan your trip at low tide.

From the tide pools, follow the main road up the incline of the cliffs to the parking area across Paseo Del Mar, returning to the trailhead in the nature preserve.

Miles and Directions

0.0 From the nature preserve parking area, hike east along the roadway that is now designated as the main trail through the preserve.

0.2 Turn left and hike north along the road. Next, turn left and hike west along the bluff.

0.5 Turn left and head south toward the ocean.

0.7 Cross Paseo Del Mar and enter White Point/Palms Beach Park. Turn right (west) and walk down the pavement to the beach.

1.0 Turn left (southeast) and walk toward the tide pools.

1.5 Reach White Point. Explore the tide pools, then turn around and walk back toward the parking area at White Point Nature Preserve.

2.6 Arrive back at the trailhead and parking area.

Hike Information

Local information: Palos Verdes Peninsula Land Conservancy, 916 Silver Spur Rd., Suite 207, Rolling Hills Estates, CA, 90274; 310-541-7613

42 Portuguese Bend

An easy stroll inland above the bluffs overlooking the Palos Verdes Peninsula, this trail presents the perfect opportunity to marvel at the lush landscape of one of several nature preserves on the peninsula while spotting unique wildlife endemic to this area.

Start: At the parking area at the end of Main Sail Drive
Distance: 1.9 miles out and back
Hiking time: About 1 hour
Difficulty: Easy
Trail surface: Dirt trail and dirt road
Nearest town: Rancho Palos Verdes
County: Los Angeles
Other trail users: Equestrians
Canine compatibility: Leashed dogs permitted

Trailhead facilities/amenities: None
Land status: Los Angeles city park
Fees and permits: None
Schedule: Open year-round, sunrise to sunset
Maps: USGS San Pedro, CA; www.pvplc.org/_lands/docs?Portuguese_Bend_Trail_Map.pdf
Trail contact: Palos Verdes Peninsula Land Conservancy, 916 Silver Spur Rd., Suite 207, Rolling Hills Estates, CA, 90274; 310-541-7613; www.pvplc.org

Finding the trailhead: From Los Angeles, take I-110 south to its terminus. Turn left onto North Gaffey Street and drive for 0.2 mile. Turn right onto West 1st Street and drive for 1 mile. Turn left onto Western Avenue and drive for 1.7 miles. Turn right onto 25th Street/Palos Verdes Drive and drive for 2.2 miles. Turn right onto Forrestal Drive and drive for 0.7 mile. Turn left onto Main Sail Drive and drive to its end and park. GPS: 33°44'26.7"N 118°21'08.7"W

The Hike

One of the lesser-used trails on the Palos Verdes Peninsula, Portuguese Bend provides a brisk hike through coastal chaparral, winding up to a summit that provides a dramatic view of the Pacific Ocean and, on clear days, Santa Catalina Island. Portuguese Bend is the largest area of undeveloped land on the Palos Verdes Peninsula, largely due to its geologic significance as one of the most unstable land areas in California. The land is perpetually in a state of landslide and has been determined to be so since the 1950s. Because the land is considered unstable for large developments, the nature preserve has flourished.

This trail is teeming not only with native flora but is also home to several species of wildlife that are unique to this area. Several species of bird can only be found in this part of California and on the Channel Islands, such as the Allen's hummingbird, the orange-crowned warbler, and the Pacific slope flycatcher.

Parking is free and easy because there is plentiful space around the trailhead on surface streets to park. From the parking area, follow the wide dirt road called Klondike Canyon Trail, which takes a steep decline into a dry watershed and wraps up around a bend, beginning a moderate incline.

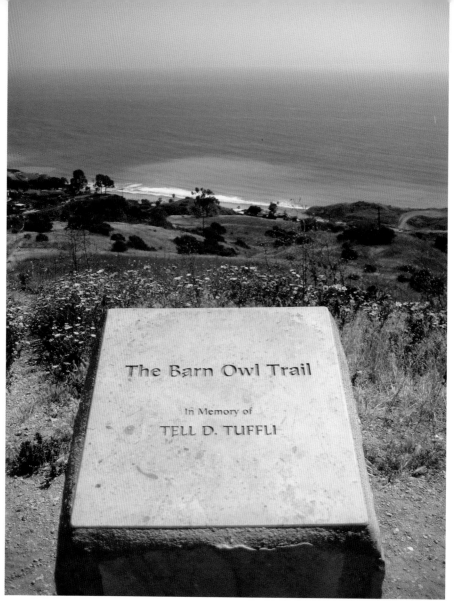

Some trails are marked better than others. Photo by Monique Riedel.

At 0.3 mile, turn right onto the Barn Owl Trail. The trail steadily makes an ascent up the bluffs of the nature preserve. At times the trail, although relatively wide, may become overgrown with verdant chaparral and wildflowers. Be prepared to navigate your way through dense foliage during springtime. At 0.6 mile, follow the Burma Road Trail to a summit overlooking the bluffs, affording you the opportunity to revel in captivating views of the Pacific Ocean and the coastline of the peninsula.

Although fauna is plentiful on the trail, there are little or no shade trees. For the majority of the hike, you will be in wide-open space, akin to meadowlands on a hillside. This is advantageous for catching glimpses of the coastline and Catalina Island

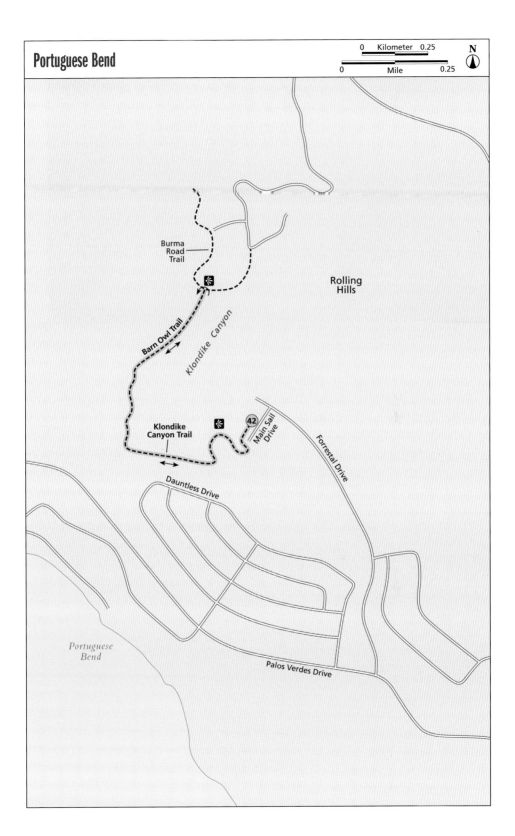

Portuguese Bend

0   Kilometer   0.25

0   Mile   0.25

N

Burma Road Trail

Rolling Hills

Barn Owl Trail

Klondike Canyon

Klondike Canyon Trail

42 Main Sail Drive

Forrestal Drive

Dauntless Drive

Portuguese Bend

Palos Verdes Drive

In spring, trails are loaded with wildflowers. Photo by Monique Riedel.

from different perspectives along the trail. The ocean breeze is a constant companion on your trek, and even on warm days offers a bit of respite from the sun.

From the top of Burma Road Trail, head back down the same way you came to Main Sail Drive at 1.6 miles. Turn left onto Main Sail Drive and follow this wide dirt path upward toward another small summit that provides yet a different and spectacular perspective of the coastline. From this summit, continue on Main Sail Drive to the parking area and arrive back at the trailhead at 1.9 miles.

Miles and Directions

0.0 Start hiking west down the dirt roadway near the end of the street, following the Klondike Canyon Trail.

0.3 Turn right onto the Barn Owl Trail.

0.6 Continue up on the Burma Road Trail.

0.8 Arrive at the top of the trail. Return via the same route.

1.6 Turn left onto Main Sail Drive.

1.7 Turn left onto a use trail to the top of the hill.

1.8 Arrive on top of an unmarked summit. Retrace your steps toward the parking area.

1.9 Arrive back at the trailhead and parking area.

Hike Information

Local information: Palos Verdes Peninsula Land Conservancy, 916 Silver Spur Rd., Suite 207, Rolling Hills Estates, CA, 90274; 310-541-7613

43 Point Vicente

Walk leisurely atop dramatic bluffs overlooking the Pacific Ocean. Explore fascinating geologic formations and enjoy the scenery of Point Vicente Lighthouse on the site of historic Marineland of the Pacific, once the largest oceanarium in the world.

Start: At the parking lot along the west side of Calle Entradero

Distance: 2 miles out and back

Hiking time: 1 to 2 hours

Difficulty: Easy

Trail surface: Dirt and pavement

Nearest town: Rancho Palos Verdes

County: Los Angeles

Other trail users: Bicyclists

Canine compatibility: Leashed dogs permitted

Trailhead facilities/amenities: All facilities available

Land status: Los Angeles city park

Fees and permits: None

Schedule: Open year-round, sunrise to sunset

Maps: USGS Redondo Beach, CA

Trail contact: Palos Verdes Peninsula Land Conservancy, 916 Silver Spur Rd., Suite 207, Rolling Hills Estates, CA, 90274; 310-541-7613; www.pvplc.org

Finding the trailhead: From Los Angeles, take I-110 south. Take Exit 4 for CA 1/Pacific Coast Highway, turn right, and follow signs for Harbor City/Lomita. Merge onto CA 1/Pacific Coast Highway, heading west. Drive for 3 miles. Turn left onto Crenshaw Boulevard and drive for 3.4 miles. Turn right onto Crest Road and drive for 1.6 miles. Turn left onto Hawthorne Boulevard and drive for 2.1 miles. Continue on Via Vicente/Calle Entradero for 0.8 mile. Park in the lot on the ocean side of the road. GPS: 33°45'19.7"N 118°24'54.1"W

The Hike

Some may consider this trail to be a mild stroll rather than a traditional "hike." The dramatic ocean views and plummeting seaside bluffs provide an enchanting jaunt laden with opportunities to view ancient geologic formations and sea life. You can check out views of the Channel Islands and explore the historic sites of Marineland of the Pacific and Point Vicente Lighthouse, nestled on the bluffs of the Palos Verdes Peninsula.

Point Vicente Lighthouse is a fully operational lighthouse owned and operated by the US Coast Guard and is registered on the *National Register of Historic Places.* The lighthouse has been operational since March 1926. There is also a Coast Guard museum on the premises. Visiting hours to the lighthouse are limited to the second Saturday of the month, and admission is free.

Be prepared to catch an ocean breeze on this well-maintained path. From the parking area, follow the paved walkway south toward the lighthouse. The first part of the trail is in an upscale residential area and

▶ **The lighthouse at Point Vicente is open for tours on the second Saturday of every month, except for March when it is open on the first Saturday.**

237

The lighthouse at Point Vicente can be toured on the second Saturday of every month. Photo by Monique Riedel.

PACIFIC
OCEAN

Pointe Vicente

POINTE VICENTE
COUNTY PARK

Marineland
(defunct)

Long Point

follows along steep ocean bluffs. There is a plethora of viewpoints at which to stop and soak in the panoramic ocean views. It is common to see a pod of dolphins chasing waves playfully along the shores of the coves. Farther up the trail, at the Point Vicente Interpretive Center, watching for whales is a popular pastime. Point Vicente Interpretive Center is located adjacent to the lighthouse. From December to May, the annual migration of the gray whale is a focal point of activity around the center. The interpretive center is also endowed with other attractive features, such as a native plant garden and museum. The interactive museum features a life-size model of a gray whale, historical information and memorabilia of Marineland of the Pacific, and displays of the native settlers of the Palos Verdes Peninsula.

The Palos Verdes Peninsula is a tectonic fault block that rose out of the sea floor more than a million years ago. Palos Verdes, which in Spanish translates to "range of green trees," was inhabited by the Tongva/Gabrieleno natives for thousands of years before the arrival of the Spanish and Mexican explorers, and eventually US developers. From the bluff trail, fascinating geologic formations can be spotted, giving a snapshot of the rich history of this colorful locale.

Whether exploring historic sites or reveling in natural splendor, once you have imbued your senses along this splendid trail, head back on the path north toward the parking area via the same route.

Miles and Directions

0.0 From the parking area on Calle Entradero, hike along the paved path toward the lighthouse.

0.9 Arrive at the interpretive center.

1.0 Arrive at the entrance to the Point Vicente Lighthouse. Access is restricted. Retrace your steps toward the trailhead.

2.0 Arrive back at the trailhead and parking area.

Hike Information

Local information: Palos Verdes Peninsula Land Conservancy, 916 Silver Spur Rd., Suite 207, Rolling Hills Estates, CA, 90274; 310-541-7613

Santa Catalina Island

Santa Catalina Island is one of the Channel Islands, located 26 miles off the coast of California and is the only island populated with permanent residences and various attractions. On November 24, 1602, Spanish explorer Sebastian Viscaino visited the island and aptly named it Santa Catalina in honor of Saint Catherine's Day, the day he happened on this 22-mile-long, 8-mile-wide jewel of the Pacific Coast.

The trail that heads toward East Peak gains awe-inspiring views along the ridgeline. Photo by Allen Riedel.

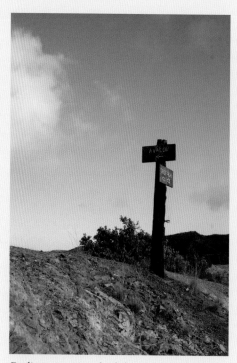

Catalina, as the island is most often referred to, was a part of the original land grant awarded by Governor Pio Pico of Mexico. And as such, much like the rest of the California coast, it has changed ownership several times over the last century. In the late 1800s George Shatto, a real estate developer, purchased the land with the intention of creating a resort and getaway for the people of Los Angeles. His sister-in-law, Etta Whitney, is credited with coming up with the name Avalon after reading Tennyson's poem, "Idylls of the King," in honor of King Arthur. Despite changes of ownership over the years, the name Avalon endured. Modern-day Avalon is a hub of activity and is the main launching point for all excursions around the island.

Rudimentary signs lead the way on Catalina Island. Photo by Allen Riedel.

Eventually, chewing gum tycoon William Wrigley obtained majority ownership of the island, with the ambition of transforming the island into a major resort attraction. He is credited with the development of the Catalina Casino, a unique art deco architectural structure on the shore north of Avalon. The casino is purported to be the "only building of its size erected in a full circular pattern."

Today, Avalon is a bustling yet quaint town free of traffic because there are only a limited number of vehicles permitted on the island. The most popular modes of transportation, aside from walking, are golf carts and bicycles.

44 Avalon Canyon–Wrigley Gardens

Explore spectacular botanic gardens and a majestic historic monument memorializing a world-renowned chewing gum tycoon and entertainment entrepreneur while hiking to one of the most breathtaking peaks on Santa Catalina Island. From a leisurely stroll to steep switchbacks, this trail offers something for everyone.

Start: Entrance to Wrigley Memorial & Botanical Gardens
Distance: 6.5 miles out and back
Hiking time: About 2.5 hours
Difficulty: Moderate
Trail surface: Dirt and pavement
Nearest town: Avalon
County: Los Angeles
Other trail users: Bicyclists
Canine compatibility: Leashed dogs permitted
Trailhead facilities/amenities: All available
Land status: Land conservancy

Fees and permits: Free permit from the Catalina Island Conservancy is required (see below); fee is charged to enter the botanic garden
Schedule: Open year-round, 8 a.m. to 5 p.m. daily
Maps: USGS Santa Catalina East, CA
Trail contact: Catalina Island Conservancy, 708 Crescent Ave., Avalon, CA, 90704; 310-510-2595 or 320 Golden Shore, Suite 220, Long Beach, CA, 90802; 562-437-8555; www.catalinaconservancy.org/

Finding the trailhead: From Avalon, take a bus, drive a car, or walk north on Avalon Canyon Road for 1.2 miles to the entrance of the Wrigley Memorial & Botanical Gardens. Passage to Catalina Island must be arranged in Long Beach Harbor. GPS: 33°19'35.4"N 118°20'25.1"W

The Hike

The Wrigley Memorial was constructed in 1933–1934 in honor of William Wrigley, whose devotion to the island is memorialized in the monument honoring his legacy. In 1935 Wrigley's widow, Ada, added the botanical garden to the premises with the help of horticulturist Albert Conrad.

The Wrigley Memorial is administered and governed by the Catalina Island Conservancy. Admission to the memorial and hiking trails requires a permit and a fee is charged at the entrance to the botanical garden. The botanical gardens offer an opportunity to stroll among rare and endangered plant species, most of which are endemic to Catalina Island. The facilities are beautifully manicured and offer restrooms, informational postings, and a kiosk. This is a perfect way to begin your expedition up the trail to the monument and the summit of East Peak.

From the botanic gardens, follow the road up toward the base of the monument and turn right. Pass through a gate onto a dirt road that follows the ridgeline of the island. The trail is wide but begins a steady and sometimes steep incline up toward the imposing monument. You will easily spot the bright blue flagstone and clay embellishment to the ornate monument once you round the corner. At the monument, you can take time to explore the intricacy and detail of the craftsmanship used in its construction. From different vantage points on the monument, you can capture spectacular views of Avalon Bay—and the mainland coastline on clear days.

From the monument, prepare to begin a steady climb up toward East Peak. The trail is wide but, at times, is rocky and uneven. There is little or no shade, so on a hot day make sure to have ample water for the ascent.

The trail follows the ridgeline to 2.1 miles and reaches a high point. Continue to the 2.5-mile mark and turn right at the junction of the fire road and the trail. Follow the trail to the 2.9-mile mark and turn right, continuing up to East Peak.

At 1,684 feet in elevation, East Peak bestows a breathtaking view of the entire island. It is common to find yourself a lone traveler on this part of the trail because the most popular destination is the Wrigley Memorial. Only the most dedicated excursionists will find themselves at the summit of East Peak. Here, you will be able to view both sides of the island and contrast the hustle and bustle of Avalon to the unpopulated pristine coast just over East Peak.

From East Peak, follow the road back to the trailhead, descending the ridgeline toward the Wrigley Memorial and through the botanical gardens to the gate and trailhead.

The Wrigley Memorial was originally intended for the interment of William J. Wrigley. Photo by Allen Riedel.

Miles and Directions

0.0 Walk up the road toward the Wrigley Memorial. Enjoy the paths through the botanic gardens as well.

0.3 Turn right at the monument and pass through the gate. Continue on the fire road/trail to the ridgeline of the island.

1.4 Turn left and follow the trail along the ridgeline.

2.1 Reach a high point along the ridge.

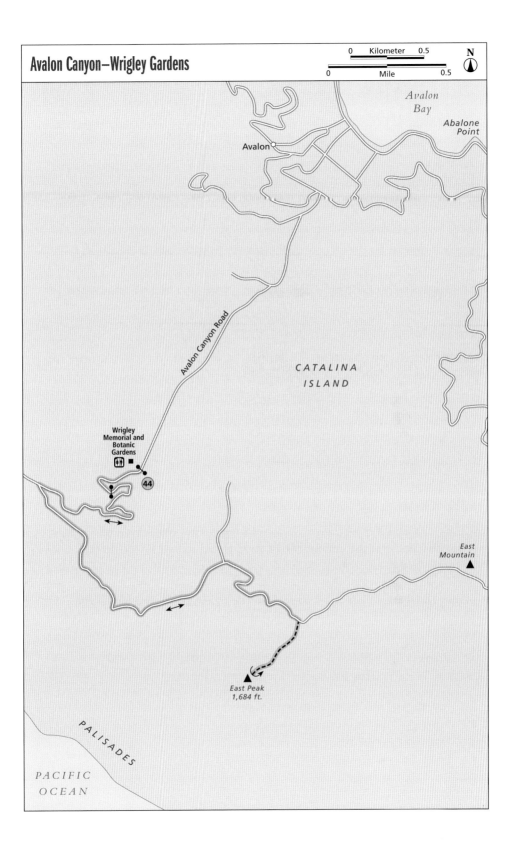

0   Kilometer   0.5

0   Mile   0.5

N

Avalon Bay

Abalone Point

Avalon

Avalon Canyon Road

CATALINA ISLAND

Wrigley
Memorial and
Botanic
Gardens

44

East Mountain

East Peak
1,684 ft.

PALISADES

PACIFIC
OCEAN

WILLIAM WRIGLEY JR.

William Wrigley Jr. followed in the footsteps of his father and became a businessperson. He had a penchant for sales and began his career selling his father's brand of soap. Wrigley was an expert marketer and is known for creating standards in advertising that are second nature to business owners today. He had the idea of selling his product and adding bonus incentive "premiums" to the sale. First, he tried adding baking powder bonuses to his soap sales, and the baking powder proved to be more popular than the soap itself. So Wrigley entered into the baking powder business. With the baking powder, he added chewing gum as the bonus, and again, the gum was the more popular item. Eventually, he rearranged his company to focus on chewing gum sales, and that is where he built his fortune and empire.

Wrigley advertised in every possible manner—in newspapers, magazines, and even on posters—nearly bankrupting himself and his company many times in the process. He believed in the products so much that he was willing to do whatever it took to get the name of the product into the minds of the consumers. It worked. By the late 1800s, his company had created its two most popular flavors, Juicy Fruit and Spearmint, adding Doublemint in 1914. By that time, he had already become the top-selling gum manufacturer in the world. He purchased the companies that had been making and distributing his gum, renaming the resulting corporation after himself. He eventually took his products to Australia, England, and New Zealand.

Wrigley had been a fan of baseball his whole life; the Chicago Cubs were his favorite team. He began to buy stock in the Cubs in 1916, gaining control of the team by 1921. He purchased two other baseball teams as well as redesigned the Cubs' stadium, which was eventually named after him and is one of the oldest still in use in Major League Baseball.

In 1919, he bought Catalina Island. He built a resort and invited many Hollywood celebrities to visit. He lived there off and on with his family in a vacation home and developed the island. He loved the island and brought many improvements, such as public utilities, to the residents. He set aside nearly 90 percent of the island to remain free and pure of development. His family donated the remaining land in 1975 to the Catalina Island Conservancy, which protects the island to this day. The memorial that bears his name is right next to a botanic garden and a hiking trail that leads to the crest of the island.

2.5 Turn right and follow the trail at the junction where the fire road and trail split.

2.9 Turn right and follow the trail to East Peak.

3.25 Arrive atop East Peak. Return via the same route.

6.5 Arrive back at the trailhead.

Hike Index

Avalon Canyon/Wrigley Gardens, 243

Backbone Trail–Malibu Springs, 44

Big Horn Mine, 139

Calabasas Peak, 63

Castle Rock, 173

Charmlee Wilderness Park, 52

Chiquito Trail, 222

Cougar Crest/Bertha Peak, 177

Dawson Peak, 145

Eaton Canyon Falls, 111

Echo Mountain, 103

Ernie Maxwell Scenic Trail, 195

Etiwanda Peak, 160

Franklin Canyon, 81

Fuller Ridge/Marion Mountain/Devil's
    Slide/Cactus to Clouds Trails to
    Mount San Jacinto, 214

Grays Peak, 213

Griffith Park, 93

The Grotto, 39

Heart Rock Falls, 169

Jepson Peak, 181

La Jolla Valley Loop, 29

Lion Peak, 208

Mishe Mokwa, 34

Monrovia Canyon Falls, 121

Mount Baden-Powell, 133

Mount Baldy, 150

Mount Hawkins, 127

Mount Islip, 165

Mount Williamson, 165

Nicholas Flat, 48

Paradise Falls, 23

Paramount Ranch, 57

Pine Knot Trail to Grand View
    Point, 213

Point Vicente, 237

Portuguese Bend, 233

Red Tahquitz, 198

Rubio Canyon, 107

Runyon Canyon, 89

San Jacinto Peak, 186

San Juan Loop Trail, 226

Satwiwa/Rancho Sierra Vista, 99

Sitton Peak, 226

Solstice Canyon, 68

Spitler Peak, 203

Sturtevant Falls, 116

Suicide Rock, 191

Temescal Gateway Park, 72

Tenaja Falls, 218

Timber Mountain, 155

White Point, 229

Wilacre Park, 85

Will Rogers State Historic Park, 77

About the Authors

Allen Riedel, MSE, is a photographer, journalist, author, and educator. He has authored multiple hiking guides, including *100 Classic Hikes in Southern California, Best Hikes with Dogs in Southern California,* and a number of Best Easy Day Hikes guides.

Monique Riedel, JD, is an author, businessperson, and outdoor enthusiast. She is also the author of *Best Easy Day Hikes Ventura.*

Monique and Allen live in the Sierra National Forest.

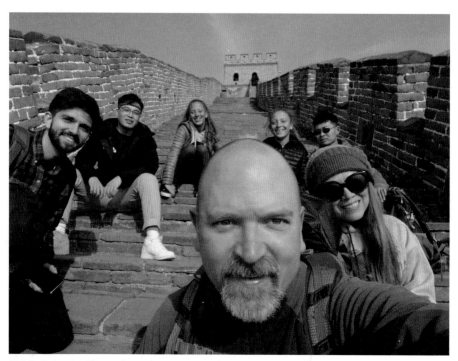

While living in China, the authors got to explore with their children and friends. Left to right Michael, Will, Makaila, Allen, Sierra, Rocky, and Monique.